CORNERSTONE

BUILDING ON YOUR BEST FOR CAREER SUCCESS

ROBERT M. SHERFIELD

THE COMMUNITY COLLEGE OF SOUTHERN NEVADA

RHONDA J. MONTGOMERY

THE UNIVERSITY OF NEVADA, LAS VEGAS

PATRICIA G. MOODY

THE UNIVERSITY OF SOUTH CAROLINA

PEARSON

Prentice
Hall

Upper Saddle River, New Jersey
Columbus, Ohio

Library of Congress Cataloging in Publication Data

Sherfield, Robert M.

    Cornerstone : building on your best for career success / Robert M.
Sherfield, Rhonda J. Montgomery, Patricia G. Moody.

      p. cm.

    ISBN 0-13-195825-9

    1. Career development. 2. Vocational guidance. 3. Success in
business. I. Montgomery, Rhonda J. II. Moody, Patricia G. III. Title.

HF5381.S5428 2006

650.1--dc22

                               2005021850

Photo Credits, by page number

2, Corbis; **4,** Comstock Images; **8,** Patrick
White/Merrill; **12,** Laima Druskis/PH College;
19, Frank LaBua/PH College; **22,** George Henry
Storey/Corbis/Bettmann; **32,** Dynamic Graphics;
34, Patrick White/Merrill; **40,** Scott Cunningham/
Merrill; **46,** Stockbyte; **48,** AP Wide World
Photos; **54,** Corbis; **56,** PhotoDisc;
60, © Bob Daemmrich; **69,** Peter Kramer/
Getty Images; **78,** Dynamic Graphics;
80, Esbin/Anderson/Omni-Photo
Communications; **86,** HBO/Worldwide Pants
Inc./The Kobal Collection; **90,** Patrick
White/Merrill; **100,** Corbis; **102,** Dynamic
Graphics; **106,** Arthur Torr-Brown © Dorling
Kindersley; **110–111,** Hemera Technologies;
112, ROTA/Getty Images; **126,** Dynamic
Graphics; **128,** Anthony Magnacca/Merrill;
132, Patrick White/Merrill; **133,** Dynamic
Graphics; **138,** PH College; **139,** Eric Lessing/Art
Resource, NY; **150,** Corbis; **152,** PhotoDisc;
156, Patrick White/Merrill; **158,** Comstock;
162, Scott Gries/Getty Images; **174,** Corbis;
176, Patrick White/Merrill; **180,** Patrick
White/Merrill; **191,** Getty Images; **198,** Corbis;
200, Dynamic Graphics; **204,** Patrick White/
Merrill; **207,** J. Nourok/Photo Edit; **213** (top),
Laima Druskis/PH College, (bottom), Joel
Saget/Agence France Presse/Getty Images;
220, Corbis; **222,** Dynamic Graphics;
226, PhotoDisc; **242,** PhotoDisc; **245,** KELD
NAVNTOFT/AFP/Getty Images.

Vice President and Publisher: Jeffery W. Johnston
Executive Editor: Sande Johnson
Editorial Assistant: Susan Kauffman
Production Editor: Holcomb Hathaway
Design Coordinator: Diane C. Lorenzo
Cover Designer: Jeff Vanik
Cover Photos: Corbis
Production Manager: Pamela D. Bennett
Director of Marketing: Ann Castel Davis
Marketing Manager: Amy Judd
Compositor: Carlisle Communications, Ltd.
Cover Printer: Phoenix Color Corp.
Printer/Binder: Courier Kendallville, Inc.

All chapters have been adapted for use in this book from *Cornerstone:
Building on Your Best*, Fourth Edition, by Sherfield, Montgomery,
Moody, © 2005 by Pearson Education, Inc.

Pearson Education Ltd.
Pearson Education Singapore Pte. Ltd.
Pearson Education Canada, Ltd.
Pearson Education–Japan

Pearson Education Australia Pty. Limited
Pearson Education North Asia Ltd.
Pearson Educación de Mexico, S.A. de C.V.
Pearson Education Malaysia Pte. Ltd.

10 9 8 7 6 5 4

ISBN 0-13-195825-9

Contents

1   CHANGE   3

Dealing with Change, Setting Goals, and Getting Motivated

2   PERSIST   33

Things You Need to Know About Succeeding But Might Never Ask

3   PRIORITIZE   55

Managing Your Time and Money Wisely

4 READ 79

Building Active Reading and Comprehension Skills

5 LEARN 101

Multiple Intelligences, Learning Styles, and Personality Typing

6 RECORD 127

The Art of Active Listening and Note Taking

7 REMEMBER 151

Empowering Your Memory

Today, you will begin preparing for the many opportunities that lie ahead. You might think of this time as "the first day of the rest of your life." Regardless of what you have experienced in the past—good or bad—this is a new day and it brings many exciting opportunities and challenges. It might take a while, but soon you will begin to understand yourself better, and as a result, you will also begin to understand others.

The secret to life is not **finding** yourself. The secret to life is **creating** yourself. —GEORGE BERNARD SHAW

Chances are good that you have already faced many changes. All your life you have been evolving and becoming. The pace is about to pick up! Some days you may feel like you are on a runaway train. At first, you might think you can't keep up. Be patient with yourself as you focus on discovering your greatest strengths and shaping your ambitions.

Throughout your educational experience, you will always be changing and creating yourself anew. As you work toward becoming who and what you want to become—the person you were meant to become—we invite you to *build on your best*.

We also invite you to . . .

BUILD ON YOUR OPEN-MINDEDNESS

A truly educated person learns to consider a person's character rather than the color of one's skin, or one's religion, or sexual orientation, or ethnic background. As you become more open-minded, you will begin to work on understanding before judging, reasoning before reacting, and delving deeper before condemning. As you build on your best character, strive hard to develop a habit of practicing open-mindedness.

BUILD ON YOUR COMPETENCE

You have already established a certain level of competence or you wouldn't be here. Now is the time to push yourself to learn more than you ever have before. Your future depends on the knowledge you are gaining today. Work to acquire knowledge about the world, other cultures, and events that impact and shape humanity, and most important,

work hard to understand yourself and your place in the world.

BUILD ON YOUR ABILITY TO QUESTION

It has been said, "Sometimes, the question is more important than the answer." As you move through the coming months and years, don't be afraid to ask questions of others, especially your instructors. Questioning is the first step in becoming a more critical and logical thinker.

BUILD ON YOUR SUPPORTIVE NATURE

Education is more than facts and figures. It involves learning how to support others in the world around you—learning how to be a member of a larger community than your own. An ancient Chinese quote may help you in building on your best supportive nature: "Help thy brother's boat across and lo, Thine own has reached the shore."

BUILD ON YOUR ABILITY TO GIVE

As you build on your best, you will have more to give than ever before. Writer and educator Leo Buscaglia once said that you want to make yourself the most creative, educated, wonderful, caring person in the world so that you can give it away. Strive hard to find a need in the world and devote your best to it. It's a strange but true phenomenon—the more you give, the more you get.

BUILD ON YOUR NEED TO BE CHALLENGED

The easy road will never lead to greatness or to your best. Winston Churchill said, "It is from adversity that we gain greatness." When you are struggling, remember that you are getting stronger. You are preparing for becoming the person you were meant to be. As you register for classes, search for instructors, volunteer for projects, and explore internships, choose those that will challenge you, make you stretch, and ultimately lead you to another level in the search to be your best.

BUILD ON YOUR CREATIVITY

In building on your best, don't forget to let your creativity shine. You may say that you are not a "creative person," but that would be an unfair statement. Everyone has creative genius on some level. By allowing yourself to wander, dream, explore, and yes, even fail, your creativity will develop and soar. Try new ideas, experience new adventures, engage in activities with new people. Build your creativity!

BUILD ON YOUR ABILITY TO BALANCE

No ONE thing will ever bring you joy, peace, or prosperity. Try to include family, friends, cultural events, social activities, work, and service in your daily life. Seek balance between work and play. You will never be happy unless there is a sense of balance in your life. Harmony and balance in life help you to be your best.

BUILD ON YOUR PROSPERITY

While money won't make you happy, you need a certain amount to take care of yourself and your family. Your definition of success may or may not involve money and material possessions. It is not a sin, however, to pursue financial success. Prosperity can afford you the opportunity to give back to your community, your family, and fellow citizens in need. Money, used properly, can bring great happiness if you share it with others.

BUILD ON YOUR SUCCESS

You need to define exactly what success means to you so you know what you are working toward. Whatever success is for you, pursue it with all of the passion and energy you have. Set your goals high and work hard to create a life that you can ultimately look back on with pride, satisfaction, and joy and be able to say, "I did my best. I have no regrets."

Yes! You Can.

To Our Students

We chose the title *Cornerstone* because a cornerstone is the fundamental basis for something—the first building block—laid to establish a firm foundation. Often, a ceremony takes place when a cornerstone is laid, and sometimes treasured documents and valuables are placed within the cornerstone of the building. A celebration usually accompanies the laying of the cornerstone. *Today is a celebration; a celebration of your success,* your future, your hopes, your challenges, your potential and, yes, a celebration for building on your best.

It is our hope that this book will help you to see the possibilities of your future, anticipate and cope with new situations, guide you through difficult days, discover more about yourself and your unique gifts, develop study and learning habits that help you succeed in every class, come to understand and appreciate more about diverse cultures, hone your creative and critical-thinking skills, and learn more about careers and the countless opportunities available to you. It is our ultimate hope that you will use this book as a stepping-stone to obtain your degree or certificate.

As you begin reading *Cornerstone,* pay special attention to the features because these will assist you in mastering the content and applying the information to other classes and "real world" situations.

Critical Thinking. This chapter will help you prepare for classes and projects. It will also help you think more critically when making major purchases, establishing relationships, and making major life decisions regarding your future.

Reading Comprehension. This chapter will help you learn to read faster and more efficiently. As the semester progresses and assignments pour in, learning to read more effectively and better comprehend the texts, journals, magazines, and the Internet will be essential. This chapter can literally turn your academic life around.

Real Stories. Academic concepts make more sense when put into real life situations. *Cornerstone* provides two features that show how these concepts relate directly to your life. Each chapter contains a "Case Study" that shares the stories of actual students and a "World of Work" feature that allows you to interact with professionals from companies across the country.

What *Cornerstone* can do for your students . . . We have spent the past 10 years researching, reading, exploring, and, most important, listening. We have listened to colleagues at our respective institutions, to students from around America, and we have listened to *you,* our colleagues in America's career colleges and schools. We are honored and privileged that you have chosen to use *Cornerstone: Building on Your Best for Career Success.* We thank you for your confidence in this book, in the *Cornerstone* program, and in us. We think that you will be excited and pleased with the results from your advice.

You will find exciting features and tested material. The focus of *Cornerstone* is:

- Self-discovery
- Change
- Motivation
- Goal setting
- Personal responsibility

We believe that the fundamental success of any first-year course is helping students understand the importance of being responsible for their own learning, their own success, and indeed, their own actions. We have included activities to help students *build on their best.* The following sections discuss the salient features of this edition.

Critical Thinking

Chapter 9, "Think: Critical- and Creative-Thinking Skills," includes these important tools:

- **practical applications** for critical and creative thinking
- **specific examples** of when critical and creative thinking are needed in college, work, and life
- information about how critical thinking can assist with **decision making, problem solving, and conflict management**
- applications for distinguishing **fact from opinion**

Retention

Chapter 2, "Persist: Things You Need to Know About Succeeding But Might Never Ask," grew from listening to students and colleagues across the United States discuss the challenges that first-year students face beyond academics. This chapter deals frankly with the topics of:

- college policy
- grading
- success centers on campus
- personal decorum
- counselor–student relationships
- faculty–student relationships
- financial aid
- campus safety

Chapter 4, "Read: Building Active Reading and Comprehension Skills," was developed to help students cope with one of the fastest growing and most serious academic problems on campus today—comprehension and reading speed. For years, we have heard colleagues across the country lament students' inability to read and comprehend texts. This chapter covers material such as:

- dictionary usage
- vocabulary building
- finding main ideas
- improving concentration

This chapter also includes a reading speed calculator.

Application

Materials and activities at the end of each chapter include the following:

- **Case Study:** Real college students from across the United States have contributed their stories related to the chapter content. Students will have the opportunity to read the case study, answer questions about the situation, and apply the case to their own lives.
- **Online Journal:** By visiting the *Cornerstone* Companion Website at www.prenhall.com/sherfield, students will be able to submit journal entries directly to you related to pre-set questions or questions/situations that you assign.
- **Advice to Go, Cornerstones:** This succinct poster offers one-sentence summary statements of the chapter's most important points.

Again, it is with sincere gratitude that we welcome you to the *Cornerstone* program. Thank you for choosing *Cornerstone* and know that we wish you much success in your course.

About the Authors

ROBERT M. SHERFIELD, PH.D.

Robert Sherfield has been teaching public speaking, theater, and student success and working with first-year orientation programs for over 20 years. Currently, he is a professor at the Community College of Southern Nevada, teaching courses in student success, public speaking, technical writing, and drama.

An award-winning educator, Robb was recently named Educator of the Year at the Community College of Southern Nevada. He twice received the Distinguished Teacher of the Year Award from the University of South Carolina at Union and has received numerous other awards and nominations for outstanding classroom instruction and advisement. In 1998, 1999, and 2000, he was nominated by students for, and named to, *Who's Who Among American Educators.*

Robb's extensive work with student success programs includes experience with the design and implementation of these programs—including one program that was presented at the International Conference on the Freshman Year Experience in Newcastle upon Tyne, England.

In addition to his coauthorship of *Cornerstone: Building on Your Best for Career Success,* he has also coauthored *Cornerstone: Building on Your Best* (Prentice Hall, 2005), *Roadways to Success* (Prentice Hall, 2001), the trade book *365 Things I Learned in College* (Allyn & Bacon, 1996), *Capstone: Succeeding Beyond College* (Prentice Hall, 2001), *Case Studies for the First Year: An Odyssey into Critical Thinking and Problem Solving* (Prentice Hall, 2004), and *The Everything® Self-Esteem Book* (Adams Media, 2004).

Robb's interest in student success began with his own first year in college. Low SAT scores and a mediocre high school ranking denied him entrance into college. With the help of a success program, Robb was granted entrance into college, and he went on to earn a doctorate and become a college faculty member. He has always been interested in the academic, social, and cultural development of students, and sees this book as his way to contribute to the positive development of first-year students across the nation.

Visit **www.robertsherfield.com.**

RHONDA J. MONTGOMERY, PH.D.

Rhonda Montgomery is an associate professor in the William F. Harrah College of Hotel Administration at the University of Nevada, Las Vegas, and has been teaching in higher education for 18 years. Rhonda has been responsible for developing and incorporating first-year orientation/study skills curricula into existing introductory courses and programs.

Currently, Rhonda is teaching a first-year orientation/student success course as well as hospitality education. Because she believes in the holistic development of first-year students, she volunteers to teach first-year students each semester and uses a variety of experiences such as field trips, exercises, and case studies to aid in their retention and success.

Rhonda has received several awards for her teaching and advising. She is also an active member of Phi Eta Sigma, a National Freshman Honorary Association. Rhonda is the coauthor of seven texts, including *Cornerstone: Building on Your Best* (Prentice Hall, 2005), *Roadways to Success* (Prentice Hall, 2001), *365 Things I Learned in College* (Allyn & Bacon, 1996), *Capstone: Succeeding Beyond College* (Prentice Hall, 2001), and *Case Studies for the First Year: An Odyssey into Critical Thinking and Problem Solving* (Prentice Hall, 2004). She has also presented at The National Conference on the Freshman Year Experience and spoken extensively to first-year students and educators about building success into their curriculum.

PATRICIA G. MOODY, PH.D.

Patricia G. Moody is dean of the College of Hospitality, Retail and Sport Management at the University of South Carolina, where she has been a faculty member for over 25 years. An award-winning educator, Pat has been honored as Distinguished Educator of the Year at her college and as Collegiate Teacher of the Year by the National Business Education Association, and has been a top-five finalist for the Amoco Teaching Award at the University of South Carolina. In 1994, she was awarded the prestigious John Robert Gregg Award, the highest honor in her field of over 100,000 educators.

Pat frequently speaks to multiple sections of first-year students, incorporating personal development content from her trademark speech "Fly Like an Eagle," as well as numerous strategies for building self-esteem and for achieving success in college. She also works with first-year classes on subjects such as goal setting, priority management, and diversity.

A nationally known motivational speaker, Pat has spoken in 42 states, has been invited to speak in several foreign countries, and frequently keynotes national and regional conventions. She has presented "Fly Like an Eagle" to thousands of people, from Olympic athletes to corporate executives to high school students. Her topics include Thriving in the Changing Corporate Environment, Perception Is Everything: Powerful Communications Strategies, Gold Star Customer Service, and The Great Balancing Act: Managing Time at Home and at Work.

An avid sports fan, she follows Gamecock athletics and chairs the University of South Carolina Athletics Advisory Committee.

Acknowledgments

National Advisory Board Members

We would like to sincerely thank the members of our National Advisory Board for their support and assistance: Paula Campbell, International Education Corporation; Starr Eaddy, William Paterson University and PCI Health Training Institute; Karen McGrath, PIMA Medical Institute; Darlla Roesler, Vocational Nursing Program Director, Western Career College; Pam Rushing, PIMA Medical Institute; and Mary Weizmann, Florida Metropolitan University.

Professional Acknowledgments

First, we would like to thank the following individuals for their support: Dr. Carol Harter, President, University of Nevada–Las Vegas; Rose Hawkins, Department Chair, Community College of Southern Nevada; Dr. Joan McGee, Interim Vice President, Community College of Southern Nevada; Dr. Stuart Mann, Dean, University of Nevada–Las Vegas; Dr. Mark Becker, Provost, University of South Carolina; Dr. Richard Carpenter, President, Community College of Southern Nevada; Professor Patti Shock, Department Chair, University of Nevada–Las Vegas; Carlos Campo, Interim Dean, Community College of Southern Nevada; Dr. Andrew A. Sorensen, President, University of South Carolina.

Contributor Acknowledgments

Our sincere thanks to Paul Billings, Community College of Southern Nevada, for *At This Moment* assessments; Janet Lindner, Midlands Technical College, for developing the *Companion Website*; Kateri Drexler, for consulting on the development of the *Online Class Component* and *Success Website*; and Angela McGrady, PIMA Medical Institute, for creating a curriculum to accompany this book.

Our sincere thanks also to the following faculty, who recommended students for the case studies: Julie Boch, Massasoit Community College; Irma Camacho, El Paso Community College; Chloe Carson, Southwest Texas State University; Sharon Cordell, Roane State University; JoAnn Credle, Northern Virginia Community College; Roy Hurd, Empire College; Sherie Hurd, Empire College; Faye Johnson, Middle Tennessee State University; Janet Lindner, Midlands Technical College; Cheryl Rohrbaugh, Northern Virginia Community College; JoAnne Reinke, Central Missouri State University; Pat Thomas, Middle Tennessee State University; Brad Waltman, Community College of Southern Nevada; Anna E. Ward, Miami-Dade Community College; Kay Young, Jamestown Community College; Marie Zander, New York Institute of Technology.

We offer our heartfelt thanks to our contributors for *World of Work*: Brian Epps, Barona Valley Ranch Resort and Casino; Darlla Roesler, Western Career College; Tim Rice, Waddell and Reed Financial Services; Robin Baliszewski, Pearson Education/Prentice Hall; Dr. Starr Eaddy, William Paterson University; Maritza Rudisill, Disneyland; Coleman Peterson, Wal-Mart Stores, Inc.; Mary Weizmann, Florida Metropolitan University; James Farmer, General Motors; and Tonya Overdorf, Attorney, Indianapolis, IN.

And thanks to our students who shared their real-life stories for *Case Studies*: Sonia Armfield, The Art Institute of Las Vegas; Vanessa Santos, Miami-Dade Community College; Coretta Hooks, University of South Carolina; Candice Guasco, Empire College; Joey Luna, El Paso Community College; LaDondo Johnson, Houston Community College; Oscar Bowser, Midlands Technical College; Damion Saunders, Western Career College; Nailah Robinson, Northern Virginia Community College; and Steve Rodriguez, Community College of Southern Nevada.

Our Wonderful and Insightful Reviewers

For this new book: Christian M. Blum, Bryant & Stratton College; James Briski, Katherine Gibbs School; Pela Selene Terry, Art Institute of NYC; Christina Donnelly, York Technical College; Connie Egelman, Nassau Community College; Amy Hickman, Collins College; Beth Humes, Pennsylvania Culinary Institute; Kim Joyce, Art Institute of Philadelphia; Lawrence Ludwig, Sanford-Brown College; Bethany Marcus, ECPI College of Technology; Kate Sawyer, Pittsburgh Technical Institute; Patricia Sell, National College of Business and Technology; Janis Stiewing, PIMA Medical Institute; and June Sullivan, Florida Metropolitan University.

For their help with previous *Cornerstone* projects, thus strengthening the foundation of the entire program: Fred Amador, Phoenix College; Kathy Bryan, Daytona Beach Community College; Dorothy Chase, Community College of Southern Nevada; JoAnn Credle, Northern Virginia Community College; Betty Fortune, Houston Community College; Doroteo Franco Jr., El Paso Community College; Cynthia Garrard, Massasoit Community College; Joel Jessen, Eastfield College; Peter Johnston, Massasoit Community College; Steve Konowalow, Community College of Southern Nevada; Janet Lindner, Midlands Technical College; Carmen McNeil, Solano College; Joan O'Connor, New York Institute of Technology; Mary Pepe, Valencia Community College; Bennie Perdue, Miami-Dade Community College; Ginny Peterson-Tennant, Miami-Dade Community College; Anna E. Ward, Miami-Dade Community College; Wistar M. Withers, Northern Virginia Community College; Marie Zander, New York Institute of Technology; Joanne Bassett, Shelby State Community College; Sandra M. Bovain-Lowe, Cumberland Community College; Carol Brooks, GMI Engineering and Management Institute; Elaine H. Byrd, Utah Valley State College; Janet Cutshall, Sussex County Community College; Deborah Daiek, Wayne State University; David DeFrain, Central Missouri State University; Leslie L. Duckworth, Florida Community College at Jacksonville; Marnell Hayes, Lake City Community College; Elzora Holland, University of Michigan, Ann Arbor; Earlyn G. Jordan, Fayetteville State University; John Lowry-King, Eastern New Mexico University; Charlene Latimer; Michael Laven, University of Southwestern Louisiana; Judith Lynch, Kansas State University; Susan Magun-Jackson, The University of Memphis; Charles William Martin, California State University, San Bernardino; Jeffrey A. Miller; Ronald W. Johnsrud, Lake City Community College; Joseph R. Krzyzanowski, Albuquerque TVI; Ellen Oppenberg, Glendale Community College; Lee Pelton, Charles S. Mott Community College; Robert Rozzelle, Wichita State University; Penny Schempp, Western Iowa Community College; Betty Smith, University of Nebraska at Kearney; James Stepp, University of Maine at Presque Isle; Charles Washington, Indiana University–Purdue University; and Katherine A. Wenen-Nesbit, Chippewa Valley Technical College.

The Creative and Supportive Team

Without the support and encouragement of these people at Prentice Hall, this book would not be possible. Our sincere thanks to Robin Baliszewski, Jeff Johnston, Sande Johnson, Amy Judd, Susan Kauffman, Debbie Ogilvie, Walt Kirby, Alan Hensley, Steve Whitehead, Toni Payne, Wendy DiLeonardo, Angie Smajstrla, and Pam Jeffries.

And finally, to a few people whose creative talents have helped us greatly over the years: Nancy Forsythe of Pearson Education/Allyn and Bacon, who gave us a chance; Gay Pauley of Holcomb Hathaway and John Wincek and Rhonda Wincek of Aerocraft Charter Art Service, who continually amaze us with their design and production talents; and Amy Gehl and others at Carlisle Communications, our typesetter.

CORNERSTONE

BUILDING ON YOUR BEST
FOR CAREER SUCCESS

1 Change

ark was the son of textile workers. Both of his parents had worked in the cotton mill for almost 30 years. They lived in the rural south about 35 miles from the nearest metropolitan area. His high school graduated a small number of students yearly. Mark had decided to attend a community college some 30 miles from home for his first two years and then transfer to a larger, four-year college. Money, time, grades, goals, and family commitments led to his decision.

Mark was not a good student in high school. He finished with a D— average and his SAT scores and class rank *were in the lowest 25th percentile.* In fact, initially he had been *denied entrance to the community college.* The college granted him provisional acceptance only if he enrolled in, and successfully completed, a summer preparatory program. During the summer, Mark enrolled in the prep program, *never realizing what lay ahead.*

Mark's first class that semester was English. The professor walked in, handed out the syllabus, called the roll, and began to lecture. Lord Byron was the topic for the day. The professor sat on a stool by the window, leaned his elbow on the ledge, and sipped a cup of coffee as he told the story of how Byron's foot had been damaged at birth. He continued to weave the details of Byron's life poetically, through quotes and parables, until the 50-minute period had quietly slipped away. After an hour's break, Mark headed across campus for history. The professor entered with a dust storm behind her. She went over the syllabus, and before the class had a chance to blink, she was involved in the first lecture. "The cradle of civilization," she began, "was Mesopotamia." The class scurried to find notebooks and pens to begin taking notes. *Already they were behind, Mark included.* Exactly 47 minutes after she had begun to speak, the professor took her first breath. "You are in history now. You elected to take this class and you will follow my rules," she told the first-year students sitting in front of her. "You are not to be late, you are to come to this class prepared, and you are to read your homework. If you do what I ask you to do, you will learn more about Western civilization than you ever thought possible. *If you do not keep up with me, you will not know if you are in Egypt, Mesopotamia, or pure hell!* Class dismissed!"

Without a moment to spare, Mark ran to the other end of campus for his next class. He walked into the room in a panic, fearing he was late. To his surprise, the instructor was not yet in class. *The class*  *waited for more than 10 minutes before the professor entered.* "You need to sign this roster and read chapter one for Wednesday," he said. "You can pick up a syllabus on your way out." *Mark was shocked. Was the class over?* What about the bell? The students in the class looked at each other with dismay and quietly left the room, wondering what Wednesday would hold. On the 30-mile trip home, Mark's mind was filled with new thoughts . . . *Lord Byron, Mesopotamia, professors who talked too fast, professors who did not talk at all, the cost of tuition, the size of the library.* He knew that something was different, *something had changed.* He couldn't put his finger on it. It would be years later before he would realize that the change was not his classes, not his schedule, not the people, not the professors—but himself; *Mark had changed.* In one day, he had tasted something intoxicating, something that was addictive. *He had tasted a new world.*

> *Mark was not a good student in high school. He finished with a D— average . . .*

Mark had to go to work that afternoon, and even his job had changed. He had always known that he did not want to spend the rest of his life in the factory, but this day the feeling was stronger. His job was not enough, his family was not enough, the farm on which he had been raised was not enough anymore. *There was a new light for Mark, and he knew that because of one day in college, he would never be the same.* It was like tasting Godiva chocolate for the first time—Hershey's kisses were no longer enough. It was like seeing the ocean for the first time and knowing that the millpond would never be the same. *He couldn't go back. What he knew before was simply not enough.*

My name is Robert Mark Sherfield, and 27 years later, as I coauthor your text, I am still addicted to that new world. Spartanburg Methodist College changed my life, and I am still changing—with every day, every new book I read, every new class I teach, every new person I meet, and every new place to which I travel, I am changing.

QUESTIONS FOR REFLECTION

Consider responding to these questions online in the Questions for Reflection module of the Companion Website.

1. Mark knew that his life was changed from the first day of college. You may not have experienced this type of change yet, but look ahead a few months or even years. What changes do you hope college will help make in your life?

2. What were your expectations for your first days of college? Contrast your expectations of your first days with what you actually experienced.

3. Discuss the class you currently take that most excites you about learning.

Before reading this chapter, take a moment and respond to the following 10 questions. Consider each one carefully before answering, and then respond by circling the number in the appropriate box. When you have answered the questions, add your points and find your total score on the feedback chart below.

STATEMENT	STRONGLY DISAGREE	DISAGREE	DON'T KNOW	AGREE	STRONGLY AGREE	SCORE
1. I am aware of the expectations that my school and teachers have of me.	1	2	3	4	5	
2. I am enthusiastic about the challenges and opportunities that will be presented to me in my program.	1	2	3	4	5	
3. I have difficulties adapting and adjusting to changes in my life.	5	4	3	2	1	
4. I have thought about what it means to be a "successful" student.	1	2	3	4	5	
5. I know where to get help with problems related to school.	1	2	3	4	5	
6. I have not set goals for my future.	5	4	3	2	1	
7. I actively work toward the goals I have set for my future.	1	2	3	4	5	
8. I am motivated by goals that are challenging.	1	2	3	4	5	
9. I tend to give up easily when frustrated.	5	4	3	2	1	
10. The fear of failure usually stops me from even trying.	5	4	3	2	1	
TOTAL VALUE						

SUMMARY

43–50   You are exceptional in your ability to adapt to changes, set clear and realistic goals, and recover from setbacks. You likely have a clear understanding of what continuing education has in store for you, and because of your exceptional motivational level, you are eager to meet those experiences head-on.

35–42   Your ability to deal effectively with life changes and goal setting is above average. You likely have a solid sense of why you are continuing your education and what you want to get out of being in school. You are self-motivated most of the time.

26–34   You are average in your level of coping skills for dealing with life changes and setting goals. You likely have a general notion of what you want to get for yourself as a result of your continuing education. Some fine-tuning of your expectations and motivational level would likely be helpful.

18–25   Your expectations for your continuing education experiences are somewhat unclear, and your ability to prepare for and adjust to change is limited. Your goals need refinement, and you'd benefit from having strategies to help cope with the changes you will face, the motivation you will need, and the goals to make it happen.

10–17   Your ability to cope with change is limited, and your expectations of your continuing education experiences are unfocused. You will need to spend significant time exploring your expectations for your career, as well as developing strategies to help cope with the coming life changes.

Goals . . .

Based on the summary above, what is one goal you would like to achieve related to making a positive change and setting realistic goals in your life?

Goal Statement _____

_____

Think of three actions you can take that might help you move closer to realizing this goal.

1. _____
2. _____
3. _____

Questions FOR BUILDING ON YOUR BEST

As you read this chapter, consider the following questions. At the end of the chapter, you should be able to answer all of them. We encourage you to ask a few questions of your own. Consider turning to your classmates or instructors to assist you.

1. Why is it important to accept change in my life and cope with the unexpected changes that may come my way?
2. Why is thinking about and preparing for change a positive way to handle and cope with some of the negative side effects that may accompany change?
3. What attitudes and/or behaviors do I currently have that hinder my ability to change, set realistic goals, and be motivated?
4. How has adversity strengthened or discouraged me in my life?
5. How will goal setting help me be a better student?
6. How does self-esteem impact my ability to achieve my goals?

What additional questions might you have about change, motivation, and goal setting in college and life?

1. _____
2. _____
3. _____

Your Career College Experience

Those who choose to further their educational experience soon understand that education is a two-way street. Not only do you have expectations of your college and program of study—your college and program also have expectations of you. Successful completion requires that you accept substantially more responsibility for your own learning. By accepting admission into the institution you are attending, you have voluntarily agreed to be a part of their community. This agreement means that you have a responsibility to follow the institution's codes of academic and moral conduct. You have also committed yourself to the pursuit of knowledge and respecting your fellow classmates, faculty, administrators, and staff while adhering to the institution's procedures and guidelines.

Before reading further, jot down some thoughts about what you want to achieve in your program and career, what you value about continuing your education, what you expect from your institution, and what your institution expects from you.

Regardless of your background or reasons for continuing your education, the experience of change is something you'll share with everyone. Will you be able to open yourself up to new people and new situations?

1. *While in school, I want to achieve . . .*

   ■ _____

   ■ _____

2. *When I complete my program, I want to . . .*

   ■ _____

   ■ _____

3. *I feel continuing my education is significant to my life because . . .*

   ■ _____

   ■ _____

4. *From my program, I expect . . .*

   ■ _____

   ■ _____

5. *The people who will be able to help me are . . .*

   ■ _____

   ■ _____

Education is the knowledge of how to use the whole of oneself. Many use one or two faculties out of a score with which they are endowed. One is educated who knows how to make a tool of every faculty; how to open it, how to keep it sharp, and how to apply it to all practical purposes.   —H. W. BEECHER

6. *To achieve my goals, I may have to change . . .*

    ▪ _____

    ▪ _____

My program expects me to . . .

_____

_____

_____

_____

What Do You Want?
THINKING ABOUT YOUR CHOICES

Today, you face many decisions. Some of them will affect the rest of your life. Some changes and decisions will be of your own making; others will be beyond your control. Some will be easily altered; others will hold for the long run.

Before you read further, think about where you are at this very moment and where you want to be in the coming years. Remember that planning, focusing, and hard work can help you reach your goals.

The following activity is one of the first cornerstones of this book. It asks you to look at your current status, your peers, your past, and your aspirations and is intended to guide you in evaluating your life, attitudes, and thoughts. Take your time, be honest with yourself, and think in terms of realistic goals.

1. *What are the characteristics of a successful person?*

    _____

    _____

2. *Name one person you think of as successful. Why is that person successful?*

    _____

    _____

3. *List one accomplishment that might signify your success.*

    _____

    _____

Continuing your education is an instrumental change in your life. It is preparing you for all the possibilities ahead, but it cannot prepare you for the personal knowledge that you will gain as you mature and grow. When I consider how change has affected me, I realize that my career did not progress as I had planned while in school. During that time, I thought the changes I was experiencing were incredible and some of the most difficult of my life. But by enduring those changes, and accepting some of the hard lessons I've learned along the way because of them, I realize how much they helped me grow personally and professionally.

Change is such an important thing in our lives. Our whole destiny is affected by it. I think it is important that we consider change a friend, not an enemy. Sometimes, things that occur in our lives seem cruel, overwhelming, or hopeless, but learning to deal with change can help us survive them. In my experience, change has always brought something positive. Sometimes, you have to look a little harder and give it time, but the growth experience is rewarding.

A career in the hospitality industry has always been something I have enjoyed. Years ago, many people believed that their careers would be like their fathers' and grandfathers'—they worked their entire lives at one company and then they retired with the gold watch. However, that is not the case anymore. I read lately in the *Wall Street Journal* that the average adult will experience 7 to 10 career changes during their work life—not just job changes, but career changes. That powerful statement indicates how necessary it is for a person to be able to adapt to change.

As I made my career choices and changes, I grew in ways I never imagined possible. For me personally, I seek knowledge. When I have mastered something in my current position, I tend to become restless and thirst for more knowledge. I think it is fine to recognize this as a need for change. If you cannot get what you are seeking in your current position, you need to explore how to achieve what you are looking for.

QUESTIONS FOR REFLECTION

Consider responding to these questions online in the World of Work module of the Companion Website.

1. What have you experienced in your life that at the time made you feel hopeless, but in reality became a growth opportunity?

2. What did this experience teach you about using change as a positive force in your life?

3. What do you have to do to prepare yourself for multiple career changes?

Brian R. Epps, *Executive Director of Hotel Operations,* Barona Valley Ranch Resort and Casino, San Diego, CA

4. *What might you have to change to achieve this accomplishment?*

_____

_____

5. *How will you approach these changes?*

_____

_____

6. *What part will your education play in helping you reach this accomplishment?*

_____

_____

_____

_____

_____

_____

So, What's This All About?

Why are you here? What is the driving force that brought you to the doors of this institution? Was it a desire to learn more about your field? Was it to fulfill a dream? Was it unemployment? Did a major change occur in your life? Did you need retraining for the world of work? Whatever the reason, you're here and that is a positive and wonderful thing for you and your family.

It is a proven fact that over 70 percent of entering students say that their primary reason for furthering their education was "to be able to get a better job" and "make more money."

Now, for the good news! According to the 2000 U.S. Census, people who further their education and training DO earn more than those who did not complete high school or those with only a high school diploma or GED. Figure 1.1 shows you the difference in earning power.

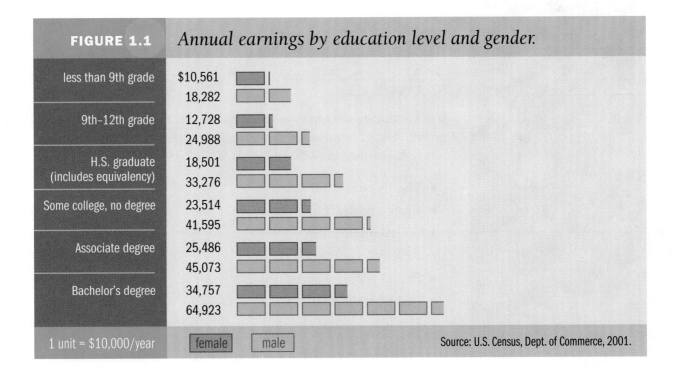

FIGURE 1.1   *Annual earnings by education level and gender.*

	female	male
less than 9th grade	$10,561	18,282
9th–12th grade	12,728	24,988
H.S. graduate (includes equivalency)	18,501	33,276
Some college, no degree	23,514	41,595
Associate degree	25,486	45,073
Bachelor's degree	34,757	64,923

1 unit = $10,000/year   female   male

Source: U.S. Census, Dept. of Commerce, 2001.

Beyond money, furthering your education can help you:

- Work in a career of your choosing (not just a job).
- Develop a healthier self-esteem.
- Strengthen your confidence in many areas of your life.
- Expand your independence (thus reducing your dependence).
- Become more knowledgeable about more things.
- Increase your options for future employment.
- Grow to be a role model and mentor for your family and friends.

Changes in the Days to Come

One of the first changes you may notice about continuing your education is that you have to learn to juggle many things at once, including your course work, your finances, your family, and perhaps job responsibilities. Learning how to set priorities for your time, money, and resources is a critical step to successfully handling this challenge. Chapter 3 will help you with priority management. Figure 1.2 offers a guide to understanding expectations.

Y ou gain strength, experience, and confidence by every experience where you really stop to look fear in the face.... You must do the thing you think you cannot.   —ELEANOR ROOSEVELT

Change can introduce you to new people, ideas, cultures, and experiences.

Attitudes That Hinder Change

It is sometimes easy to develop attitudes that hinder change and stop growth. Such attitudes are dangerous because they rob you of opportunity, happiness, growth, and goals. These attitudes include:

- The "I can't" syndrome
- Apathy, or the "I don't care" syndrome
- Closed-mindedness
- Unfounded anxiety
- Fear of taking chances
- Loss of motivation
- The "let someone else deal with it" syndrome

If you can learn to watch out for and control these negative attitudes, you will begin to view change as a wonderful and positive lifelong event.

FIGURE 1.2	*A guide to understanding expectations.*		
	HIGH SCHOOL	**POST SECONDARY**	**WORK**
PUNCTUALITY AND ATTENDANCE	Expectations: • State law requires attendance • The hours in the day are managed for you • There may be some leeway in project dates Penalties: • You may get detention • You may not graduate • You may be considered truant • Your grades may suffer	Expectations: • Attendance and participation in class are enforced by some instructors • Some instructors will not give you an extension on due dates • You decide your own schedule and plan your own day Penalties: • You may not be admitted to class if you are late • You may fail the assignment if it is late • Repeated tardiness is sometimes counted as an absence • Most instructors do not take late assignments, especially if prior arrangements have not been made	Expectations: • You are expected to be at work and on time on a daily basis Penalties: • Your salary and promotions may depend on your daily attendance and punctuality • You will most likely be fired for abusing either
TEAMWORK AND PARTICIPATION	Expectations: • Most teamwork is assigned and carried out in class • You may be able to choose teams with your friends • Your grade reflects your participation Penalties: • If you don't participate, you may get a poor grade • You may jeopardize the grade of the entire team	Expectations: • Many instructors require group work • Your grade will depend on your participation • Your grade may depend on your entire team's performance • You may have to work on the project outside of class Penalties: • Lack of participation will probably lower your grade • Your team members will likely report you to the instructor if you do not participate and their grades suffer as a result	Expectations: • You will be expected to participate fully in any assigned task • You will be expected to rely on co-workers to help solve problems and increase profits • You will be required to attend and participate in meetings and sharing sessions • You will be required to participate in formal teams and possess the ability to work with a diverse workforce Penalties: • You will be "tagged" as non-team player • Your lack of participation and teamwork will cost you raises and promotions • You will most likely be terminated

(continued)

FIGURE 1.2	*A guide to understanding expectations, continued.*

	HIGH SCHOOL	POST SECONDARY	WORK
PERSONAL RESPONSIBILITY AND ATTITUDE	Expectations: • Teachers may coach you and try to motivate you • You are required to be in high school by law regardless of your attitude or responsibility level Penalties: • You may be reprimanded for certain attitudes • If your attitude prevents you from participating, you may fail the class	Expectations: • You are responsible for your own learning • Instructors will assist you, but there may be little "hand holding" or personal coaching for motivation • Continuing education did not choose you, you chose it, and you will be expected to hold this attitude toward your work Penalties: • You may fail the class if your attitude and motivation prevent you from participating	Expectations: • You are hired to do certain tasks and the company or institution fully expects this of you • You are expected to be positive and self-motivated • You are expected to model good behavior and uphold the company's work standards Penalties: • You will be passed over for promotions and raises • You may be reprimanded • You may be terminated
ETHICS AND CREDIBILITY	Expectations: • You are expected to turn in your own work • You are expected to avoid plagiarism • You are expected to write your own papers • Poor ethical decisions in high school may result in detention or suspension Penalties: • You may get detention or suspension • You will probably fail the project	Expectations: • You are expected to turn in your own work • You are expected to avoid plagiarism • You are expected to write your own papers • You are expected to conduct research and complete projects based on higher education and societal standards Penalties: • Poor ethical decisions may land you in front of a student ethics committee or a faculty ethics committee, or result in expulsion from the institution • You will fail the project • You may fail the class • You may face deportation if your visa is dependent on your student status	Expectations: • You will be required to carry out your job in accordance with company policies, laws, and moral standards • You will be expected to use adult vision and standards Penalties: • Poor ethical decisions may cause you to be severely reprimanded, terminated, or in some cases could even result in a prison sentence if your unethical behavior was also illegal.

So, I Want to Change
HOW DO I DO IT?

After reading and reflecting thus far, you may have identified several changes that you need to make to be successful. Further, changes may have been thrust upon you by choices you or those around you have made. The model on the following page provides a method for dealing with and implementing change in your life and might be helpful in bringing about positive results.

The Role of Change
IN MOTIVATION, GOAL SETTING, AND SELF-ESTEEM

The transition from one place to another is seldom easy, even when the transition is what you want. Accepting that your life is going to change and working hard to deal with those changes will afford you the opportunity to see your continuing education experience, and indeed your future, with new eyes.

In the past, you may not have associated change with motivation, goal setting, and self-esteem; however, you may find it necessary to change your behaviors and attitudes when it comes to achieving your goals.

The remainder of this chapter will assist you in understanding more about motivation, goal setting, and self-esteem and will give you a blueprint for setting realistic goals and working toward self-motivation.

The Impact of Values
ON MOTIVATION, GOAL SETTING, AND SELF-ESTEEM

If you have been highly motivated to accomplish a goal in the past, this achievement was probably tied to something you valued a great deal. Most of what you do in life centers around what is truly important to you. You cannot get excited about achieving a goal or be disciplined enough to stick to it unless you definitely want to make it happen. If you really want to run a marathon, for example, you have to pay the price of long hours of practice, getting up early in the morning, and running when others are sleeping or playing. If you hate running, but you set a goal to complete a marathon in record time because your father was a champion runner and expects the same of you, you are not likely to achieve this goal. Your goals must relate to your personal value system.

Values, self-esteem, motivation, and goal setting are all mixed up together, making it difficult to separate one from the other. What you try to accomplish is directly connected to those things, ideas, and concepts that you value most. Values are central beliefs and attitudes that make you a unique person, while greatly impacting your choices and your personal lifestyle. If you cherish an attitude or belief, many of your actions will be centered around this ideal.

THE CHANGE IMPLEMENTATION MODEL

Determine what you need or want to change and why.

Research your options for making the desired changes and seek advice and assistance from a variety of sources.

Identify the obstacles to change and determine how to overcome them.

Establish a plan by outlining several positive steps to bring about the changes you identified.

Implement your plan for bringing about the desired change:

- Focus on the desired outcome.
- View problems as positive challenges.
- Turn your fears into energy by reducing anxiety through physical exercise, proper nutrition, and stress-management strategies.
- Associate with positive and motivated people.

The Change Implementation Model: *Example*

Consider the following example, in which you use the Change Implementation Model to bring about positive change in your life.

You entered your Accounting 101 class eager to take the first course in your major field. You were shocked to find that your instructor began lecturing on the first day. Not only was the material difficult to understand, so was the instructor. He clearly knew the world of accounting but was not a good teacher.

The instructor assigned two chapters per session, but the lectures were not based on material found in the text. You tried to study as you had previously done and felt overwhelmed and isolated.

After three weeks and a failed first test, you noticed that the students who passed the test had formed study groups, something that you once thought only the brightest students practiced.

Using the *Change Implementation Model,* you decide to make positive changes in your study habits. Your plans for change are shown in the chart on the following page.

(continued)

1	Determine what you need or want to change and why.	You realize that you must change your study habits or fail the class. Your old study methods are not working.
2	Research your options for making the desired changes and seek advice and assistance from a variety of sources.	You look around campus to determine what services are available to you such as tutoring, learning centers, and learning communities. You also make an appointment to speak with the instructor. You talk to one of the members of a study group in class to see what benefits she is getting from the group.
3	Identify the obstacles to change and determine how to overcome them.	In the past, you have been afraid to get involved. You realize that you have never adjusted your time-management practices to post-secondary life; you are still studying on a "high school time frame." You realize that you have never reached out to classmates before. By listing the problems on paper, you see that you have to change your habits and take a risk by asking to join a study group.
4	Establish a plan by outlining several positive steps to bring about the changes you identified.	You spend a quiet evening thinking about steps that you can take to become a better student. You decide that you need to (1) approach members of the study group to ask permission to join, (2) make an appointment at the tutoring center, and (3) make a commitment to reading the assigned material every night.
5	Implement your plan for bringing about the desired change: • Focus on the desired outcome.	You know that you want and need to pass the class. This is the ultimate desired outcome, but you also know that you must change your study habits for other classes and this group may help you do so. You realize that if you can change your time and study practices, you will be successful in other areas.
	• View problems as positive challenges.	Instead of concentrating on the amount of time and energy required for the study group, you decide to look at it as a way to learn more, study better, and make new friends who have the same goals.
	• Turn your fears into energy by reducing anxiety through physical exercise, proper nutrition, and stress-management strategies.	You learn that two people from the study group also run every other morning. You decide to ask them if you can join them. You also decide that instead of going off campus to the Burger Hut, you will bring your own lunch and use this time to study for other classes.
	• Associate with positive and motivated people.	You notice that your attitude toward the class and life in general is improving because of the positive attitudes in the group. You can't believe how much you have changed in a few short weeks just by concentrating on the positive and associating with people who are motivated to succeed.

The Change Implementation Model: *Activity*

Now, choose one of the major changes you wish to incorporate into your life. Using the Change Implementation Model, devise a strategy to effect this change. Write your steps for implementing change below.

1 What do you need or want to change? Why?

_____

_____

2 Research your options for making the desired changes and seek advice and assistance from a variety of sources. List possible options here.

_____

_____

3 Identify the obstacles to change. How will you overcome them?

_____

_____

4 Establish a plan: Outline several positive steps to bring about the changes you identified.

_____

_____

5 Implement your plan for bringing about the desired change.

a. Focus on the desired outcome. List it here.

_____

_____

b. View problems as positive challenges. Summarize them here.

_____

_____

c. Turn your fears into energy by reducing anxiety through physical exercise, proper nutrition, and stress-management strategies. List your strategies here.

_____

_____

d. Associate with positive and motivated people. Who are they?

_____

_____

You were not born with your basic values. Your values were shaped to a great extent by your parents, the school you attended, the community where you grew up, and the culture that nourished you. Because of your personal background, you have developed a unique set of values. To make good decisions, set appropriate goals, and manage your priorities, you must identify those values that are central to who you are today. Until you clarify what you really value, you may try to accomplish what is important to someone else, and you will tend to wander around and become frustrated. Values, goals, and motivation bring direction to your life and help you get where you want to go.

The Impact of Attitude
ON MOTIVATION, GOAL SETTING, AND SELF-ESTEEM

Have you met people who turned you off immediately with their negative attitudes? They whine about the weather or their jobs, they verbally attack people who differ from them; they degrade themselves with negative remarks. Listen for the negative comments people make, and the messages they send out about themselves. When people continually feed their brains negative messages, their bodies respond accordingly. If you are one of these people, you can change this behavior.

The impact of a bad attitude on your motivation and self-esteem is overpowering, and the importance of a good attitude should not be underestimated. Focusing on the positive can bring dramatic changes in your life.

We all know that life sometimes deals bad blows, but your goal should be to be positive much more often than you are negative. Positive attitudes go hand in hand with energy, motivation, and friendliness. People with positive attitudes are more appealing; negative people drive others away. By continuing your education, you are bringing more positive energy to your life.

Listen to yourself for a few days. Are you whining, complaining, griping, and finding fault with everything and everybody around you, including yourself? Is your bad grade the instructor's fault? Is your family responsible for everything bad that ever happened to you? If these kinds of thoughts are coming out of your mouth or are in your head, your first step toward improved motivation and self-esteem is to develop a positive attitude about yourself and your future.

To be successful at anything, you have to develop a winning attitude. You have to eliminate negative thinking. Begin today: Tell yourself only positive things about yourself; build on those positives; focus on the good things; work constantly to improve. Winners get up early with an attitude of "I can't wait for this day to start so I can have another good day." OK, OK—so you may not get up early, but you can get up with a positive attitude. Tell yourself things that will put you in the right frame of mind to succeed. When you are talking to yourself—and everybody does—feed your brain positive thoughts: "I am going to complete my program and find a great job."

How are the friends you are making in school influencing your decisions?

Overcoming Doubts and Fears

Fear is a great motivator; it probably motivates more people than anything else. Unfortunately, it motivates most people to hold back, to doubt themselves, to accomplish much less than they could, and to hide the person they really are.

One of the biggest obstacles to reaching your potential may be your own personal fears. If you are afraid, you are not alone; everyone has fears. It is interesting to note that our fears are learned. As a baby, you had only two fears: a fear of falling and a fear of loud noises. As you got older, you added to your list of fears. And, if you are like most people, you let your fears dominate parts of your life, saying things to yourself like: "What if I try and fail?" "What if people laugh at me for thinking I can do this?" "What if someone finds out that this is my dream?"

You have two choices where fear is concerned. You can let fear dominate your life, or you can focus on those things you really want to accomplish, put your fears behind you, and go for it. The people most successful in their fields will tell you that they are afraid, but that they overcome their fear because their desire to achieve is greater. Barbra Streisand, recording artist and stage performer, becomes physically nauseated with stage fright when she performs, yet she faces these fears and retains her position as one of the most popular entertainers of our time.

They who have conquered doubt and fear have conquered failure.   —JAMES ALLEN

MOVING OUT OF YOUR COMFORT ZONE

Successful people face their fears because their motivation and ambition force them out of their comfort zones. Your comfort zone is where you know you are good, you feel confident, and you don't have to stretch your talents far to be successful. If you stay in your comfort zone, you will never reach your potential and you will deny yourself the opportunity of knowing how it feels to overcome your fears.

Deciding to continue your education probably caused you some level of discomfort and raised many fears: "What if I flunk out?" "What if I can't do my job, go to school, and manage a family at the same time?" The mere fact that you are here is a step outside your comfort zone—a very important step that can change your life dramatically.

Everyone has a comfort zone. When you are doing something that you do well, and you feel comfortable and confident, you are in your comfort zone. When you are nervous and afraid, you are stepping outside your comfort zone. When you realize you are outside your comfort zone, you should feel good about yourself because you are learning and growing and improving. You cannot progress unless you step outside your comfort zone.

DEALING WITH HARDSHIP AND FAILURE

To be motivated, you have to learn to deal with setbacks. Have you ever given up on something too quickly, or gotten discouraged and quit? Can you think of a time when you were unfair to yourself because you didn't stay with something long enough? Did you ever stop doing something you wanted to do because somebody laughed at you or teased you? Overcoming failure makes victory much more rewarding. Motivated people know that losing is a part of winning: the difference between being a winner and being a loser is the ability to try again. If you reflect on your life, you may well discover that you gained your greatest strengths through hardships. Difficult situations make you tougher and more capable of developing your potential. Overcoming hardships is an essential part of success in school and in life. Think of a time in your life when you faced difficulties but persisted and became stronger as a result. This was one of your "yes I can" moments.

Yes You Can!
IDEAS FOR SUCCESS

Consider the following ideas for dealing with adversity and failure:

- Accept the fact that EVERYONE experiences failure and adversity.

- Make a commitment to yourself that you will not walk away when things get tough.

- Identify the reasons that you have experienced adversity or failure.

- Determine if a certain person or people in your life contributed to this failure.

- Be honest and truthful with yourself and determine what role, if any, you played in bringing about this adversity or failure.

- If you played a role in your own failure, devise a plan or set a goal to eliminate the behavior that caused the problem.

Motivation
WHAT IS IT AND HOW CAN I GET IT?

Quite often you hear people talk about their lack of motivation or you hear someone else referred to as a "motivated person." You might wish you were more motivated, but aren't sure how to get to that point. You see people who are highly self-disciplined and you would like to be more like them, but you don't have a clue how to get started. You've probably heard that old cliché, "A journey of a thousand miles begins with a single step." It may be old and sound a little corny, but actually, it's the truth, and you have already taken the first step.

Becoming motivated is a process—it's not one giant leap to becoming something you want to be. Motivation rarely comes overnight; rather, you become motivated by experiencing one small success after another as your confidence grows, and gradually, you try something bigger and more challenging. There are only two broad categories that will ever motivate you: a **dream** you have or a **problem** you are trying to overcome. Every goal and everything regarding motivation will fit into one of these two categories. Either dreaming of something or wanting to solve a problem is the first part of the formula for motivation. The other part is about making it happen—an action plan. Dreaming or wanting to solve a problem without action will get you nowhere. Nothing works unless you do! Motivation can be broken down into:

Desire + Courage + Goals + Discipline = Motivation

Abraham Lincoln

was raised in great poverty, lost the love of his life when he was 26, suffered a nervous breakdown at age 27, failed in business twice, lost eight elections, and suffered the death of two children . . . all *before* he became our president and changed the face of the world.

In order to stay motivated, you have to become committed to doing something. You need to face your fears and not let them become bigger than your dreams. You need to be willing to write your dream or desire down as a goal and say it out loud to your friends and family. You need to put those goals or commitments somewhere you can see them often in order to keep you on track. You need to take the initiative to get started. You have to be willing to form good habits and replace bad habits. For example, if you are a procrastinator, you have to work hard to change the habit that gets you in trouble over and over and over again. You need to be determined to take responsibility for yourself and your habits. In other words, you need to discipline yourself. If you can keep up a good practice for 21 days, it usually becomes a habit. Tell yourself, "I can do anything for 21 days."

No one can do any of this for you. Motivation comes from within, and you are the only one in control of your personal motivation. The choice to be motivated, to be successful, to reach your potential is up to you. Blaming others, making excuses, using difficult circumstances as a crutch, or quitting will never get you anywhere. If you want to be motivated and successful, *get up and get started*.

When you are sure that you are becoming more disciplined, that your work habits are getting better, your grades are improving, and you are focused on success, reward yourself. Do something that you have really wanted to do for a long time. Share your successes with a few people who really care. Be careful not to boast. If you are good, people will know it. As you grow and become more successful, you will begin to make wiser choices; you will reach bigger goals; you will be on your way to accomplishing your dreams!

Becoming Who You Want to Be
THE GOAL-SETTING PROCESS

Goal setting itself is relatively easy. Many people make goals but fail to make the commitment to accomplish those goals. Instead of defining their goals in concrete, measurable terms, they think of them occasionally and have vague, unclear ideas about how to attain them. The first step toward reaching a goal is the commitment to pay the price to achieve it. Opportunities abound everywhere; commitment is a scarce commodity.

There is only one definition of success . . . to be able to spend your life in your own way.
—CHRISTOPHER MORLEY

All things are possible until they are proved impossible—and even the impossible may only be so, as of now. —PEARL S. BUCK

HOW TO WRITE GOALS

According to Boldt (2001), "It is difficult to act without a clear picture of where you are going." The process of goal setting involves deciding what you want and working to get it. Goals can be short term or long term. Short-term goals can usually be accomplished within six months or a year, although they could be accomplished in a much shorter time. "Within six months, I will save enough money to take my family on a weekend vacation" is a short-term goal; "Within two years, I will become a graphic artist" is a long-term goal.

When you write goals, you need to include a *goal statement, action steps, target dates,* and a *narrative statement.* The *goal statement* should be specific and measurable; that is, it should entail some tangible evidence of its achievement. An example of a goal statement is "I will lose 10 pounds in six weeks." You can make goal statements from intangibles if you can devise a way to measure the desired outcome. For example, "I will develop a more positive attitude by the end of six weeks as evidenced by at least three people commenting on my improved attitude and by my dealing positively with at least three negative situations weekly."

After you write the goal statement, you'll need to create specific *action steps* that explain exactly what you are going to do to reach your goal. Then, decide on a target date for reaching your goal.

The next step is to write a *narrative statement* about what your goal accomplishment will mean to you and how your life will change because of reaching this goal. For example, if your goal is to lose 50 pounds, paint a "verbal picture" of how your life is going to look once this goal has been reached. Your verbal picture may include statements such as: "I'll be able to wear nicer clothes." "I'll feel better." "I'll be able to ride my bicycle again." "My self-esteem will be stronger." If your goals don't offer you significant rewards, you are not likely to stick to your plan. Finally, write down *two reasons why* you deserve this goal. It may seem simple, but this is a complex question. Many people do not follow through on their goals because deep down, they don't feel they deserve them. The narrative statement helps you understand why you deserve this goal.

When you have accomplished your goal, you need to begin the process again. Successful people never get to a target and sit down; they are always becoming. They reach one goal and begin dreaming, planning, preparing for the next accomplishment. Goal setting and follow-through are major components of your personal staying power.

Loving Yourself More
TEN WAYS TO INCREASE YOUR SELF-ESTEEM

If you were asked to name all the areas of your life that are impacted by self-esteem, what would you say? The correct answer is, "Everything. All areas of

Name _____

GOAL STATEMENT _____

_____

ACTION STEPS

1. _____

2. _____

3. _____

4. _____

TARGET DATE _____

NARRATIVE STATEMENT

_____

_____

_____

_____

_____

_____

_____

_____

_____

_____

_____

I DESERVE THIS GOAL BECAUSE:

1. _____

_____

2. _____

_____

I HEREBY MAKE THIS PROMISE TO MYSELF. _____

date _____ signature _____

your life." Self-esteem and self-understanding are two of the most important components of your personal makeup! In other words, you have got to know and love yourself! Did you know that your IQ score might not be as important as knowing your own talents and strengths and having healthy self-esteem? A student can be brilliant in terms of mental ability, but may perform at a very low capacity because of unhealthy self-esteem. Unhealthy self-esteem and a lack of self-understanding are also connected to loneliness and depression. "Self-esteem is the armor that protects kids from the dragons of life: drugs, alcohol, delinquency and unhealthy relationships" (McKay and Fanning, 2000).

- **Take control of your own life.** If you let other people rule your life, you will always have unhealthy self-esteem. You will feel helpless and out of control as long as someone else has power over your life. Part of growing up is taking control of your life and making your own decisions. Get involved in the decisions that shape your life. Seize control—don't let life happen to you!

- **Adopt the idea that you are responsible for you.** The day you take responsibility for yourself and what happens to you is the day you start to develop your self-esteem. When you can admit your mistakes and celebrate your successes knowing you did it your way, you will learn to love yourself much better.

- **Refuse to allow friends and family to tear you down.** You may have family or friends who belittle you, criticize your decisions, and refuse to let you make your own decisions. Combat their negativity by admitting your mistakes and shortcomings to yourself and by making up your mind that you are going to overcome them. By doing this, you are taking their negative power away from them. Spend less time with people who make you feel small and insecure and more time with people who encourage you.

- **Control what you say to yourself.** "Self-talk" is important to your self-esteem and to your ability to motivate yourself positively. Your brain is like a powerful computer and it continually plays messages to you. If these self-talk messages are negative, they will have a detrimental impact on your self-esteem and on your ability to live up to your potential. Make a habit of saying positive things to yourself: "I will do well on this test because I am prepared." "I am a good and decent person, and I deserve to do well." "I will make it through my program, no matter what anyone tells me."

- **Take carefully assessed risks often.** Many people find risk taking very hard to do, but it is one of the very best ways to raise your self-esteem level. If you are going to grow to your fullest potential, you will have to learn to take some calculated risks. While you should never take foolhardy risks that might endanger your life, you must constantly be willing to push yourself out of your comfort zone. Every day, force yourself to take a little step outside your comfort zone.

- **Don't compare yourself to other people.** You may never be able to "beat" some people at certain things. But it really does not matter. You only have to beat yourself to get better. If you constantly tell yourself that you are not "as handsome as Bill" or "as smart as Mary" or "as athletic as Jack," your inner voice will begin to believe these statements, and your body will act accordingly. One of the best ways to improve self-esteem and to accomplish goals is simply to get a little better every day without thinking about what other people are doing. If you are always practicing at improving yourself, sooner or later you will become a person you can admire—and others will admire you, too!

- **Develop a victory wall or victory file.** Many times, you tend to take your accomplishments and hide them in a drawer or closet. Put your certificates, letters of praise, trophies, and awards out where you can see them on a daily basis. Keep a file of great cartoons, letters of support, or friendly cards so that you can refer to them from time to time.

- **Keep your promises and be loyal to friends, family, and yourself.** If you have ever had someone break a promise to you, you know how it feels to have your loyalty betrayed. The most outstanding feature of one's character is one's ability to be loyal, keep one's promises, and do what one has agreed to do. Few things can make you feel better about yourself than being loyal and keeping your word.

- **Win with grace—lose with class.** Everyone loves a winner, but everyone also loves a person who can lose with class and dignity. On the other hand, no one loves a bragging winner or a moaning loser. If you are engaged in culinary competitions, art shows, or other competitions, you will encounter winning and losing. Remember, whether you win or lose, if you're involved and active, you're already in the top 10 percent of the population.

- **Set goals and maintain a high level of motivation.** Find something that you can be passionate about; set a realistic goal to achieve this passion, and stay focused on this goal every day. By maintaining a high level of motivation, you will begin to see your goals come to fruition and feel your self-esteem soar. Setting a goal and achieving it is one of the most powerful ways to develop healthy self-esteem.

The better you become at dealing with change, deciding what you want out of your continuing education experience, setting realistic goals, and forcing yourself out of your comfort zone, the more your self-esteem and indeed your outlook will improve.

Making goal setting a part of your life can help you succeed in school and in the workplace. Very few people actually set goals, write them down, and refer to them on a daily basis. You are guaranteed to see progress in yourself in many areas if you will follow the strategies suggested for motivation and goal setting in this chapter.

Now is the time for you to seek new truths, associate with new and different people, read books that you will never have time to hold in your hands again, develop a solid philosophy of life, explore new religions and cultures, go to plays, take your family to the park or out to dinner, laugh, cry, write to friends, and love much. The winds of change are coming—*FLY!*

what's it ALL ABOUT?

In the space below, pretend that you have to write an advertisement for yourself to appear in a newspaper. This advertisement will feature all of your positive qualities and outstanding characteristics. Think about all of the good and positive things that you have to offer to others and your community.

_____

_____

_____

_____

_____

_____

_____

_____

_____

_____

_____

_____

_____

_____

_____

_____

_____

_____

_____

_____

_____

_____

_____

_____

NAME: Sonia Armfield

SCHOOL: The Art Institute of Las Vegas, Las Vegas, NV

MAJOR: Graphic Design   AGE: 35

Below is a real-life situation faced by Sonia. Read the brief case and respond to the questions.

I moved to the United States from Colombia almost eight years ago. No one could have ever told me about the massive changes that were about to come my way. I never thought that locating to a different country and a different culture would be easy, but I never expected that my entire world would change.

In Colombia, I received a bachelor's degree in Journalism from a university. After graduation, I began to work as a reporter for a TV station. I met an American in Colombia and he asked me to marry him, so I decided to change locations and come to America. I had heard of many wonderful opportunities in the United States and thought that my education and training would help me.

Upon entering the United States, I had to learn an entirely new language, I had to learn how to drive, I had to learn a new currency, and I had to learn how to live in a new culture. Change was all around me and all that I could think was what a terrible mistake I had made.

I searched the city for employment. To my surprise, there were no Spanish networks in the city. I could not find any employment that would utilize my skills. Even though I held a degree in Journalism, I could only get offers to become a housekeeper in one of the hotels. One look at me and upon hearing my dialect, everyone immediately assumed that I was unskilled.

At this point in my life, the changes from Colombia to America were enormous. I was so upset, frightened, and unsure that I cried every day. I knew that I had the qualifications and personality to make a difference, but no one would give me the opportunity.

A friend advised me to take a job as a housekeeper to get my foot in the door at one of the hotels. After a few months there, I posted for another position in another department. I was able to move out of housekeeping and into another job. After a few years, my life began to change for the better. We had a son, and I began my new education in graphic design at the Art Institute.

The changes that happened to me from one country to another were huge, but I now know that with persistence, courage, and determination, change in a person's life can actually help him or her become a better individual. Change became my friend.

What is the most major change in your life and how did it affect your life and emotions?

_____

_____

What is the very best change that has ever happened to you? Why? How did this affect your life?

_____

_____

If Sonia had been enrolled in your school, where could she have gone on campus to find help or to talk to someone about all of the changes in her life?

_____

_____

_____ Phone # _____

How can adversity and discrimination affect your life in a *positive* way?

_____

_____

_____

If you were to face the major roadblocks that Sonia faced, to whom could you turn in your life for help? Why?

_____

_____

What changes do you think that you are going to have to personally make in your life to assure your success?

_____

_____

_____

_____

ADVICE TO GO
CORNERSTONES

Get *involved* and direct the changes in your life.

Keep a sense of *humor* and *joy*.

Use the power of *positive thinking*.

Work hard to step *outside* your comfort zone.

Base your goals on what you *value*.

Focus on the *positive* aspects of change and growth.

Talk to family and friends.

Don't give in to adversity or defeat.

Be *courageous* and *objective*.

Believe in yourself.

CHANGE

2

Persist

onda was beyond excited. She had waited for this day for 15 years. Today was the day that she had set aside to visit New England Technical Institute and tie up all of the loose ends that might hinder her from being successful in her first quarter of training as a legal assistant.

Vonda had begun college 15 years ago, but dropped out to marry her high school sweetheart. Shortly after their marriage, she found herself pregnant with their first child. When Ben was only one and a half, she found herself pregnant with Jannyce. For the past 14 years, Vonda had been a mother, a wife, a daughter, a clerk at the grocery store, and a dreamer.

She dreamed of working in a law office, but her dreams were put on hold while her husband completed his engineering degree and they raised Ben and Jannyce. *But she never let go of the dream that one day she would have a career in which she helped people.*

Today was that day. Vonda had received her acceptance letter to NETI last week. Her dream was really going to happen. Ben and Jannyce had started high school, her husband was behind her, she had given notice at the grocery store, and finally, the dream was no longer deferred.

Vonda drove to NETI with more excitement than she had felt in years. If the truth was known, more excitement than she had ever felt, with the exception of having her children. Her plans for the day were to attend the early morning orientation session, drop by financial aid to apply for a work-study position, meet her program advisor, pick up her schedule and books, find her classrooms, and have lunch in the canteen. *She just wanted things to go smoothly.*

> **Vonda never let go of the dream that one day she would have a career in which she helped people.**

When Vonda turned onto the main drive of NETI, she was stunned to see so many people. *Stunned!* She had arrived almost an hour early, but the student parking lot was beyond full. She drove to the back of the building only to find that lot full as well. She circled for a while and finally decided to park down the road in an overflow lot. By the time she parked and walked back to the institute, she only had five minutes before orientation started.

She ran to the auditorium, checked in, received her packet, and  entered to find that there was standing room only, and not much of that. Shortly after she entered, the session began. The students were welcomed and for the next hour, person after person stood before them talking about policies, financial aid, parking, academic success, and student responsibilities. Vonda thought that her head would explode with so much new information. *But she was elated to be in this atmosphere of learning and growing.*

After the session was over and she had located her program advisor, Vonda decided to have lunch before going to the financial aid office. She found the canteen, purchased her lunch, and decided to sit at an outside table to soak in the environment. *"I'm here,"* she thought. She was ready to scream with joy.

Sitting there on that concrete bench, Vonda knew that things were not going to be easy. "I couldn't even park," she laughed to herself. "But *nothing is going to stop me now."* She watched other students moving about, talking, laughing—some walking alone, others with rolling suitcases full of books and fliers and dreams.

As she sat there, her mind wandered. "Fifteen long years I've waited. I don't know what is down the road, but I'm ready to take the drive. I'm ready to jump any hurdle that is in front of me." She finished her lunch, looked around at everyone, and in her mind, she knew that she was home.

QUESTIONS FOR REFLECTION

Consider responding to these questions online in the Questions for Reflection module of the Companion Website.

1. Have you ever put a dream on hold? How did this affect your life?

2. Vonda was shocked over the parking situation. What is the biggest shock you've had since beginning your program?

3. Do you feel "at home" at your institution like Vonda does? Why or why not?

Before reading this chapter, take a moment and respond to the following 10 questions. Consider each one carefully before answering, and then respond by circling the number in the appropriate box. When you have answered the questions, add your points and find your total score on the feedback chart below.

STATEMENT	STRONGLY DISAGREE	DISAGREE	DON'T KNOW	AGREE	STRONGLY AGREE	SCORE
1. I have read and understand my school's catalog.	1	2	3	4	5	
2. I am uncomfortable talking with instructors.	5	4	3	2	1	
3. When I need help with my studies, I don't really know where to go to get that help.	5	4	3	2	1	
4. I do not enjoy participating in class discussions.	5	4	3	2	1	
5. I know what my instructors' office hours are, and how to contact them.	1	2	3	4	5	
6. If I must stop attending a course, I know what actions I should take.	1	2	3	4	5	
7. I have spoken with an academic advisor or counselor more than once.	1	2	3	4	5	
8. I know what it means to be prepared to attend class.	1	2	3	4	5	
9. I do not know how the courses I intend to take will or will not help me in the future.	5	4	3	2	1	
10. I have investigated my options for financial aid, scholarships, grants, and loans.	1	2	3	4	5	
TOTAL VALUE						

SUMMARY

43–50 You are exceptional in your knowledge of your school's support services and relate well with your instructors. When you need assistance, you're not afraid to seek it out and use it to your maximum benefit.

35–42 You likely have an above average knowledge of how your school operates and how to get assistance when you need it. Continue to access the people and services at your school for ongoing guidance and success.

26–34 You are average in your knowledge of what it takes to successfully stay in school. You likely have had successful school experiences, but some additional guidance and knowledge about your school's policies would benefit you.

18–25 Your level of preparedness for continuing education is limited; additional skills for successfully staying in school are needed. Make connections with your teachers and academic advisors and listen carefully to their suggestions.

10–17 You seem to be lacking many of the skills and strategies necessary to successfully stay in school. You need to pay careful attention to the ideas and exercises you will encounter in this course, as well as visit your school's academic counseling department for additional guidance.

Based on the summary above, what is one goal you would like to achieve related to persisting in school?

Goal _____

_____

_____

List three actions you can take that might help you move closer to realizing this goal.

1. _____

2. _____

3. _____

Questions
FOR BUILDING ON YOUR BEST

As you read this chapter, consider the following questions. At the end of the chapter, you should be able to answer all of them. You are encouraged to ask a few questions of your own. Consider asking your classmates or instructors to assist you.

1. How can I establish a positive relationship with my instructors?

2. Where can I go at school if I need some serious academic help?

3. What do drugs have to do with financial aid?

4. Where can I go to learn more about financial aid and scholarships?

5. Why is it important to get involved and where can I go to find more information about student chapters of professional organizations?

What additional questions might you have about the nuts and bolts of persisting in school?

1. _____

2. _____

3. _____

To Be Successful, You Have to Last

PERSISTENCE IN CONTINUING EDUCATION

Have you ever given up on something in the past and regretted it later? Do you ever think back and ask yourself, **"What would my life be like if only I had done X or Y?"** Have you ever made a decision or acted in a way that cost you dearly? If you see yourself in any of these statements, then you now know the value of persistence.

Persistence. The word itself means that you are going to stay—that you have found a way to stick it out, found a way to make it count, and found a way *to not give up*. That is what this chapter is all about—finding out how to make career college work for you. It is about giving you advice up front that can save your education and your future dreams. It is about helping you "make it."

Dropping out of school is not uncommon. As a matter of fact, over 40 percent of the people who begin their continuing education never complete their programs. Don't be mistaken in thinking that they dropped out because of their inability to learn. Many leave because they made serious and irreparable mistakes early.

Before everything else, **getting ready** is the secret to success. —HENRY FORD

Some students leave because they did not know how to manage their time. Some leave because they could not manage their money and didn't know how to look for other funding sources. Some leave because they couldn't get along with an instructor. And still, some leave because they simply could not figure out how "the system" worked, and frustration, anger, disappointment, and fear got the better of them. **You do not have to be one of these students.** This chapter and *indeed this book* are geared to help you NOT make those mistakes. They are geared to help you make the decisions that will lead to successful completion of your course.

What You Need to Know Up Front

POLICIES AND PROCEDURES OF YOUR INSTITUTION

Familiarizing yourself with the policies and procedures of your institution can save you a great deal of grief and frustration in the long run. Policies and procedures vary from institution to institution, but regardless, it is your responsibility to know what you can expect from your institution and what your institution expects from you. These policies can be found in the school catalog (traditional and online) or student handbook or schedule of classes, depending on your institution.

Some universal policies include:

- Most institutions adhere to a strict drop/add date. Always check your schedule of classes for this information.
- Most institutions have an attendance policy for classroom instruction (also lab and clinical).
- Most institutions have a strict refund policy.
- Most institutions have an Academic Dishonesty Policy.
- Most institutions have a standing drug and alcohol policy.
- Institutions do not put policies into place to hinder your degree/certificate completion; rather, the purpose is to ensure that all students are treated fairly and equitably.

F? WHAT DO YOU MEAN AN F?

There will be times when you are disappointed with a grade that you receive from an instructor. What do you do? Threaten? Sue? Become argumentative? Those techniques usually cost you more than they gain for you.

First, remember that the grade you earn from an instructor is seldom changeable. If you made a less than sterling grade, there are several things that you need to do. First, be truthful with yourself and examine the amount of time you spent on the project. Did you really give it your best? Next, review the requirements for the assignment. Did you miss something? Did you take an improper or completely wrong focus? Did you omit some aspect of the project? Did you turn the project in late?

Next, consider the following questions, as they can contribute to your total understanding of material, projects, and expectations.

- Did you attend class regularly?
- Did you come to class prepared and ready for discussion?
- Did you ask questions in class for clarification?
- Did you meet with the instructor during office hours?
- Did you seek outside assistance in places such as the writing center or math lab?
- Did you ask your peers for assistance or join a peer study/focus group?

These activities can make the difference between success and failure with a project or a class.

If you are truly concerned about the grade, talk to the instructor about the assignment. Ask him or her what is considered to be the most apparent problem with your assignment, and ask how you might improve your studying or preparing for the *next* assignment.

Above all, don't get into a verbal argument over the grade. In 99 percent of the cases, this will not help. Also, make sure that *the instructor is your first point of contact*. Unless you have spoken with him or her *first* and exhausted all options with him or her, approaching the department chair, the dean, the vice president, or the president will more than likely result in your being sent directly back to your instructor.

CLASSROOM CHALLENGES

When instructors don't speak English well. Yes, you will have instructors who do not speak English well. Institutions often hire instructors from around the world because of their expertise in their subjects. You may be shocked to find that it is difficult to understand an instructor's dialect or pronunciation. If you have an instructor with a foreign accent, remember these hints:

- Sit near the front of the room.
- Watch the instructor's mouth when you can.
- Follow the instructor's nonverbal communication patterns.
- Use a tape recorder if allowed.
- Read the material beforehand so that you will have a general understanding of what is being discussed.
- Ask questions when you do not understand the material.

Large lecture classes often have a lab component, also, in which instruction is much more focused.

Understanding what instructors want. Instructors are unique. They all value and appreciate different things. What makes one instructor the happiest person on earth will upset another. One instructor may love students who ask questions and another instructor will think these students are trying to be difficult. One instructor may enjoy students who have opposing points of view, while the next instructor may consider them troublemakers. One instructor may be stimulated when students stop by the office to chat, while another may consider this an infringement on his or her time.

The best way to deal with your instructors is as individuals, on a one-to-one, class-by-class basis. Take some time at the beginning of the semester to make notes about what you see in class, how students are treated who do certain things, and how the instructor reacts in certain situations. This exercise will assist you in decoding your instructors and in making the most out of your relationship with them.

There are, of course, certain characteristics that all instructors cherish in students, so

Yes You Can!
TIPS FOR SUCCESS

Consider the following tips for making the most of your relationships with your instructors:

- Make an effort to get to know your instructor outside the classroom if possible.
- Come to class prepared, bringing your best to the table each class session.
- Answer questions and ASK questions in class.
- Ask for help if you see things getting difficult.
- Never make excuses; talk and act like an adult.
- Volunteer for projects and co-curricular opportunities.
- Be respectful, and it will most likely be returned.

keep in mind that all instructors like students who read the text, come to class and come on time, and hand in assignments on time.

The Golden Rule—or Just a Crock?

CLASSROOM ETIQUETTE AND PERSONAL DECORUM

You may be surprised, but the way you act in (and out of) class can mean as much to your success as what you know. No one can make you do anything or act in any way that you do not want. The following tips are provided from years of research and actual conversations with thousands of instructors teaching across the United States. You have to be the one who chooses whether to use this advice.

- Bring your materials to class daily: texts, notebooks, pens, calculators, and syllabi.

- Come to class prepared: read your text and handouts, do the assigned work at home, bring questions to be discussed.

- Turn in papers, projects, and assignments on time. Many instructors do not accept late work.

- Participate in class. Ask questions, bring current events to the discussion, and contribute with personal experiences.

- Ask your instructor about the best time to come in for help. The time before and after class may not be the most appropriate time. Your instructor may have "back-to-back" classes and may be unable to assist you.

- If you are late for class, enter quietly, DO NOT walk in front of the instructor, don't let the door slam, don't talk on your way in, and take the seat nearest the door. Make every effort not to be late to class.

- Wait for the instructor to dismiss class before you begin to pack your bags to leave. You may miss important information or you may cause someone else to miss important information.

- Never carry on a conversation with another student while the instructor or another student is talking.

- Do not sleep in class.

- If for any reason you must leave during class, do so quietly and quickly. It is customary to inform the instructor that you will be leaving early before class begins.

- If you make an appointment with an instructor, keep it. If you must cancel, a courtesy call is in order.

- If you don't know how to address your instructor, that is, by Mr., Mrs., Miss, Ms., or Dr., ask them which they prefer.

- You should not wear sunglasses, oversized hats, strong cologne or perfume, skates, or earphones to class.

- Be respectful of other students. Treat diversity with dignity and respect.

- Mind your manners. Profanity and obscene language may offend some people. You can have strong, conflicting views without being offensive.

- Turn off your cell phone or beeper. If you have a home or work situation that requires that you "stay connected," put the device on vibrate.

- Remember that respect for others on your part will afford you the opportunity to establish relationships that otherwise you might never have had.

- Call your instructor or program to notify them if you are going to be late or absent. Remember this is your job and you need to be accountable.

- Come dressed in uniform (per dress code). Dress for success! Most schools have some type of dress code for classes.

Where Is It Written?
YOUR INSTITUTION'S CATALOG

Every institution has a different catalog. Don't make the mistake of thinking that these catalogs are advertising tools and not that important. Your institution's catalog is one of the most important publications you will read during your education. It describes the rules, regulations, policies, procedures, and requirements of the institution and your program. It is imperative for you to keep the catalog that was issued when you begin because program requirements can sometimes change. Most institutions require that you graduate under the rules and requirements stated in the catalog under which you entered. This policy is sometimes referred to as the grandfather clause.

The catalog includes information about adding and dropping classes, probation, plagiarism, attendance, course descriptions, program requirements, faculty credentials, and school accreditation. It is an important tool.

Pennies from Heaven
THE SECRET WORLD OF FINANCIAL AID

You may feel that it is crazy to talk about financial aid at this point. After all, you had to have found the money to enroll or you would not be reading this. Still, financial aid comes in many forms, and there may be some sources of aid you have not yet thought about that can help you through the rest of your continuing education. The most well-known sources of financial assistance are the federal and state governments. Federal and state financial aid programs have

WORLD OF WORK

As a nursing student, there was a single incident that occurred that might have thrown me off course, but I refused to give in to another person's will for me. I was in my third semester of the RN program when one of my instructors called me into her office and asked the reasons why I wanted to pursue nursing. I told her that I was already an LPN (licensed practical nurse) and wanted to continue my education and become an RN. I felt that I was good at it! I believed that I possessed the important qualities that were required, such as compassion, caring, and true empathy for my patients. I knew that I was young (only 19 at the time), but I was also driven to complete the program no matter what. She said that I didn't have what it takes academically or technically. She told me that I should drop out of the program and find some other profession. The instructor continued to tell me that I would never pass the licensing exam, so why prolong my inevitable failure by continuing? She was very negative in her attitude toward me.

At that time in my life I was devastated and actually considered giving up and dropping out. I was a C student and often required tutoring to pass a course. I studied really hard, never missed class, read the book, and took notes. However, my study skills were less than adequate, which made the program even more difficult. I passed up the parties and focused on my goal; I wasn't going to fail. I think I stayed motivated mainly due to the positive people in my life. Their encouragement and support helped me to stay focused on my goal! I constantly tried to surround myself with positive influences. I passed the program and graduated with an Associate of Science in Nursing. I also passed the RN licensing exam on the very first try!

I tell you this personal story to say, "Keep your goals foremost in your mind!" I often ask myself what I want from the situation or experience. What will be the end result? What am I willing to do to achieve it? I am a great list maker and oftentimes will write down my goal and the current path I need to take to get there. I have even posted it around the house, bathroom, or office so that I don't lose sight of what I want or where I am going. I think fear was perhaps the biggest obstacle for me. What would I do if I failed? What would people think of me? Do I really deserve this? To counter these negative or fearful thoughts, I often asked myself, "What would you do if you were not afraid?" By removing the fear, the true goal emerges and you are able to see that it is attainable and you deserve to succeed. Another strategy that I use is time management. I schedule everything! I take my books and materials everywhere with me and use every minute of the day to my advantage, wasting none of it. It is important to remember to schedule some fun and relaxation in there, too.

I constantly have used the strategies that I developed as a student in the workplace, and even have developed new ones. I have never stopped learning and growing! I tried to learn everything I could at a job and seemed to always be promoted for my efforts. I took a job as a nursing director for a large multispecialty outpatient clinic, and at the age of 38 was informed that in order to keep my job, I needed a baccalaureate degree. So, with grave doubts as to my ability (remember, I was never a great student) and a lot of fear, I went back to school. By this time in my life I had a husband and two children. Life got very chaotic and hard, but I never gave up, and two years later I received a B.A. in Health Service Administration.

There were many times after a 10-hour workday that I didn't want to go to class or write one of the many papers that were due. Believing in myself, taking fear out of the equation, and keeping the end result in front of me helped to keep me motivated. I am the only one of my siblings to ever receive a degree of any kind, and I think that my persistence is what prompted my son to pursue his dream of attending Cal Poly (his is a mechanical engineering major).

When the clinic closed four months after receiving my degree and I was laid off, I knew it was time to do something different. I was excited to have the whole world open to me! My persistence in getting my degree would open doors that previously would have been closed. I obtained a position as the director of a vocational nursing program, and now at the age of 43, I am working on a master's degree in Educational Management.

If I could impart one piece of advice, it would be, "Believe in yourself and believe in your goal." Never give up. Never let other people tell you that you cannot achieve it. Had I listened to that person so long ago, where would I be? How my life would have been different! Sometimes life takes over and we end up postponing our goals for a while, but we must never let them go. If you truly want to achieve something and you put your heart and soul into it, you will succeed.

The following quote by Robert F. Kennedy has helped me stay positive and focused over the years:

"There are those who look at things the way they are, and ask why . . . I dream of things that never were, and ask why not?"

 **QUESTIONS** FOR REFLECTION

Consider responding to these questions online in the World of Work module of the Companion Website.

1. Compare your level of motivation and persistence to that of Darlla Roesler.

2. Discuss one time in your life when you persisted against all odds and won.

3. How can you use Ms. Roesler's story to help you increase your "staying power" in school?

Darlla Roesler, Program Director, Vocational Nursing, Western Career College, Sacramento, CA

been in place for many years and are a staple of assistance for many students. Sources of aid include:

Federal and state loans

Federal and state grants

Scholarships (local, regional, and national)

Work study (if your institution participates in this program)

Not every school takes part in every federal assistance program. To determine which type of aid is available at your school, you need to contact the financial aid office. Some students may be confused about the differences among loans, grants, and work-study programs. The following definitions are supplied by *The Student Guide,* published by the U.S. Department of Education:

- Grants—Monies that you don't have to repay
- Work Study—Money earned for work that you do at the institution that does not have to be repaid
- Loans—Borrowed money that you must repay with interest

One of the biggest mistakes students make when thinking about financial aid is forgetting about scholarships from private industry and social or civic organizations. Each year, millions of dollars are unclaimed because students do not know about these scholarships or where to find the necessary information. Below, you will find resources that can help you research and apply for all types of financial aid.

When planning for an education, students should include the hidden cost of such things as tuition, books, and supplies in their spending budget. These costs are usually to be expected. What is often overlooked are the hidden expenses of continuing education. These hidden expenses include such things as eating out, trips to the hairdresser, phone bills, toiletries, and money spent on recreational activities. The amount of money each student spends per week varies greatly depending upon the student's interests and habits as well as the cost of living if the school is not located in the local area.

Establishing a realistic monthly budget is essential to financial health. Beware of offers too good to be true. Avoid the temptation to use credit cards to purchase items you are unable to afford right now. And, become a wise consumer in selecting financial institutions.

FEDERAL FINANCIAL AID TYPES

All accredited schools can participate in the following financial aid programs. Again, check with your financial aid office for details and forms.

Pell Grant.   This is a need-based grant awarded to qualified undergraduate students who have not been awarded a previous degree. Amounts vary based on need and costs.

Federal Supplemental Educational Opportunity Grant (FSEOG).   This is a need-based grant awarded to institutions to allocate to students through their financial aid offices.

Stafford Loan   (formerly known as the Guaranteed Student Loan).   The Stafford Direct Loan Program is a low-interest, subsidized loan. You must show need to qualify. The government pays the interest while you are in school, but you must be registered for at least half-time status. You begin repayments six months after you leave school.

Unsubsidized Stafford Loan.   This Stafford Loan is a low-interest, NON-subsidized loan. You DO NOT have to show need to qualify. You are responsible for the interest on the loan while you are enrolled. Even though the government does not pay the interest, you can defer the interest and the payments until six months after you have left school.

PLUS Loan.   This is a federally funded, but state-administered, low-interest loan to qualified parents of students in school. The student must be enrolled at least half-time. Parents must pass a credit check and payments begin 60 days after the last loan payment.

Work Study.   Work study is a federally funded, need-based program that pays students an hourly wage for working on (and sometimes off) campus. Students earn at least minimum wage.

Hope Scholarship Tax Credit.   This tax credit is for students in their first two years of school and who are enrolled at least half-time in a degree or certificate program. For each student, taxpayers may receive a 100 percent tax credit for each year for the first $1,000.00 of qualified out-of-pocket expenses. They also may claim a 50 percent credit on the second $1,000.00 used for qualified expenses.

Perkins Loan. This is a need-based loan where the amount of money you can borrow is determined by the government and the availability of funds. The interest rate is 5 percent and repayment begins nine months after you leave school or drop below half-time status. You can take up to 10 years to repay the loan.

There are three ingredients in the good life: learning, earning, and yearning. —CHRISTOPHER MORELY

TIPS FOR APPLYING FOR FINANCIAL AID

- Do not miss a deadline. There are *no* exceptions for making up deadlines for federal financial aid!
- *Read all instructions* before beginning the process.
- Always fill out the application completely and have someone proof your work.
- If documentation is required, submit it according to the instructions. Do not fail to do all that the application asks you to do.
- Never lie about your financial status.
- Begin the application process as soon as possible. Do not wait until the last moment. Some aid is given on a first-come, first-served basis. Income tax preparation time is usually financial aid application time.
- Talk to the financial aid officer at the institution you will attend. Person-to-person contact is always best. Never assume anything until you get it in writing.

Research all possible avenues of financial aid.

LOANS

The majority of today's students who receive some type of financial assistance receive it in the form of a student loan. Unfortunately, not all students understand the ramifications of financing education with the assistance of student loans.

Student loans are a type of student aid that must be repaid. There are very few ways to avoid repaying this type of debt. It cannot be forgiven in bankruptcy proceedings. And, it does appear on credit history reports.

A knowledgeable consumer investigates fully all alternatives to borrowing money for continuing education before accepting a loan. When you have to utilize a student loan to finance your education, it is best to research each lender and their policies regarding student loans. Some lending institutions routinely sell student loan accounts to other account administrators. Others will permit you to consolidate several years' worth of loans into one so that you only have one payment. As students become more savvy student loan consumers, the competition for student loan customers among financial institutions has increased. With this healthy competition, it pays to shop around for the best interest rates and repayment agreements. It also pays to know all the terms of your account and to manage your loans wisely.

Because a student loan is a long-term commitment, they should be taken out by students only after they have exhausted every other possible form of financial aid, such as scholarships or grants. The reason for this is that a student loan must be paid back and more often than not, you will have to pay for interest accumulated on these loans. Interest is the "price" of money. When you take out a loan, you have to pay to borrow that money.

OTHER SOURCES OF FINANCIAL AID

You should attempt to locate and secure as many possible forms of free aid as you can. Free aid is aid that does not require payments from you in the future. These financial aid sources can include grants, scholarships, and work-study. Although some of these sources of financial aid require additional work on your part, they are well worth the effort.

Most students can take advantage of grants or scholarships offered by the federal government or their school. Most scholarships are provided by private organizations, so it will be crucial to look into this type of aid early in the financial aid process as many of the private organizations establish very early deadlines.

If you currently hold a job, perhaps your employer has a tuition assistance program that could contribute to your education. Many students who excel in their field of study are eligible for work related Co-op positions. Private or government employers outside of the school environment offer Co-op positions. Co-op positions may enable a student to earn extra money for working in their field of study outside of the normal school environment.

DECIDING HOW MUCH TO BORROW

When you have considered all other financial aid alternatives and still find yourself a little short on funds to pay for school, a student loan is a reasonable alternative. Now the question is, "How much do I need to borrow?" The key to borrowing is to *limit* your borrowing.

Limiting your borrowing is extremely crucial since you will eventually have to repay the loan amount in full plus any interest accumulated on the loans . . . this interest adds up quickly! How can you limit your borrowing? First you should consider the actual costs of continuing education. Making a budget is extremely valuable in determining your needs as a student. A budget will allow you to see on paper where you will spend your money.

ESTIMATING YOUR INCOME AND REPAYMENT

Although it is difficult to determine your future salary, your school's career services office should have data or information about what you can expect to earn in the future based on your field of study.

Estimating your future income allows you to determine how much you can afford to spend in paying back student loans. Although many student loan repayment options exist today, you can still estimate your student loans payments based on your total amount of loans, your current interest rate, and how long you want to pay back the loans.

Monthly payments between 8 percent and 10 percent of your future earnings are considered average payments for student loan debt. Monthly payments above 10 percent approach what is considered to be high.

DRUGS AND MONEY

What do drugs and money have in common? More than you might think! Did you know that when applying for federal financial aid, you must complete a drug conviction worksheet? This worksheet will be used to determine if you can receive ANY type of federal aid. Be warned!

The questions on the worksheet include:

- Have you ever been convicted of selling or possessing drugs?
- Have you completed an acceptable drug rehab program since your last conviction?
- Do you have more than two convictions for possessing drugs?
- Do you have more than one conviction for selling drugs?

DID YOU KNOW?

Katie Couric

was fired from CNN. The president of the network said that he never wanted to see her on TV again. Now, she anchors NBC's *Today* show and makes a reported $15 million a year.

Won't You Stay for a While?

PERSISTING IN SCHOOL

The age-old "scare tactic" for first-time students, "Look to your left, look to your right—one of those people will not graduate with you," is not far from the truth. But the good news (actually, the great news) is that you do not have to become a statistic. You do not have to drop out of classes. You have the power to get through your program. Sure, you may have some catching up to do. You may have to work harder and longer, but the beauty of continuing education is that if you want help, you can get help.

Below, you will find some powerful, helpful tips for persisting in school. Using only a few of them can increase your chances of graduating. Using all of them virtually assures it!

- **Visit your advisor or counselor** frequently and establish a relationship with him or her. Take his or her advice. Ask him or her questions. Use him or her as a mentor.

- **Make use of every academic service** that you need that the institution offers, from tutoring sessions to writing centers; these are essential tools to your success.

- **Work hard to learn and understand your "learning style."** This can help you in every class in which you enroll.

- **Work hard to develop a sense of community**. Get to know a few fellow students or a special faculty member, a secretary, or anyone to whom you can turn for help.

> *Striving for success without hard work is like trying to harvest where you have not planted.* —DAVID BLY

- **Join a club or an organization**. Research proves that students who are connected to school through activities drop out less often.

- **Watch your finances carefully**. Don't get "credit-carditis." If you see yourself getting into financial trouble, seek counseling immediately! Poor financial management can cost you success as quickly as failing classes.

- Concentrate on setting realistic, achievable goals. **Visualize your goals**. Write them down. Find a picture that represents your goal and post it so that you can see your goal every day.

- Work hard to develop and **maintain a sense of self-esteem and self-respect**. The better you feel about yourself, the more likely you will reach your goals.

- **Learn to budget your time** as wisely as you budget your money. You've made a commitment to continuing education and it will take a commitment of time to bring your dream to fruition.

- If you have trouble with an instructor, don't let it fester. Make an appointment to **speak with the instructor** and work through the problem.

- If you get bored in class or feel that the class is not going to benefit you, remember that it is a required class and **you will always have a few boring classes** during your school experience. Stick to it and it will be over soon.

- **Attend classes regularly**—if you're not there, you can't learn and will quickly fall behind.

- Seek help with academic issues **early on in the term**, when they first arise. Don't wait until the end of term to try and turn around poor grades.

Continuing your education can be hard and trying, especially if you have been out of school for a while. There has never been a time when the old saying "knowledge is power" is more true. The more you know and understand about your institution, the less likely you will make mistakes that can cost you time, emotional distress, money . . . and your degree or certificate.

When you go to purchase a car, you spend time researching and considering. You want to make sure that you know as much as you can before you "take the leap." You should approach your education with the same type of understanding.

By simply taking the time to familiarize yourself with the workings of your institution, you can eliminate many of the hassles that students face. By doing this, you can enjoy your experience with more energy, excitement, and optimism. Good luck.

what's it ALL ABOUT?

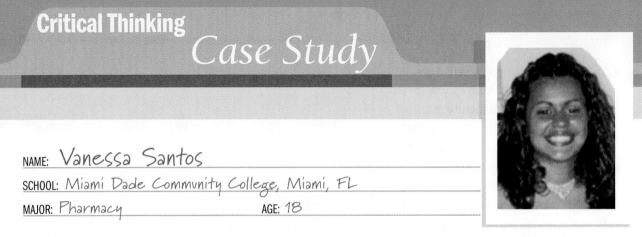

NAME: Vanessa Santos

SCHOOL: Miami Dade Community College, Miami, FL

MAJOR: Pharmacy   AGE: 18

Below is a real-life situation faced by Vanessa. Read the brief case and respond to the questions.

The first two weeks of school were really bad for me. I wasn't actually prepared for the first day of classes. As a matter of fact, my mother had scheduled the "family vacation" on the weekend before classes started. I was not prepared or focused, and I missed the first week of classes. This set me apart from other students in my classes.

The first day that I did go to classes, I was so lost that I left. I went home and asked my mom to come with me to help me find my classes and get my books and supplies. She agreed to help me.

I also work full-time until six o'clock in the evening. This is really tough for me. I scheduled my classes for evenings and Saturdays, but I found that many things I need are closed on Saturday or when I get to the campus after six thirty. I was not able to get my ID card, which I needed for the library and to take my midterm exams. I did not get off to a great start.

What was Vanessa's first mistake?

_____

_____

Where could she have turned for help at your institution?

_____

_____

_____

Why is preparation for your educational experience necessary to your success?

_____

_____

_____

How can your work schedule affect your performance?

_____

_____

_____

If you hold a job, how can you make sure you have the correct balance to succeed at both work and school?

_____

_____

_____

_____

What advice would you give to an entering student from your experience dealing with the first weeks of classes?

_____

_____

_____

_____

What preparation did you make for your educational experience that really helped you in your first few weeks? What do you wish you had done differently to prepare yourself?

_____

_____

_____

_____

ADVICE TO GO

CORNERSTONES

for persisting in school

Concentrate on your future.

Use *personal decorum* in and out of the classroom.

Establish a *relationship* with your instructors.

Speak with your *advisor or counselor* frequently.

Know the *rules and policies* of your institution.

Seek *academic assistance* when needed.

Join a *career club* and get involved.

Apply for *financial aid* early and often.

Make use of *student services*.

Keep a *journal* of your experiences.

PERSIST

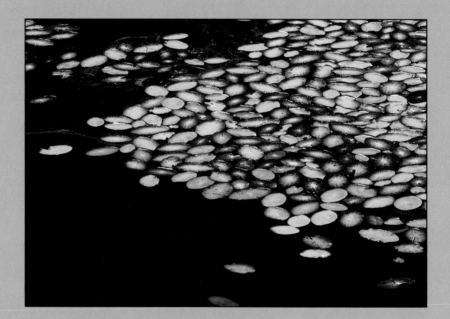

This chapter offers some pointers for getting things accomplished. Some of them will work for you and some of them won't, but when you have finished the chapter, *you should have a better handle on how to get the job done and still have time for family and friends.*

If you can't follow a schedule as rigid as Yolandra's, that's fine. Design a schedule you can follow. You might have heard the old saying, *"All work and no play makes Jack a dull boy."* This statement is true, but so is *"All play and no work will make Jack flunk out of school."* The trick is to find a happy medium.

f you really want to know what you value, look at your calendar and your check book.

—HERB KELLEHER

QUESTIONS
FOR REFLECTION

Consider responding to these questions online in the Questions for Reflection module of the Companion Website.

1. Would any of Yolandra's time-management techniques work for you? Why or why not?

2. How could you alter your current habits to maximize the use of your time?

3. Yolandra rewarded herself after she completed her assignments. What two rewards can you think of to give yourself after you have completed your assigned work for classes?

Before reading this chapter, take a moment and respond to the following 10 questions. Consider each one carefully before answering, and then respond by circling the number in the appropriate box. When you have answered the questions, add your points and find your total score on the feedback chart below.

STATEMENT	STRONGLY DISAGREE	DISAGREE	DON'T KNOW	AGREE	STRONGLY AGREE	SCORE
1. I am aware of when my "prime time" is (that time of day when I am most alert and productive).	1	2	3	4	5	
2. I don't schedule my hardest tasks during my prime time.	5	4	3	2	1	
3. I balance the time I spend for work, school, and play.	1	2	3	4	5	
4. I never use an organizer or a calendar to plan my time.	5	4	3	2	1	
5. I have a history of being late in turning in assignments for school.	5	4	3	2	1	
6. When it comes to my work habits, I am an organized person.	1	2	3	4	5	
7. I never rely on credit cards and loans to cover my regular expenses.	1	2	3	4	5	
8. I feel that I need to work more and more hours to pay for my expenses.	5	4	3	2	1	
9. I make it a habit to put aside a portion of my earnings into a savings account.	1	2	3	4	5	
10. I avoid buying things I don't need when my budget is tight.	1	2	3	4	5	
TOTAL VALUE						

SUMMARY

43–50 You are exceptional in your ability to set priorities and keep to them. You have an organized system in place for managing your time and money. You have struck a balance in your time for all the different facets of your life, including work and play.

35–42 You have an above average level of skill in determining your financial and scheduling priorities. You probably plan ahead for important tasks and have established a routine for study habits that others are aware and respectful of.

26–34 You are average in your ability to set priorities and stick to them. You have a fair sense of how to manage your time and balance the demands of your life. More consistent use of your skills would be beneficial.

18–25 Your skills in planning and prioritizing are somewhat low, and you probably have difficulty in organizing your time and budget. Additional learning in how to better schedule your time and set priorities is needed.

10–17 You have little skill in setting priorities for yourself. You usually under plan, give in to distractions, and are impulsive. Significant changes need to be made in order to keep yourself on track and headed in the right direction.

Based on the summary above, what is one goal you would like to achieve related to managing your time or money more wisely?

Goal _____

_____

List three actions you can take that might help you move closer to realizing this goal.

1. _____
2. _____
3. _____

Questions FOR BUILDING ON YOUR BEST

As you read this chapter, consider the following questions. At the end of the chapter, you should be able to answer all of them. You are encouraged to ask a few questions of your own. Consider turning to your classmates or instructors to assist you.

1. How can I determine exactly how I am spending my time?
2. How can I manage a reasonable balance between school, work, family, and social life?
3. What techniques can I use to help me stop procrastinating?
4. How can I learn financial-management strategies that will help me now and after school?
5. How can I learn to control my spending habits?

What additional questions might you have about time management and financial planning?

1. _____
2. _____
3. _____

You Have All the Time There Is
TAKING CONTROL OF YOUR TIME AND YOURSELF

Have you ever tried to define time? This is an interesting exercise. If you stop now and try to define exactly what time is, you will probably find it difficult. Time is elusive and flexible and also restrictive and binding. Yet, we all know that time exists, and we all know how much trouble we can bring down on our heads when we use it poorly or waste it. The truth is, many students' worst problems start with poor use of time. Staying power actually begins with how you manage your time and get control of your life.

Some people seem to be born with the ability to get so much more done than most other people. They appear to always be calm and collected, to have it together, to reach lofty goals. Many people from this group work long hours in addition to going to school. They never appear to be stressed out, and they seem to attend all the social functions.

You are probably aware of others who are always late with assignments, never finish their projects on time, rarely seem to have time to study, and appear to have no concrete goals for their lives. Many people from this second group never make it past their first class of continuing education. There is no guarantee that you will finish your program just because you have enrolled. Some students lack staying power because they have no concept of how to manage themselves. Obviously, all these people have the same amount of time in their days and nights. The secret is that one group organizes for success, whereas the other never knows what happened to them.

Staying power begins with how you manage your time. Strive to build on your best in all areas of your life—school, work, family, and friends.

Sometimes, we get the idea that one group of people accomplishes more because they have more time or because they don't have to work or they don't have children or they are smarter or wealthier. Actually, all of these reasons may be true, but it doesn't change the facts. We all have the same amount of time each week, and we decide how to spend most of it. Even if you are rich, you can't buy more time than the allotted 10,080 minutes that each of us is given every week.

Time is an unusual and puzzling resource. You can't save it in a box until you need it. You don't feel it passing by like wind in your face. It has no color. If you are in a hurry or if you are pressured to reach a deadline, time seems to fly. If you are bored or have nothing to do, it seems to creep at a very slow pace. Time is an invisible commodity. You can't get your arms around it; yet, you know it exists.

Corporate managers realize the value of time because they pay consultants millions of dollars to teach their employees how to use their time more wisely. *Time is money in the business world;* employees who can produce excellent work by established deadlines are highly valued. Time must be considered one of your most valuable resources while you are in career college and after you complete your program. Time management is actually about managing you, taking control. The sooner you get control of how you use your time, the quicker you will be on your way to becoming successful in your program and at work. Learning to manage your time is a lesson that you will use throughout your learning endeavors and beyond. Actually, you can't control time, but you can control yourself. Time management is really about self-management. Time management is paying attention to how you are spending your most valuable resource and then devising a plan to use it more effectively.

The "P" Word: Procrastination

HOW TO QUIT AVOIDING THE HARD JOBS AND GET YOUR PRIORITIES IN ORDER

We all procrastinate, then we worry and promise we'll never do it again if we can just get through this day. We say things to ourselves like, "If I can just live through this test, I will never wait until the last minute again." But something comes along and we put off our school work. "My son is sick." "I'm tired from working eight hours today." "I need to do laundry." Life happens, but with hard work and planning, most students learn to deal with life and family and school and work.

Some people don't have a clue how they spend their time. Many convince themselves they are working very hard; yet, the bottom line doesn't prove this to be true. Students need to learn early on that their programs will probably require a lot of time outside of class. Some experts advise students to count on spending at least three hours outside of class for every hour spent in class.

Some people actually do work hard, but their work habits are so poor that they still don't produce very much. Others try to work while they are simultaneously entertaining themselves. For example, they watch TV while they read. Doesn't work! If you want to watch your favorite television show, you need to work in a quiet place where you can concentrate. Then, reward yourself with 30 minutes to watch your program.

The truth is simple: We all tend to avoid the hard jobs in favor of the easy ones. Even many of the list makers fool themselves. They mark off a long list of easy tasks while the big ones still loom in front of them. Many of us put off unpleasant tasks until our back is against the wall. So, why do we procrastinate when we all know how unpleasant the results can be? Why aren't we disciplined and organized and controlled so we can reap the rewards that come from being prepared?

Procrastination is quite simply a bad habit formed after many years of practice. There are reasons, however, that cause us to keep doing this to ourselves when we all know better.

WHY IS IT SO EASY TO PROCRASTINATE?

Procrastination for most people is a habit that has been formed by years of perfecting the process. There are reasons, however, that some students procrastinate:

- **Superhuman expectations.** You simply overdo and put more on your calendar than Superman or Superwoman could accomplish.
- **Whining.** You tell yourself that smart people don't have to study, and everybody is smart but you. Smart people are studying or they have studied in the past and have already mastered the material you are struggling with now. Sooner or later, you must pay the price to gain knowledge. So, the sooner you quit whining, the sooner you will begin to master time management.
- **Fear of failing.** You have failed a difficult subject in the past, and you are scared it is going to happen again, so you do the natural thing and avoid unpleasant experiences.
- **Emotional blocks.** It is time to get started and you have no routine and no past regimen to get you started. You are already feeling guilty because you have wasted so much time. You feel tired, depressed, and beaten.

We have only this moment, sparkling like a star in our hand . . . and melting like a snowflake. Let us use it before it is too late.   —MARIE RAY

HOW TO BEAT PROCRASTINATION

Not only is it important that you overcome procrastination for the sake of your education, but it is also equally crucial to your success at work. Procrastination is a bad habit that will haunt you until you make up your mind to overcome it. The chart on pages 63 and 64 offers 25 tips that might help.

Managing Time So You Can Have More Fun

WONDERFUL WORK = WONDERFUL EXPERIENCES

As you focus on managing and organizing your time, remember that you are not learning to manage yourself and your time just so you can do more work. Of course, you want to be more productive while using less time. But the real benefit of managing your time is so you can have more fun.

So how do you do this? Every 15 minutes for one week, you will record exactly how you spent that time. This exercise may seem a little tedious at first, but if you complete the process over a period of a week, you will have a much better concept of where your most precious resource—time—is being used. Yes, that's right—for a week, you need to keep a written record of how much time you spend sleeping, studying, eating, working, getting to class and back,

25 Ways to Beat Procrastination

- **Face up to the results of procrastination.** What will happen if you procrastinate? How will you feel if you fail the test? How miserable will you be over the weekend if you have to write a last-minute paper while your family and friends get to go see a movie?

- **Concentrate on the rewards of managing yourself and your time.** Think about the rewards that you will get when you finish a difficult task. You can go to a movie or relax or spend time with your children. You can get a good grade. Think about how good you will feel when the weekend comes and your paper is finished and you don't have to spend all your time working on a project. Focus on how good you will feel when you did well on a project. While you are working, stop periodically and focus on the rewards.

- **Break up big tasks into small ones.** If you have to write a paper, can you work on one segment tonight and another one tomorrow? If you start early and finish a small segment each day, a big paper is just a series of small tasks.

- **Give yourself a time limit to accomplish a task.** Work will expand to take up as much time as we allow it to. Push yourself to work faster and more efficiently.

- **Set a regular time for study, and do not vary from it.** Determine your personal "best time" and "best place."

- **Start studying with positive, realistic thoughts.** Push negative thoughts out of your mind. Tell yourself that you are growing and becoming more competent. Remember, "You can do this."

- **Establish study habits.** See Chapter 7 for a thorough discussion of study habits.

- **Set reasonable, concrete goals that you can reach in about 20 to 25 minutes.** Then, set others for the next block of time.

- **Face fear; look it right in the face.** Make up your mind you are going to overcome fear by studying and preparing every day.

- **Get help from your instructor.** Show the instructor what you have done and ask if you are on the right track.

- **Avoid whining and people who whine and complain.** You have this job to do, and it is not going away.

- **Allow yourself more time than you think you need to complete an assignment or to study for a test.**

- **Practice your new study habits for 21 days.** By then, you will have gone a long way toward getting rid of your procrastination habits.

- **Actually reward yourself when you have accomplished an important body of work.** Perhaps you spent two hours looking for research articles on the Internet. Now, you deserve a reward. Watch a TV program; visit a friend for a few minutes; talk on the phone; answer your e-mail; read a book to a child. If you have not finished your work, push yourself to go back to work for a few more minutes. When you do this, you are building your discipline and staying power. Ask yourself: "Can I work just fifteen more minutes?"

- **Look at this task in terms of your long-range goals.** Where does it fit in your plans of getting what you want? Does passing this test get you admitted to the job you want? Does making a B+ on this test take you one step closer to your career? Does making a good grade on this speech move you toward overcoming your fear of public speaking?

(continued)

25 Ways to Beat Procrastination, *continued*

- **Avoid getting involved in too many organizations, accepting too many commitments, or overextending yourself.** Stop and think about how much you really want to do something before you accept. How much time will it take? Does it help you grow and learn? Does it fit with your goals? It's better to say "no" than to accept something that will make you miserable before you finish. "NO!" is a powerful word—use it! Weed out activities that take too much of your time and provide you very little personal reward. You only have so much personal time. Fill that time with activities that give you pleasure and energy.

- **Force yourself to jump in.** Even if your initial work is not satisfactory, you have made a start, and chances are you will get focused as you progress. Sometimes, you just have to plunge in. You can't jump off the high dive in small steps. Just do it!

- **Start on the difficult, most boring tasks first.** Sometimes, it is effective to do these difficult tasks early in the morning before breakfast. This depends on your personal "best time" to work.

- **Practice "do it now."** Do simple tasks as you get them. Practice multitasking. What things can you do at the same time? For example, you can read a chapter while the clothes are washing. You can take your children on a walk and get your own exercise at the same time.

- **Find a quiet place to study and concentrate.** Small children might not understand that Mommy or Daddy needs to study very badly. You may need to make regular visits to the library or to a computer laboratory so you can focus on your work.

- **Gain the support of your family and/or friends.** Talk to the important people in your life and let them know how important your education is to you. Ask them to help and support you.

- **Weed out your personal belongings and living space.** Clean out and organize your closets and drawer space. Give things you no longer wear to charity. Buy fewer things that require waxing, polishing, recharging, cleaning, or storing. Things become monsters that take up your valuable time. Live a simpler life.

- **Prepare to be successful by getting ready the evening before.** Be sure your car has gas; select and press your clothes; put all your materials in order; check to see if the children's necessities and clothes have been organized. Often, the first few minutes of every day determine if you are going to have a good day. Program yourself for success!

- **Take time to smell the roses.** Part of every day should belong to you to do what you want. We all need to find time for regular exercise; we need to spend quality time with people we love and enjoy; we need to pay attention to friends and relationships; we need time to focus on spiritual development. Don't overmanage yourself to the point that you lose sight of what is really important—friends and family and self!

- **Balance your load.** If you are working full-time and paying for all of your expenses, you may need to take a lighter load so you can have a life. If you are a nontraditional student who is working and has small children and a home to take care of, you might need to rethink your schedule. Very few people will ever lament that they didn't do more work. But many will be sorry they didn't spend quality time with their parents, grandparents, or small children when they could have. It is true that you can do it all, but most of us can't do it all at one time. This race is just yours. You are not racing everyone else around you—just yourself.

cooking, caring for children, watching television, doing yard work, going to movies, hanging out, doing laundry, whatever.

Take your plan with you and keep track of your activities during the day. To make things simple, round off tasks to 15-minute intervals. You will also want to note the activity so you can evaluate how you spent your time later. Study the example that is provided for you in Figure 3.1. Create daily time sheets for one week to use for this exercise. Remember to take these pages with you and record how you are spending your time during the day. As you progress through the week, try to improve the use of your time.

1. What was your most surprising discovery about how you spent your time?

   _____

   _____

2. On what activities should you have spent more time?

   _____

   _____

3. On what things did you waste time?

   _____

   _____

4. How could you have used your time more wisely?

   _____

   _____

FIGURE 3.1 *Evaluating how you really spend your time.*

7:00	get up & shower	7:00		12:15
	✗	7:15		12:30
		7:30	Walked to lunch	12:45
	Breakfast	7:45	Ate lunch	1:00
8:00		8:00		1:15
		8:15		1:30
	Read paper	8:30	Talked w/ Joe	1:45
	Walked to class	8:45	2:00	2:00
9:00	Class	9:00	Went to book store	2:15
		9:15		2:30
		9:30	Walked home	2:45
		9:45	3:00	3:00
10:00		10:00	Called Ron	3:15
		10:15		3:30
		10:30		3:45
	Walked to class	10:45	4:00 Watched TV	4:00
11:00	Class	11:00		4:15
		11:15		4:30
		11:30	Walked to library	4:45
		11:45	5:00	5:00
12:00		12:00		5:15

Planning and Organizing for School

Each evening, you should take a few minutes (and literally, that is all it will take) and sit in a quiet place and make a list of all that needs to be done tomorrow. Successful time management comes from planning the NIGHT BEFORE! Let's say your list includes the following:

Research project
Study, test on Friday
Read Chapter 13
Meet with study group
Attend class, 8:00
Attend class, 10:00
Help child with school project

Exercise
Buy birthday card for mom
Wash the car
Wash clothes
Buy groceries
Call Janice about weekend

Now, you have created a list of tasks that you will face tomorrow. Next, separate this list into three categories: **MUST** *Do, Would* **LIKE** *to Do,* and **FUN** *Breaks.*

MUST DO
Read Chapter 13
Meet with study group
Study, test on Friday
Exercise
Help child with school project
Attend class, 8:00
Attend class, 10:00

WOULD LIKE TO DO
Research project
Buy birthday card for Mom
Wash clothes
Buy groceries

FUN BREAKS
Wash the car
Call Janice

You have a prime time when you are most capable of performing at your peak.

Don't get too excited yet. Your time-management plan is *not* finished. You have not done the most important part yet. Now, you will need to rank the items in order of their importance. You will put a 1 by the most important, a 2 by the next most important, and so forth in each category. It may look something like this:

MUST DO
1 Read Chapter 13
1 Meet with study group
1 Study, test on Friday
2 Attend class, 8:00
2 Attend class, 10:00
2-Help child with school project
3 Exercise

WOULD LIKE TO DO
1 Research project
2 Buy birthday card for Mom
3 Wash clothes
2 Buy groceries

FUN BREAKS
2 Wash the car
1 Call Janice

WORLD OF WORK

I was fortunate in college; in addition to my academic pursuits, I was also involved in social and cultural activities. I also worked for a professor. I learned that the more I had to do, the more I could get done. The semesters that I was the busiest were the semesters that my grades were the highest. You have to learn how to do what you have to do, and when you have to do it. In college, there can be so many distractions. You have to deal not only with your schedule, but with the schedules of those around you.

As a Financial Advisor, I continually employ many of the *priority management skills* I learned in college. With the amount of information circulating around, you learn that you can't pay attention to everything. You quickly learn to prioritize and do the things that have to be done. I learned in college that you may not be able to do it tomorrow; tomorrow may be worse than today.

Technology has greatly impacted the way I conduct my personal and professional life. Learning to use this technology to help me prioritize has been both a challenge and a blessing. Technology is always changing. We had to upgrade our entire system in the office recently. This caused our customer service to suffer somewhat, but in the long run, it will be worth it. It sometimes amazes me that we functioned without e-mail and ATMs. With each new invention, we wonder how we ever survived without it. However, technology can't replace human contact.

QUESTIONS FOR REFLECTION

Consider responding to these questions online in the World of Work module of the Companion Website.

1. Why do you think Mr. Rice was able to get more accomplished during the times that he had the most to do?

2. According to Mr. Rice, why is it risky to put things off until tomorrow? Do you agree or disagree?

3. In your opinion, why can't technology replace human contact?

Timothy Spencer Rice, Financial Advisor, Waddell & Reed, Inc., Shawnee Mission, KS

Planning and Organizing for Work

Some supermen and superwomen work full-time and go to school full-time while they juggle families and other responsibilities. If kept up for a long period, you will burn out from the stress that such a pace imposes on your mind and body, and if you have children, they may be adversely affected by your over-full schedule. If you work less and, if necessary, take longer to get through your program, you will have more opportunity to savor your college experience.

IMPORTANT PRINCIPLES FOR PRIORITY MANAGEMENT AT WORK

- Organize your materials at work as they are organized at home. If you have a desk in both places, keep your supplies in the same place in both desks. Simplify your life by following similar patterns at work and at home. Make your office or work space inviting, attractive, and stimulating. If you are a visual thinker and need to see different assignments, be considerate of others who may work close to you. Use clear plastic boxes, colored file folders, and colored file boxes to organize your projects.

- Write directions down! Keep a notebook for repetitive tasks. Keep a calendar, and be on time to meetings.

- Learn to do paperwork immediately rather than let it build up. File—don't pile!

- Never let your work responsibilities slide because you are studying on the job. Employers always notice.

- Leave the office for lunch, breaks, and short walks.

- When you are given projects that require working with others, plan carefully to do your work well and on time.

- Keep an address book (electronic or paper) handy with important phone numbers and addresses that you use frequently.

- Perform difficult, unpleasant tasks as soon as you can so you don't have them hanging over your head.

- When you plan your work schedule, allow for unexpected problems that might interfere with the schedule.

- Practice detached concern—care about your work but don't take it home with you.

> The more time we spend . . . on planning . . . a project, the less total time is required for it. Don't let today's busy work crowd planning time out of your schedule.
>
> —EDWIN C. BLISS

Planning and Organizing at Home

Some people organize effectively at work and school but allow things to fall apart at home. Your home should be a place where you can study, relax, laugh, invite your friends, and find solitude. The following ideas about home organization will help you maximize your time.

IMPORTANT PRINCIPLES FOR PRIORITY MANAGEMENT AT HOME

- Organize as effectively at home as you do at work.
- If applicable, divide the chores. Insist on everyone doing his or her share.
- Plan a rotation schedule for major household chores and stick to it—do laundry on Mondays and Thursdays; clean bathrooms on Saturdays; iron on Wednesdays; and so on.
- Organize your closet and your dresser drawers. Get rid of clothes you don't wear. Put a sign by your telephone that reads "TIME" to remind yourself not to waste it on the phone. If you can't study at home because of drop-in visitors or other housemates, go to the library.

- Pay bills twice monthly. Pay them on time so you don't ruin your credit rating.

- Manage your money wisely so you are not stressed by too many bills and too little money.

- If you drive to class or work, fill up your tank ahead of time so you won't be late.

- Keep yourself physically fit with a regular exercise plan and nutritious meals.

- Get out of the house. Take a walk. Visit a friend.

- If you have children, teach them to be organized so they don't waste your time searching for their shoes, books, and assignments. Help family members take responsibility!

- You can't work, go to school, and hold everybody's hand all the time. Give each of your children a drawer in a filing cabinet. Show them how to organize their work. You will be preparing them to be successful.

- If you are a perfectionist and want everything in your home to be perfect, get over it!

- Get rid of the clutter in your home or apartment, basement, and closets.

- Establish a time for study hall in your home. Children do their homework, and you do yours.

- If you have a family, insist that all of you organize clothes in advance for school or work for several days.

- Put a message board in a convenient place for everyone to use.

- If your children are old enough to drive, have them run errands at the post office and grocery store.

- Carpool with other parents in your neighborhood.

- Delegate, delegate, delegate! You are not Superwoman or Superman. Tell your family you need help. Children can feed pets, make their own beds, fold clothes, vacuum, sweep, and cut the grass if they are old enough.

- Schedule at least one hour alone with each of your children each week. Make this a happy, special time—a fun break!

- Make meals happy, relaxed times when each person's successes are shared and celebrated. Discuss current events.

- Plan special times with your spouse or partner if you have one so that he or she does not get fed up with your going to school.

- Tell your family and friends when you have to study; ask them to respect you by not calling or dropping by at this time.

- Post a family calendar where everyone can see it. Put all special events on it—for example, Janie's recital, Mike's baseball game, Jasmine's company party.

- Put sacred days on this calendar so that your entire family has something to look forward to.

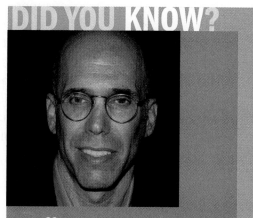

DID YOU KNOW?

Jeffrey Katzenberg

Walt Disney fired Jeffrey Katzenberg in 1994. He went on to co-create Dream-Works Studio. DreamWorks now produces movies such as *Shrek, Shark Tale, Collateral, Anchorman,* and *Madagascar.*

Practicing Fiscal Fitness

ARE YOU MANAGING YOUR MONEY OR IS IT MANAGING YOU?

Practicing fiscal fitness is as important as incorporating a regimen of physical fitness into your daily life! A very small percentage of the population learns to manage their money well, and many get themselves into serious trouble because of financial ignorance. According to the Federal Reserve, we have become a nation of debtors. Outstanding nonsecured debt rose from $805 billion in 1990 to $1.65 trillion in 2001. The worst kind of debt is credit card debt! The sooner you learn this lesson and put it into practice, the better!

Credit card companies have been waiting on you to arrive. Many have your name and address on file, and they will start sending you credit card applications right away. They want you to begin the dangerous habit of living off borrowed money. Don't let them get their tentacles wrapped around you and your money! Getting yourself too deeply in debt by abusing credit cards can bring you many sleepless nights and years of debt with high interest rates. Most credit card companies charge a very high rate of interest—18 to 21 percent or higher. For every $1,000 you charge, you will pay from $180 to $210 each year. If you make only the minimum required payment, you will begin paying interest on interest before the debt is paid off. If you have an extra $180, invest it. Years from now, it most likely will have doubled and even tripled. On the other hand, if you owe $1,000 and make only minimum payments, you will probably still owe $1,000 at the end of a year of making payments. Credit cards are a bad trap for people who use them unwisely. Also, avoid payday loans and rent-to-own traps; they are great wasters of your precious money.

Instead of using credit cards to pay for the expenditures that cause you to go over your budget, modify your expenditures. Almost every line on the expenditure chart can be modified. For example, adding a roommate or moving can lower your housing expense. You can change your car to a less expensive one or consider using public transportation or carpooling with colleagues. List five ways you can modify your expenditures.

Hints for cutting your expenses:

- Control impulse buying. (Don't buy anything that costs more than $15 until you have waited 72 hours; it is amazing how often you decide you don't need the item that you thought you had to have.)
- Carpool, take public transportation, or walk to classes.
- Don't eat out as often. Make your own meals. Make meals for several days on weekends to save time.
- Use coupons and buy during sales.
- Live more simply by cutting down on items like cell phones, beepers, and cable television.

Facts You Need to Know About Credit Cards and Loans

WHAT YOU DON'T KNOW CAN WRECK YOUR CREDIT RATING AND RUIN YOUR LIFE

Listed below are some of the most important things you can learn about managing money:

- Understand that credit cards are nothing more than high interest loans—in some cases, very high!

- Carry only one or two credit cards so you can manage your debt and not get in over your head.

- Avoid the temptation to charge. You should use credit cards only when you absolutely must and only when you can pay the full amount before interest is added. "Buy now, pay later" is a dangerous game.

- When you pay off a card or loan, celebrate and don't use that as a reason to charge again.

- If you have credit card debt, always try to pay more than the minimum.

- Pay your credit payment early enough to avoid late charges, which now average $29.84. Send the payment at least five days in advance. Late fees now represent the third-largest revenue stream for banks. If you are assessed a late fee, call and complain. If you normally pay on time and don't max out your limit, you will probably get it removed. If you get more than two late fees in a year, you could be assessed a higher interest rate on your balance.

- Call the credit company and negotiate a better rate. If they won't give you a better rate, tell them you are going to transfer the debt.

- If you have several credit debts, consolidate all the amounts into a simple payment where you have the lowest balance. Ask for a lower rate when you do. Destroy all the other cards so you don't accumulate debts again.

- If you pay off the full amount every month, some credit card companies allow you only 20 days from a purchase before they charge interest. If you carry a debt with them, however, they will allow you to have 25 days before your payment is due.

- Having a large number of credit cards with balances can seriously impact your credit rating. For example, what you do today may inhibit your ability to buy a car, purchase a house, and even get some jobs!

- You only need one or two credit cards. Destroy all applications that come to you in the mail.

- Handle your credit cards carefully. Write down the card account numbers and the phone numbers of the issuing company in case your cards are lost or stolen. Contact the company immediately if you cannot find your cards.

- Do not leave any personal information (credit cards, Social Security numbers, checking accounts) in places where roommates or other students have access to them. Purchase a metal file box with a lock and keep it in a secure place.

- Use your credit card only for plane tickets, hotel rooms, and other travel necessities that you can pay for within 20 days.

- If you have already gotten into credit card trouble, get counseling. One of the best agencies is the National Foundation for Credit Counseling.

Your credit card past is your credit future.   —STEVE KONOWALOW

Protect Yourself from Identity Theft

LIVING LARGE ON YOUR GOOD NAME

IDEAS FOR SUCCESS

Consider the following tips for managing your time and money:

- Push yourself to use your time more wisely. Can you get more done in less time by focusing on what you have learned?

- Use your time-management practices at work and for school.

- Focus on doing hard, unpleasant jobs first, then reward yourself.

- Analyze how you are actually spending your time.

- Practice the strategies you have learned for avoiding procrastination.

- Map out your activities and tasks for a week and a month at a time.

- Think about your future and how your financial actions today are going to impact you.

- Practice delayed gratification.

- If you must use a credit card, don't charge more than you can pay off at the end of the month.

Every year thousands of people are victims of identity theft. In other words, someone uses their name and personal information and charges on their credit cards. Identity theft may also include filing fraudulent tax returns, accessing bank accounts, and committing other crimes. NEVER put any personal information in the garbage that has not been shredded. Buy an inexpensive shredder and use it! Many identity theft victims have spent over 175 hours and over $10,000 per incident to resolve their problems.

People who may steal your identity are roommates, relatives, friends, estranged spouses, and household workers who have ready access to your papers. Or they may steal your wallet, go through your trash, or take your mail. They can even legally photocopy your vital information at the courthouse if, for example, you have been divorced. The Internet provides thieves many other opportunities to use official-looking e-mail messages designed to obtain your personal information.

It is very difficult, if not impossible, to catch identity thieves. While you may not be liable, you still have to spend your time filing expensive legal affidavits, writing letters, and making telephone calls to clear your good name.

Victims of identity theft can suffer staggering consequences:

- They must resolve unauthorized debts and delinquent accounts.
- Some have lost their jobs.
- Some have faced criminal investigation, arrest, or conviction.
- Victims may not even know their identity has been stolen until, after several months, a negative situation arises and they realize they have a problem.

Order a credit report once a year to be sure you have no major problems!

HOW TO MINIMIZE IDENTITY THEFT RISK

Criminals are very clever, and many are adept at using electronic means to steal your information. Here are ways to avoid having this kind of problem:

- Carry only the ID and cards you need at any given time.
- Sign all new credit cards immediately with permanent ink.
- Do not make Internet purchases from sites that are unsecured (check for a padlock icon to ensure safety).
- Do not write your PIN number, Social Security number, or passcode on any information that can be stolen or that you are discarding.
- Try to memorize your passwords instead of recording them on paper or in the computer.
- Get someone you trust to check your mail in your absence.
- Destroy all carbons.
- Be aware of "shoulder surfers." Shield your numbers when using an ATM.
- Avoid providing your Social Security number to any organization until you have verified its legitimacy.
- Check your credit file annually by requesting a copy of your report from one or all three of the major credit reporting agencies; their websites are: Equifax.com, Experian.com, and Transunion.com.

IF YOUR CREDIT CARDS ARE STOLEN

- Contact your local police immediately.
- Notify your creditors immediately and request that your accounts be closed.
- Ask the card company to furnish copies of documents that show any fraudulent transactions.
- Refuse to pay any bill or portion of any bill that is a result of identity theft.
- Report the theft or fraud to credit reporting agencies.

IF YOU LOSE YOUR DRIVER'S LICENSE

- Notify the state office of the Department of Motor Vehicles and place a fraud alert on your license number.
- Request a new driver's license.

The Pitfalls of Payday Loans, Car Title Loans, and Rent-to-Own Contracts

THERE'S SOMEONE ON EVERY CORNER TO TAKE YOUR MONEY

Many unsuspecting consumers have been duped into signing car title loans, payday loans, or rent-to-own contracts that resulted in very high monthly payments and penalties. Some were told by their title loan broker before they signed the contract that they could make a partial payment if they needed to and this would be OK. Unfortunately, the unsuspecting victims find out too late that their car is going to be repossessed due to one late or partial payment. Others realize too late that on a loan of $400, they must pay back over $500 that month. According to recent reports from consumer affairs groups, some institutions have been charging as much as 250 percent interest on an annualized basis (Cojonet, 2003). In some instances interest rates as high as 900 percent have been charged due to poor government regulatory policies.

By using rent-to-own companies, you are paying double and sometimes triple the actual cost of the item. Try never to walk into the door of a rent-to-own company.

The main point that you need to remember is that you should only borrow money from a reputable bank or credit union. NEVER get involved in a payday loan or a car title loan. Not only could you lose your car, you can ruin your credit. There are indeed people on every corner who will take your money if you don't manage your affairs very carefully.

f you can make a million by starting to invest after 45, how much more could you accumulate if you started at 25?   —PRICE PRITCHETT

Priority and financial management are life skills that will serve you well during your studies. Learning to manage your time, stop procrastinating, control spending, and budget your money are important skills that will give you staying power as a student.

The points that have been shared with you in this chapter will serve you well all through your career. The greatest benefit of developing and improving these skills, however, will be realized when you graduate and go to work in your field. As technology and business practices continue to emerge and change, you will need to continually upgrade your personal management skills. You are at the beginning of a journey where you will learn new skills and develop practices that will guide you for the rest of your life. Managing your time and money will help you reduce stress, remain positive, and realize your goals.

what's it ALL ABOUT?

NAME: Coretta Hooks

SCHOOL: USC, Columbia, SC

MAJOR: Retail Management   AGE: 23

Below is a real-life situation faced by one of Coretta's friends. Read the brief case and respond to the questions.

During my first semester, my friends and I were bombarded with credit card applications. They were in our orientation packets and they started showing up in our mailboxes. Unfortunately, one of my friends foolishly applied for—and received—several credit cards.

Marilyn spent a great deal of her time shopping. Before she knew it, she had accumulated three large balances on credit cards. She kept buying sweaters, shoes, and makeup. She ate out frequently and even took a trip to Atlanta that she charged on her credit card. She was living large! But a day of reckoning was coming!

Marilyn had never been taught a great deal about money management and nothing about the perils of credit card debt. Each of these cards charged 18 percent interest. Since she was late several times, she acquired four late fees of $29 each. When she finally realized what was happening, she was in a big mess! She couldn't tell her parents. Her dad would kill her. And her allowance wouldn't come close to paying off this debt. Marilyn cried and said over and over, "Why was I so dumb? What can I do?"

What was the first source of Marilyn's problems?

_____

_____

_____

What do you think Marilyn should do immediately?

_____

_____

_____

What can she do to get out of debt and get out of this mess?

_____

_____

_____

How does Marilyn's story have real-world implications for you?

_____

_____

_____

If you are like Marilyn and have had little training in managing money, where can you go for assistance?

_____

_____

_____

Is using a "credit repair" agency a good idea? Why or why not?

_____

_____

_____

prioritizing & money management

Manage your *time*, *money*, and *resources* carefully.

Know exactly how you are *spending* your time and your money.

Don't get caught in the *credit card trap*.

Protect your *credit rating* by using wise money management.

Prepare for success by investing for the future.

Spend more time with those who bring you *joy*.

Include *fun breaks, rewards,*

and *sacred days* in your plans.

Plan for a *balanced life*.

Focus on *quality* and *joy*.

Make *to-do lists*.

PRIORITIZE

4 Read

Conrad wanted to go home to his wife and children, but he *just could not face them.* He couldn't. He knew that the first question out of their mouths would be, "How did you do, Daddy? How did you do?"

He had just taken his placement test at Almanac Career Institute. His wife and children were excited that he was going to school for Network Security. They were excited, and he was horrified. *They seemed to have more faith in him than he had in himself.* This placement test did not determine whether Conrad was able to enter the institute; it simply determined which courses he needed to take first.

He arrived on campus early, registered with the testing center, and took three placement tests before noon. First, he took the English placement test, then the math test, and finally the reading/vocabulary/spelling placement test. Since he had worked with numbers his whole life, he was not overly concerned with the math placement test. He was, however, very worried about the English and reading tests.

After a lunch break, Conrad was told to return to the campus for his scores and to see an advisor. He went back to the testing center and waited for his appointment time at 1:30. As he sat in the testing lobby, he saw many students—some younger, some older, some with their children in tow, and some as carefree as the wind. "I wonder how they did," he thought. "What if I'm the only one who doesn't do well on these tests?"

His name was called, and an advisor greeted Conrad and escorted him to her office. She began to speak. "Mr. Hunter, you did very well on your math placement test and you are free to register for any math course in your program. I would, however, advise you to start with the basic courses and work your way up. Math courses at Almanac are not easy. I know you'll do well." She continued, "Mr. Hunter, your scores in English and reading indicate the need for a great deal of remediation."

"What does that mean?" Conrad asked.

"It means that you will need to register for English 090 and complete that course with a C or better before you can take English 101, the course required for your program in Network Security." She continued, "You will also need to register for Reading 100. This course will help you become a stronger reader and help you use a more dynamic vocabulary."

"Can I just not take the English 090 and reading courses? Can I opt out of them and just  take the required courses?" Conrad asked.

"I'm afraid not, Mr. Hunter. These tests are very accurate when it comes to predicting your success in certain classes. In looking at your scores, you seem to have a problem with reading comprehension, analysis, and interpretation. To opt out of this reading class would be very detrimental to your success."

"But I need to finish my degree as quickly as possible because my family is depending on me," Conrad informed her.

"I do understand that, Mr. Hunter, but without this reading course, your scores indicate that you will have trouble in many of your classes. Do you realize that the books used for some courses are written on the fourteenth grade level, and you're reading at the eighth grade level?"

> **"But I need to finish my degree as quickly as possible . . ."**

Conrad knew in his heart that she was right. He had never been strong in English, reading, spelling, or vocabulary. He knew that he had trouble in these areas. He knew that he had trouble concentrating and remembering what he had just read. "But how am I going to face my wife and children?" he thought. "How can I tell them that I don't read well?"

On the drive home, he struggled mightily with the questions in his head. "Should I just forget about this degree? Should I go to the dean and ask to be placed in the curriculum courses regardless of my scores? Should I tell my wife and children what happened? Should I just admit my shortcomings to my family and show them that I'm as determined as ever?"

Conrad pulled into the driveway still unsure of what he was going to tell his family. As he walked toward the front door, he heard his children yell, "Daddy's home! Daddy's home!" At that moment, he knew what he had to do.

QUESTIONS FOR REFLECTION

Consider responding to these questions online in the Questions for Reflection module of the Companion Website.

1. What decision do you think Conrad made? Why?

2. How could this be a positive experience for Conrad's entire family?

3. Has reading ever caused you problems in your academic work? If so, how have you dealt with this problem in the past?

Before reading this chapter, take a moment and respond to the following 10 questions. Consider each one carefully before answering, and then respond by circling the number in the appropriate box. When you have answered the questions, add your points and find your total score on the feedback chart below.

STATEMENT	STRONGLY DISAGREE	DISAGREE	DON'T KNOW	AGREE	STRONGLY AGREE	SCORE
1. I usually look up definitions in a dictionary when I read words I don't understand.	1	2	3	4	5	
2. Building a larger vocabulary isn't that important to me.	5	4	3	2	1	
3. I believe I can do well in school without reading the books and papers assigned by the instructors.	5	4	3	2	1	
4. I am good at finding the main ideas of the paragraphs I read.	1	2	3	4	5	
5. When reading textbooks, I use the SQ3R strategy (or another strategy) to aid my comprehension.	1	2	3	4	5	
6. I know how to use a highlighter to aid me in my reading assignments.	1	2	3	4	5	
7. I do not usually take notes from my books while I read.	5	4	3	2	1	
8. It is not possible for me to become better at understanding what I read.	5	4	3	2	1	
9. I rarely give myself the time to reread materials that I don't understand.	5	4	3	2	1	
10. I often read books, magazines, or newspapers simply for pleasure.	1	2	3	4	5	
TOTAL VALUE						

SUMMARY

43–50   You are exceptional in your reading skills. You know how to read for comprehension by employing a variety of reading strategies and how to incorporate your reading into your larger study structure. You likely get much enjoyment from reading and use that to your advantage.

35–42   Your reading skills and habits are above average. You likely enjoy reading and know how to read for comprehension. A few additional strategies will help you get even more benefit from the time you spend reading.

26–34   Your reading skills are likely average. You probably realize how important reading is for successful progress in school. You could brush up on strategies to maximize your reading comprehension.

18–25   Your reading skills are below average, but can be improved with practice and patience. You will need to learn strategies for improving your reading skills. Your reading confidence will improve as you employ those strategies.

10–17   Your reading skills are limited. You need to learn reading strategies to help you understand what you read. Your dislike for reading doesn't mean you can't be successful in college, but it will be important to learn to get the needed information from what you read.

Based on the summary above, what is one goal you would like to achieve related to reading more effectively?

Goal _____

_____

List three actions you can take that might help you move closer to realizing this goal.

1. _____
2. _____
3. _____

Questions
FOR BUILDING ON YOUR BEST

As you read this chapter, consider the following questions. At the end of the chapter, you should be able to answer all of them. We encourage you to ask a few questions of your own. Consider turning to your classmates or instructors to assist you.

1. What is the relationship between reading and building a vocabulary?
2. Why is it important for me to read with a dictionary?
3. What role does note taking play in my reading success?
4. What is SQ3R and how can it help me read better?
5. How can I improve my concentration?

What additional questions might you have about reading and comprehension?

1. _____
2. _____
3. _____

Is Reading FUNdamental or Just Pure Torture?

THE ANSWER CAN CHANGE YOUR LIFE

Quick question: What are the top two academic problems among students today? According to faculty members, assessments, national tests, and yes, even your peers around the nation, the two greatest problems students face today are math and reading comprehension—and some of the math problems can even be attributed to poor reading skills.

"I can read," you might say. "I've been reading since I was four years old!" There is a monumental difference between knowing and reading the words on a page and being able to comprehend, interpret, analyze, and evaluate those written words. Herein lies the problem. Just because you have hands, this does not make you a mechanic. Just because you have a voice, this does not make you a singer, and just because you can read words, this does not mean that you comprehend what the author intended.

How many times have you read to the bottom of a page or completed a section in a textbook and said to yourself, "I don't know anything about what I just read, much less remember it." In actuality, all of us have done this at one time or another. This chapter is here to help you eliminate this problem from your academic studies. This chapter is here to help you learn how to read a page, a section, or an entire chapter so that when you reach the end, you will comprehend what you just read.

FINALLY! A SIX-PACK THAT CAN ACTUALLY HELP YOU: THE INGREDIENTS FOR SUCCESSFUL READING

The material you're reading

An open mind

Pencils

A highlighter

A tablet or loose-leaf paper

A dictionary

It may seem elementary, but without the tools shown above, you can't improve your reading comprehension, analysis, or speed. Enough said!

Discover If You Are a Passive or an Active Reader

Evaluate the following statements truthfully regarding your reading preferences right now.

1. I enjoy reading for pleasure. — TRUE **(FALSE)**
2. Textbooks have little connection to my real life. — **(TRUE)** FALSE
3. I look for the deeper meaning in words and phrases. — TRUE **(FALSE)**
4. I seldom visualize what I am reading. — TRUE **(FALSE)**
5. I look up words that I do not understand. — TRUE **(FALSE)**
6. I read only what I have to read, and that is a stretch for me. — **(TRUE)** FALSE
7. I stop reading to ponder what something means. — TRUE **(FALSE)**
8. I never take notes when reading. — **(TRUE)** FALSE
9. Reading brings me great joy. — TRUE **(FALSE)**
10. My mind wanders constantly when I read. — **(TRUE)** FALSE
11. I make time for reading even when I am not required to read. — TRUE **(FALSE)**
12. Words are just words—they have no real meaning to my life or work. — TRUE **(FALSE)**
13. I get excited about reading something new because I know I will learn something new and useful. — TRUE **(FALSE)**
14. When reading, I just want to get it over with. — **(TRUE)** FALSE
15. I usually have no trouble concentrating when reading. — TRUE **(FALSE)**
16. I never look up words, I just read on. — **(TRUE)** FALSE

TOTAL of *even* TRUE responses ___6___

TOTAL of *odd* TRUE responses ___0___

If you answered TRUE to more *even* numbers, you tend to be a more PASSIVE reader.

If you answered TRUE to more *odd* numbers, you tend to be a more ACTIVE reader.

Active reading is really nothing more than a mind-set. It is the attitude you have as you begin the reading process. For the next few days, try approaching your reading assignments with a positive, open-minded approach and notice the difference in your own satisfaction, understanding, and overall comprehension.

Now that you have discovered if you are an active or passive reader, the following section will help you determine your reading speed.

I Feel the Need ... for Speed!

DETERMINING YOUR PERSONAL READING RATE

DID YOU KNOW?

Ray Romano

was fired from the pilot of the TV show *News Radio*. The show that he later created, wrote, and starred in, *Everybody Loves Raymond*, ran for nine years, was number one in its time slot, and won many Emmy® Awards. Romano won an Emmy® for Best Actor.

There are people who do have an incredible gift for speed reading and a photographic memory, but those people are not the norm. Speed is not everything. Most instructors agree that comprehension is *much* more important than speed. If you are a slow reader, does this mean that you are not intelligent? Absolutely not! Reading speeds will vary from person to person depending on training, frequency in reading, comprehension, and the complexity of the material.

This section is included here to give you some idea about how long it will take to read a chapter so that you can *plan your reading time* more effectively. There are an average of 450 words on a college textbook page. If you read at 150 words per minute, each page may take you an average of 3 minutes to read.

This is a *raw number* for reading only. It does not allow for marking, highlighting, taking notes, looking up words, or reflecting. When these necessary skills are coupled with basic reading, they can sometimes triple the amount of reading time required. So, that page that you estimated would take you 3 minutes to read may actually take you 9 to 10 minutes.

If your instructor has assigned a chapter in your text that is 21 pages long and it takes you 9 minutes on average to read each page, you need to allow at least 189 minutes (or 3.15 hours) to read and comprehend the chapter. If you are reading below the average 250 words per minute rate, several factors could be contributing to this situation. They include:

- Not concentrating on the passage
- Encountering vocabulary words with which you are not familiar
- Stopping too long on any given word (called fixations; discussed later)
- Not reading often enough to build your speed

In the activity on page 87, you will find a passage from a book chapter. Read the section at your normal pace. Use a stopwatch or a watch with a second hand to accurately record your time, and then calculate your rate and comprehension level using the scales provided. Take a moment now and calculate your reading rate.

WHAT DOES IT ALL MEAN?

According to Brenda D. Smith (1999), professor and reading expert, "rate calculators vary according to the difficulty of the material. Research indicates, however, that on relatively easy material, the average adult reading speed is approximately 250 words per minute at 70 percent comprehension. For students, the rate is sometimes estimated at closer to 300 words per minute." The passage that you read in the activity would be classified as relatively easy.

Start Time _____ _____ **Minutes** _____ **Seconds**

BINGE DRINKING

Binge drinking is classified as having more than five drinks at one time. Many people say, "I only drink once a week." However, if that one drinking spell includes drink after drink after drink, it can be extremely detrimental to your liver, your memory, your digestive system, and your overall health in general.

Most college students report that they do not mean to binge drink, but it is caused by the situation, such as a ballgame, a party, a campus event, or special occasions. Researchers at Michigan State University found that only 5 percent of students surveyed say they party to "get drunk" (Warner, 2002).

In their breakthrough work, *Dying to Drink,* Harvard researcher Henry Wechsler and science writer Bernice Wuethrich explore the problem of binge drinking. They suggest, "two out of every five college students regularly binge drink resulting in approximately 1,400 student deaths, a distressing number of assaults and rapes, a shameful amount of vandalism, and countless cases of academic suicide" (Wechsler and Wuethrich, 2002).

It is a situation reminiscent of the old saying, "Letting the fox guard the hen house." After a few drinks, it is hard to "self-police," meaning that you may not be able to control your actions once the drinking starts.

Perhaps the greatest tragedy of drug and alcohol abuse is the residual damage of pregnancy, sexually transmitted diseases, traffic fatalities, verbal/physical abuse, and accidental death. You know that drugs and alcohol lower your resistance and can cause you to do things that you would not normally do, such as drive drunk or have unprotected sex.

Surveys and research results suggest that students who participate in heavy episodic (HE) or binge drinking are more likely to participate in unprotected sex with multiple sex partners. One survey found that 61 percent of men who *do* binge drink participated in unprotected sex as compared to 23 percent of men who *do not* binge drink. The survey also found that 48 percent of women who *do* binge drink participated in unprotected sex as compared to only 8 percent of women who *do not* binge drink (Cooper, 2002).

These staggering statistics suggest one thing: alcohol consumption can cause people to act in ways in which they may never have acted without alcohol—and those actions can result in personal damage from which recovery may be impossible.

(387 words)

Finishing Time _____ _____ **Minutes** _____ **Seconds**

Reading time in SECONDS = _____

Words per MINUTE (use the chart on the next page) = _____

(continued)

Example: Convert your reading time to seconds. For example, if you read this passage in **2 minutes and 38 seconds,** your reading time in seconds would be **158** (2 × 60 seconds equals 120 seconds plus 38 equals 158). Using the Rate Calculator Chart, your reading rate would be about **146 words per minute.**

RATE CALCULATOR FOR RELATIVELY EASY PASSAGES

Time in Seconds	Words per Minute
40	581
50	464
60 (1 minute)	387
120 (2 minutes)	194
130	179
140	165
150	155
160	145
170	137
180 (3 minutes)	129
190	122
200	116
210	110
220	106
230	101

Source: B. Smith. (2001). *Breaking Through,* 6th ed., Upper Saddle River, NJ: Pearson Education.

Answer the following questions with T (true) or F (false) without looking back over the material.

_____ 1. Binge drinking has resulted in the deaths of students.

_____ 2. Men who binge drink have unprotected sex more often than men who do not binge drink.

_____ 3. Women who binge drink have unprotected sex no more often than women who do not binge drink.

_____ 4. "Self-policing" means that you are able to look out for yourself.

_____ 5. Binge drinking is classified as having more than three drinks at one time.

(Answers can be found on page 89.)

Each question is worth 20 percent.   Comprehension = _____%

Example: If you answered two correctly, your comprehension rate would be 40% (2 × 20%). If you answered four correctly, your comprehension rate would be 80% (4 × 20%).

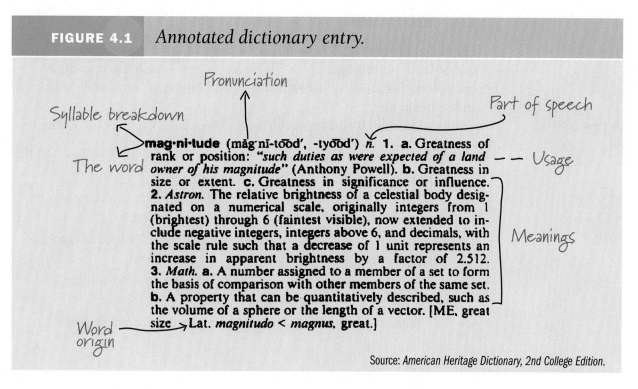

| FIGURE 4.1 | *Annotated dictionary entry.* |

Pronunciation

Syllable breakdown

Part of speech

mag·ni·tude (măg′nĭ-tōōd′, -tyōōd′) *n.* **1. a.** Greatness of rank or position: *"such duties as were expected of a land owner of his magnitude"* (Anthony Powell). **b.** Greatness in size or extent. **c.** Greatness in significance or influence. **2.** *Astron.* The relative brightness of a celestial body designated on a numerical scale, originally integers from 1 (brightest) through 6 (faintest visible), now extended to include negative integers, integers above 6, and decimals, with the scale rule such that a decrease of 1 unit represents an increase in apparent brightness by a factor of 2.512. **3.** *Math.* **a.** A number assigned to a member of a set to form the basis of comparison with other members of the same set. **b.** A property that can be quantitatively described, such as the volume of a sphere or the length of a vector. [ME. great size >Lat. *magnitudo* < *magnus*, great.]

The word

Usage

Meanings

Word origin

It's Not Just a Doorstop

USING YOUR DICTIONARY

Your dictionary will become a good friend to you. There will be many words and phrases that you will not understand when reading texts that are written on the thirteenth and fourteenth grade levels. There is nothing to be ashamed of if you resort to "looking up" a word. You'll be smarter because of it. When you look up a word in the dictionary, you are given more than just a definition. You are given the phonetic pronunciation, the spelling, the meaning, the part of speech in which the word can be used, the origin of the word, and usually several definitions (see Figure 4.1).

There are several ways to begin your collection of unfamiliar words as you read. You can write them in the margin of the page in your text, you can put the word on an index card (word on the front, definition on the back), or you can put the definition in a special column when taking notes.

Improving Speed and Comprehension

As you begin to practice your reading comprehension, review the following tips for helping you read the material more quickly and understand the material more clearly. Whenever you are faced with having to choose between comprehension and speed, choose comprehension every time.

Answers to Comprehension Test on p. 88: 1=T, 2=T, 3=F, 4=T, 5=F

CONCENTRATION

Speed and comprehension both require deep, mindful concentration. Neither can be achieved without it. Your body needs to be ready to concentrate. You need sleep, rest, and proper nutrition. It will be nearly impossible to concentrate without them.

To increase your concentration for active reading, consider the following:

- Reduce outside distractions such as people talking, rooms that are too hot or cold, cell phones ringing, etc.
- Reduce internal distractions such as fatigue, self-talk, daydreaming, hunger, and emotions that cause you to think of other things.
- Set a goal for reading "X" amount of material by "Y" time. This goal can help you focus.
- Take a short break every 20 minutes. Don't get distracted and do something else; come back to your reading in 3 to 5 minutes.
- Take notes as you read. This helps reading become an active process.

VOCABULARY

Building a strong vocabulary is not easy and it does not happen overnight. However, it is very important that you work on this aspect of reading as often as possible. If you do not know a word, you must stop and look it up. Having to stop and look up a word that you do not know will slow you down and cause you to lose concentration; however, the more words you have in your vocabulary, the fewer times you will need to stop. To increase your vocabulary for active reading, also consider the following:

- Keep those words on a list that you can review daily.
- Make time to study your vocabulary list.
- Work crossword puzzles or other word games.

FIXATION

Fixation is when your eyes stop on a single word to read it. Your eyes stop for only a fraction of a second, but those fractions add up over the course of a section or chapter. Your mind sees the words something like this:

Nutrition   is   important   to   good   health.

As you read this, you probably had six fixations because the words are spaced out. However, if they were not spaced, many people would still have six fixations. To increase your speed, try to see two words with one fixation; this will cut your reading time nearly in half. Try to see the sentence like this:

Nutrition is important   to good health.

Building a strong vocabulary does not happen overnight—it takes effort.

Smith (1999) states that "research has shown that the average reader can see approximately 2.5 words per fixation."

To reduce your fixation time for active reading, consider the following:

- Practice seeing two or more words with one fixation.

- As you practice, try to read in phrases like the example below:

Nutrition is important   to good health.   Therefore,   you should work hard   to eat   proper meals   every day.   By doing this you can maintain   good health.

FREQUENCY

Not reading often enough to build your speed is a problem with many people. In order to build your speed and work on your concentration, you must read as much as possible. The more you read, the more you improve your skills. Quite simply, nothing helps you read better than actually reading.

To increase your frequency for active reading, consider the following:

- Read every chance you get.

- Read a variety of materials (texts, magazines, newspapers, novels).

- Don't read just for learning, read for pleasure as well.

Get to the Point, Would You!

FINDING THE TOPIC AND MAIN IDEAS IN PARAGRAPHS AND SECTIONS

Typically, each paragraph has a main idea. It is usually called a topic sentence. The topic statement is what the paragraph is about. Identifying the main idea of a paragraph can greatly aid your comprehension of that paragraph and eventually the entire section or chapter. Read the following paragraph and determine the main idea—the point.

> Without exception, the conclusion should be one of the most carefully crafted components of your paper or speech. Long after your reader has finished reading or your listener has finished listening, the last part of your work is more than likely going to be the part they remember the most. Some writers and speakers suggest that you write your conclusion first, so that your paper or speech is directed toward a specific end result. That decision, of course, is up to you. However, a great piece of advice from writing experts tells us that captivating writers always know how their stories will end long before they begin writing them.
>
> —*Cornerstone: Building on Your Best*

According to Dorothy Seyler (2001), professor and reading expert, you can identify the topic of a paragraph in four easy steps:

- The topic is the **subject** of the paragraph.

- You can identify the topic by answering the question, "**What or who** is the paragraph about?"

WORLD OF WORK

I have always been struck by the power of the written word to provide insight and to transform.

Reading informs everything we do in life. Through reading and by connecting to the material, we are able to experience things we might never know. In and of itself, reading is a solitary practice. It is what you do with what you have read that matters.

In my job I read constantly, whether in the form of e-mails, financial or management reports, or product proposals. Reading is the primary vehicle for learning and it is the foundation for everything I do in business. Being able to read, extract the salient points from what I'm reading, and translate and transfer that information into action items is the basis for ensuring success in business, and indeed, for you in college.

You might say to yourself, "I'm not majoring in a field that will require me to read and analyze information every day." This may be true, but it is always better to have the skill and not need it every day than to need the skill and not have it at all.

Reading and comprehending what you have read is not a luxury; it is a demand of the modern work world. Reading is important to everyone from auto mechanics who have to read and study manuals to nurses who have to read and comprehend charts and reports to graphic artists who have to read and analyze information to enable them to create the proper message in an advertisement or a poster.

In addition to being extremely practical, reading has an emotional component. In the same way that reading books for pleasure allows us to connect with characters, I try and connect with the writer and with the material being presented. Doing this allows me to personalize the information and make it come alive in a more meaningful way.

If I could pass along one thing to you, I'd pass along the concept that reading is a gateway. It is the gateway to learning, to compassion, to understanding, to growing, to experiencing parts of the world to which we may never have the privilege of traveling, and it is the gateway to your own self-enrichment. The beauty of having this gateway is that you don't have to depend on anyone else to provide it for you—it is yours simply by doing.

QUESTIONS FOR REFLECTION

Consider responding to these questions online in the World of Work module of the Companion Website.

1. How can reading more effectively help you in your professional life like it helps Ms. Baliszewski?

2. Has reading ever taken you to another place and time? If so, how did this make you feel? If not, why?

3. What advantages do you believe improving your reading skills can have in your studies and in your future career?

Robin Baliszewski, *President,* Career, Health, Education, and Technology Division—Prentice Hall, Upper Saddle River, NJ

- The topic statement should be **general enough** to cover all of the specifics of the paragraph.

- The topic statement should be **specific enough** to exclude other paragraphs on related topics.

Doing It Right the First Time
SQ3R TO THE RESCUE

There are as many ways to approach a chapter in a textbook as there are students who read textbooks. Most would agree that there is no "right" or "wrong" way to begin the process. However, many would agree that there are a few ways of approaching a chapter that are more effective than others. One such approach is SQ3R.

The most basic and often-used reading and studying system is the SQ3R method, developed by Francis P. Robinson in 1941. This simple, yet effective, system has proved to be a successful study tool for millions of students. SQ3R involves five steps: Survey, Question, Read, Recite, and Review. The most important thing to remember about SQ3R is that it should be used on a daily basis, not as a method for cramming.

Only **you** can improve your reading skills, and reading is a skill—just like driving a car.
—DOROTHY SEYLER

Step 1: Survey   The first step of SQ3R is to survey, or pre-read, an assigned chapter. You begin by reading the title of the chapter, the headings, and each sub-heading. Look carefully at the vocabulary, time lines, graphs, charts, pictures, and drawings included in each chapter. If there is a chapter summary, read it. Surveying also includes reading the first and last sentence in each paragraph. Surveying is not a substitute for reading a chapter. Reading is discussed later.

Step 2: Question   The second step is to question. There are five common questions you should ask yourself when you are reading a chapter: Who? When? What? Where? and Why? As you survey and read your chapter, try turning the information into questions and see if you can answer them. If you do not know the answers to the questions, you should find them as you read along.

Another way to approach the chapter is to turn the major headings of each section into questions. When you get to the end of the section, having carefully read the material, taken notes, and highlighted important information, answer the question that you posed at the beginning of the section.

Step 3: Read   After you survey the chapter and develop some questions to be answered from the chapter, the next step is to read the chapter. Remember, surveying is not reading. There is no substitute for reading in your success plan.

Read slowly and carefully. The SQ3R method requires a substantial amount of time, but if you take each step slowly and completely, you will be amazed at how much you can learn.

Read through each section. It is best not to jump around or move ahead if you do not understand the previous section. Paragraphs are usually built on each other, and so you need to understand the first before you can move on to the next. You may have to read a chapter or section more than once.

Another important aspect of reading is taking notes, highlighting, and making marginal notes in your textbook. If you own your textbook, you should personalize it as you would your lecture notes. Highlight areas that you feel are important, underline words and phrases that you did not understand or that you feel are important, and jot down notes in the margins.

As you begin to read your chapter, mark the text, and take notes, keep the following in mind:

- Read the entire paragraph before you mark anything.
- Identify the topic or thesis statement of each paragraph and highlight it.
- Highlight key phrases.
- Don't highlight too much; the text will lose its significance.
- Stop and look up words that you do not know or understand.

While reading, you will want to take notes that are more elaborate than your highlighting or marginal notes. Taking notes while reading the text will assist you in studying the material and committing it to memory. There are several effective methods of taking notes while reading (see Figure 4.2). They include:

- Charts
- Outlines
- Key words
- Mind maps
- Flash cards
- Summaries
- Time lines

As you read through a chapter in your textbook, you may find that you have to use a variety of these techniques to capture information. Try them for one week. Although taking notes while reading a chapter thoroughly is time consuming, you will be amazed at how much you remember and how much you are able to contribute in class after using these techniques.

While reading, always keep a dictionary handy. It is nearly impossible to read, comprehend, and remember a paragraph or section when you don't know or understand one or more words within it. For instance, it would be difficult to get at the meaning of the following sentence if you did not understand the words. **"It is easier to answer affirmatively to a question that even an anonymous respondent knows would evoke an excruciating response."** When you look up a word, circle it and write the definition in the margin.

TRUE   UNKNOWN

a person who   It is easier to answer (affirmatively) to a question that even an (anonymous)
RESPONDS   (respondent) knows would (evoke) an (excruciating) response.

TO CALL TO MIND   PAINFUL

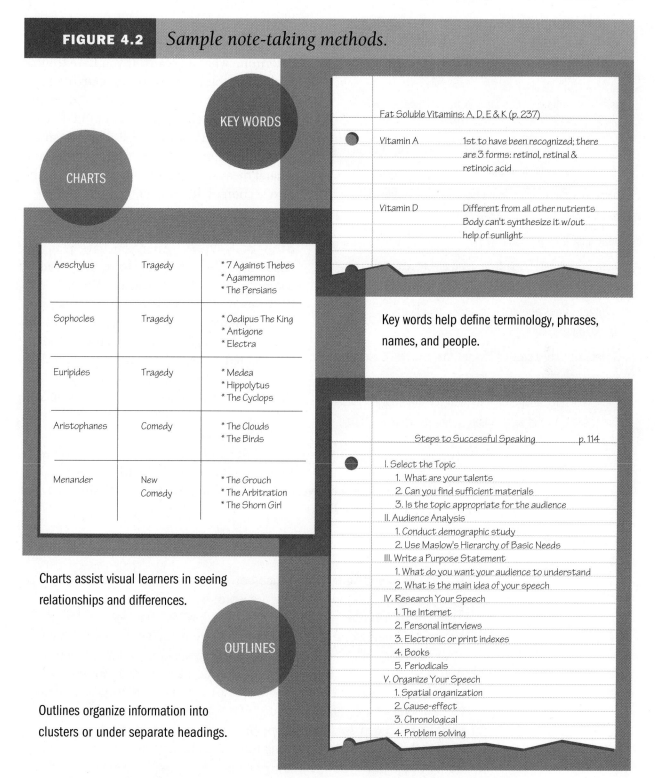

FIGURE 4.2 *Sample note-taking methods.*

KEY WORDS

CHARTS

Fat Soluble Vitamins: A, D, E & K (p. 237)

Vitamin A — 1st to have been recognized; there are 3 forms: retinol, retinal & retinoic acid

Vitamin D — Different from all other nutrients Body can't synthesize it w/out help of sunlight

Aeschylus	Tragedy	* 7 Against Thebes * Agamemnon * The Persians
Sophocles	Tragedy	* Oedipus The King * Antigone * Electra
Euripides	Tragedy	* Medea * Hippolytus * The Cyclops
Aristophanes	Comedy	* The Clouds * The Birds
Menander	New Comedy	* The Grouch * The Arbitration * The Shorn Girl

Key words help define terminology, phrases, names, and people.

Charts assist visual learners in seeing relationships and differences.

OUTLINES

Outlines organize information into clusters or under separate headings.

Steps to Successful Speaking   p. 114

I. Select the Topic
  1. What are your talents
  2. Can you find sufficient materials
  3. Is the topic appropriate for the audience
II. Audience Analysis
  1. Conduct demographic study
  2. Use Maslow's Hierarchy of Basic Needs
III. Write a Purpose Statement
  1. What do you want your audience to understand
  2. What is the main idea of your speech
IV. Research Your Speech
  1. The Internet
  2. Personal interviews
  3. Electronic or print indexes
  4. Books
  5. Periodicals
V. Organize Your Speech
  1. Spatial organization
  2. Cause-effect
  3. Chronological
  4. Problem solving

Step 4: Recite   Recitation is simple, but crucial. Skipping this step may result in less than full mastery of the chapter. Once you have read a section, ask yourself this simple question: "What was that all about?" Find a classmate, sit down together, and ask questions of each other. Discuss with each other the main points of the chapter. Try to explain the information to each other without

Consider the following tips for making the most of your reading time:

- Reduce the distractions around you. Try to find an atmosphere that is comfortable and effective for you.

- Discover what time of day is best for you to read and concentrate on your material.

- Read with a healthy snack.

- Read in sections. Don't try to read an entire chapter in one sitting. Break it down and take breaks.

- Form questions about the material from headings as you are reading.

- Never skip over words or phrases that you don't understand. Look them up in a dictionary.

- Allow yourself enough time to read the material effectively. Time management and reading comprehension go hand-in-hand.

looking at your notes. If you are at home, sit back in your chair, recite the information, and determine what it means. If you have trouble explaining the information to your friend or reciting it to yourself, you probably did not understand the section and you should go back and reread it. If you can tell your classmate and yourself exactly what you just read and what it means, you are ready to move on to the next section of the chapter.

Step 5: Review After you have read the chapter, immediately go back and read it again. "What?!! I just read it!" Yes, you did. And the best way to determine whether you have mastered the information is to survey the chapter once again; review marginal notes, highlighted areas, and vocabulary words; and determine whether you have any questions that have not been answered. This step will help you store and retain this information in your long-term memory.

SQ3R can be a lifesaver when it comes to understanding material that is overwhelming. It is an efficient, comprehensive, and DOABLE practice that can dramatically assist you in your reading efforts.

Understanding the difference between reading the words on a page and comprehending the words and their meanings can literally save your academic life. Reading, while easy and fun for some, is daunting and torturous for others. Regardless of your situation at the moment, you can improve your reading ability, your comprehension, and your speed. But you are the only person on earth who can do it. You are the only one who can make these improvements, and you are the only one who can make the commitment to yourself to improve your skills. It has been said that if you can effectively read and write the English language, there is nothing that you can't understand in the world. Good luck in your journey.

what's it ALL ABOUT?

NAME: Joey Luna

SCHOOL: El Paso Community College, El Paso, TX

MAJOR: Health Sciences   AGE: 21

Below is a real-life situation faced by Joey. Read the brief case and respond to the questions.

I have never enjoyed reading. I was not a good reader in high school and that trend continued when I first enrolled in my program. I registered for 12 hours and, soon into the semester, dropped my English class because of the reading assignments. Later in the semester, I dropped two other courses and remained only in math.

The reason I stayed in the math course was that so little reading was required. I was able to do the work without a commitment to reading a text-book or reading outside materials.

I enrolled for 12 more hours the second semester and quickly dropped them all due to the reading assignments and my frustration with reading. I know how to read, but spent so little time doing it and never really thought about comprehending what I'd read. The classes were difficult.

This semester, I am enrolled again. I am learning to read and reread the assignments for comprehension. I'm taking notes while I read. I have my first test this Monday. I have high hopes of doing very well.

What advice would you give to Joey for Monday?

_____

_____

_____

_____

If Joey were enrolled at your school, where could he have turned for help?

_____

_____

_____

_____

Why is note taking important to the reading process?

_____

_____

_____

What relationship do reading and math have with each other?

_____

_____

_____

_____

Why do you think Joey is doing better since he started taking notes while reading?

_____

_____

_____

_____

What advice would you give to a student who has struggled with reading comprehension in the past?

_____

_____

_____

_____

ADVICE TO GO

CORNERSTONES

for reading and comprehension

Commit yourself to becoming a better reader.

Approach the text, chapter, or article with an *open mind.*

Free your mind to focus on your reading.

Always read with your "*six pack*" at your side.

Underline and look up words you do not *understand.*

Write down your *vocabulary words*, and review them often.

Use *SQ3R* to increase and test your comprehension.

If you're having trouble, *get a tutor* to help you.

Understand that *the more you read,* the better you'll become at it.

READ

5

Learn

E di walked into class, and the first thing she saw when she sat down at her desk was a message on the board: "Pop Quiz Today." In her mind, she was freaking out. "I'm not ready for a quiz," she said to herself. "I did not study for a quiz today. What am I going to do?" All she could think about was the last class. "Did I miss something?" she thought. "*Did he tell us there was going to be a quiz and I just did not hear it?*"

After everyone had entered, Mr. Maughan, the instructor, said, "Calm down everyone. Yes, we're having a quiz, but I know that everyone will do very well on it." He handed out the one-page quiz, and you could almost feel the relief in the room. The pop quiz read:

Directions: *Answer the following questions:*

1. *Which business uses the slogan "Just Do It"?*

   Nike

2. *When typing, your pinky finger on your right hand is on which letter?*

   j

3. *Which TV show began with "Here's the story of a lovely lady. . ."?*

   Brady Bunch

4. *Give one example of how you might explain the word "blue" to a visually impaired person.*

   Sky

Edi completed the quiz, and the scores for the class revealed that everyone had passed the quiz with an A. "Jeez," Edi thought, "I wish that all of my classes were this easy."

> *She had always been the kind of student who had to visualize the information to understand it. Now she knew why.*

Mr. Maughan began to explain why he gave the quiz. He pointed out that everyone is always learning. "You did not have to study for this quiz because you had already learned the material through repetition, or you could think of an answer through your senses," he said. He told the class that he gave them the exam to prove that everyone learns and visualizes information differently. Some students were able to answer the "Just Do It" question by remembering the Nike commerical and the sports moves. Some were able to answer the typing question because of touch and repetition. Others could answer the *Brady Bunch* question by actually seeing the little picture boxes flash up on the screen.

This piqued Edi's interest because she knew that she always learned best by actually seeing something in her mind before doing it. She had always been the type of student who had to visualize the information to get involved with the project. And today, Edi discovered that it had to do with her learning style—visual.

Mr. Maughan explained to her that this might be one reason why she had always excelled in design. Edi is studying Fashion Design and this finally made sense to her. "Is this why I have to draw the design in my head before I can put it on paper?" she asked. "Exactly," Mr. Maughan answered. Edi smiled to herself when she finally realized why she had always outperformed in design, art, painting, and drawing and had not done so well in math and science. "I just learn by seeing and doing," she thought. "That's pretty cool."

QUESTIONS
FOR REFLECTION

Consider responding to these questions online in the Questions for Reflection module of the Companion Website.

1. How do you learn best and does this learning style match your major?

2. Can you idenfity a time when your learning style did not match your instructor's teaching style? How did this affect your learning in that class?

3. How can you work to improve your least dominant learning style?

Before reading this chapter, take a moment and respond to the following 10 questions. Consider each one carefully before answering, and then respond by circling the number in the appropriate box. When you have answered the questions, add your points and find your total score on the feedback chart below.

STATEMENT	STRONGLY DISAGREE	DISAGREE	DON'T KNOW	AGREE	STRONGLY AGREE	SCORE
1. I know which teaching styles match my learning preferences.	1	2	③	4	5	3
2. When I study, I use a variety of methods to learn new material.	①	2	3	4	5	1
3. I don't know what my strengths and weaknesses are as a learner.	5	4	3	②	1	2
4. I have devised study strategies that capitalize on my learning strengths.	①	2	3	4	5	1
5. My personality type has no impact on my study strategies.	5	4	③	2	1	3
6. There is little point in trying to improve my weaker learning styles.	⑤	4	3	2	1	5
7. I have tried using different learning strategies in my studies.	1	2	3	④	5	4
8. I do not know how I learn differently when I am seeing, hearing, or doing.	⑤	4	3	2	1	5
9. There is no way to use my strengths in music, sports, or relationships to help me learn.	5	④	3	2	1	4
10. When learning something new, I try to incorporate what I see with what I hear and to "do" or use the new information.	1	2	3	④	5	4
TOTAL VALUE						32

SUMMARY

43–50 You are exceptional in your ability to bring together your various personality traits and multiple intelligences in your studies. You have likely spent time working to improve your weaknesses, routinely trying different approaches to learning material.

35–42 You are above average in knowing how to integrate your personality traits and different aspects of intelligence into your studies. You likely try different approaches to learning, but might still need improvement in addressing your weaknesses.

26–34 You are average in your knowledge of your own learning preferences. You can see how different types of intelligence and personality affect your learning. You likely need to incorporate strategies for improving your weaknesses into your learning profile.

18–25 You have a below average knowledge of your strengths and weaknesses as a learner. You need help putting together a set of strategies to integrate your personality and intelligence strengths for learning. Giving attention to improving your weaknesses will also be helpful for you.

10–17 Your knowledge of your own strengths, weaknesses, and styles of learning is limited. You don't seem to know much about how to use your personality traits, multiple intelligences, and study strategies together to learn. You will need to spend time exploring these issues.

Based on the summary above, what is one goal you would like to achieve related to your learning style?

Goal *I would like to know how to study properly and use that to do better.*

List three actions you can take that might help you move closer to realizing this goal.

1. *studying*
2. *avoid distraction*
3. *ask questions*

Questions
FOR BUILDING ON YOUR BEST

As you read this chapter, consider the following questions. At the end of the chapter, you should be able to answer all of them. We encourage you to ask a few questions of your own. Consider turning to your classmates or instructors to assist you.

1. Why is it important for me to know my learning style?
2. How can my personality type affect my study habits?
3. What is the difference between a learning style and an intelligence?
4. How can I adapt the teaching style of my instructor to my learning style?
5. How can understanding my learning style help me become a better student?

What additional questions might you have about your learning style, primary intelligence, or personality type?

1. _____
2. _____
3. _____

Understanding Your Strengths

You may be asking yourself, "Is there one 'best' way of learning?" The answer is no. The way one learns depends on so many variables. Learning styles, your personal intelligences, personality typing, your past experiences, and your attitude all play a part in the way you process new information. While many students do not like the lecture format, others relish it. Some students learn best by touching and doing, whereas others learn best by listening and reflecting. Some students learn best with a group of people sitting outside under the trees, others must be alone in the library. There are many factors that may influence the way we learn and process information. This chapter explores the benefits of knowing your learning style and your personality type and the benefits of examining your intelligences.

To be what we are, and to become what we are capable of becoming, is the only end in life.
—ROBERT L. STEVENSON

Looking for Treasures
DISCOVERING AND POLISHING YOUR TALENTS

This section will offer you the opportunity to complete three inventories: **(1)** to assess your learning style, **(2)** to assess your personality type, and **(3)** to help you better understand multiple intelligences. These assessments are in no way intended to label you. They are not a measure of your intelligence. They do not measure your worth or your capacities as a student. The three assessments are included so that you might gain a better understanding of your multiple intelligences and identify your learning styles and your personality type. There are no right or wrong answers, and there is no one best way to learn. We hope that by the end of this section, you will have experienced a "Wow" or an "Ah-ha!" as you explore and discover new and exciting components of your education. Many students have met with great success by identifying and molding their study environments and habits to reflect their learning style and personality type.

There are many ways to learn how to ski. The learning technique that works best for you depends on many different factors, which may vary from situation to situation.

As a child, I continually conducted "natural" experiments. I wanted to see how things worked. As an adult, I find that I am most successful in learning practical things by doing them, and I tend to be a visual learner today.

As a professor, it is still most natural for me to function in the same ways as I did when I was much younger; however, I understand that my students may not all share my preferred learning style. Therefore, I provide activities that require a variety of learning styles so every student has areas of the course in which they can excel. At the same time, by forcing the use of multiple learning styles, I hope my students are developing learning styles other than the one with which they are most comfortable.

Experiential learning suits me well because I am a very active, product-oriented person. I enjoy identifying the issues, gathering the tools, and building solutions. Experiential (tactile) learning is appealing because I can see other blocks of knowledge and how they fit into solving new problems. Tactile learning reinforces and combines what I already know with what I am currently learning.

If I were giving advice to students—and I frequently do—I would encourage you to take self-tests to learn more about the areas that can help you in your career and match this with the learning styles that you are most likely to need in your chosen field. I would caution you, however, against being locked into someone else's definition of who you are. Be adventurous! Begin by transferring your class notes into a different modality. You can actually "train" other modalities by forcing yourself to rely on different senses. For example, try watching television with the screen blacked out to improve your hearing modality, or watch the screen with the sound turned down to force more effort on your visual capacity. If you write a narrative, draw a picture to accompany it so you are developing more than one capacity with the same assignment.

As a student and future employee, you might have an instructor or a boss who communicates in ways that make no sense to you. You cannot afford to close your mind to either of these people because they hold the key to your success. You must find ways to get the message despite the messenger. There are three things you can do to get the message:

1. Ask your instructor for references in your learning style. For example, ask, "Is there a diagram that illustrates the material you talked about today?"

2. Seek out someone who understands what is required and request that student's help in translating the assignment. Say to a classmate, "You seem to understand this assignment. Could you explain it to me?"

3. Finally, ask your instructor for samples of successfully completed work that other students have finished. Sometimes if you know what the outcome is supposed to look like you can figure out how to put the ingredients together. You might say to the instructor, "I want to do a good job. Could you show me an example of an excellent project?"

Students need to realize that we are all different and that each of us learns in our own ways. The important thing is for you to push yourself to develop learning styles other than the one or two that are easiest for you. The more you do this, the more successful you will be in school and at work.

QUESTIONS FOR REFLECTION

Consider responding to these questions online in the World of Work module of the Companion Website.

1. Dr. Eaddy is a visual learner and adapts her learning style to her work. What is your best learning style?

2. Dr. Eaddy became a teacher because she wanted a career that rewards her for learning. She loves to learn and to share her knowledge with students. Have you considered whether your program is in an area that matches your interests and intelligence?

3. What can you do to improve the intelligence areas where you are not as strong as you would like to be?

Starr Eaddy, Ph.D., CHES, *Assistant Professor,* William Paterson University

TAKE THE MIS

The Multiple Intelligences Survey

Robert M. Sherfield, Ph.D., 1999, 2002, 2005

Directions: Read each statement carefully and thoroughly. After reading the statement, rate your response using the scale below. There are no right or wrong answers. This is not a timed survey. The MIS is based, in part, on *Frames of Mind* by Howard Gardner, 1983.

3 = Often Applies

2 = Sometimes Applies

1 = Never or Almost Never Applies

___3___ 1. When someone gives me directions, I have to visualize them in my mind in order to understand them.

___2___ 2. I enjoy crossword puzzles and word games like Scrabble.

___2___ 3. I enjoy dancing and can keep up with the beat of music.

___1___ 4. I have little or no trouble conceptualizing information or facts.

___1___ 5. I like to repair things that are broken such as toasters, small engines, bicycles, and cars.

___2___ 6. I enjoy leadership activities on campus and in the community.

___3___ 7. I have the ability to get others to listen to me.

___2___ 8. I enjoy working with nature, animals, and plants.

___2___ 9. I know where everything is in my home such as supplies, gloves, flashlights, camera, and compact discs.

___3___ 10. I am a good speller.

___3___ 11. I often sing or hum to myself in the shower or car, or while walking or just sitting.

___2___ 12. I am a very logical, orderly thinker.

___1___ 13. I use a lot of gestures when I talk to people.

___3___ 14. I can recognize and empathize with people's attitudes and emotions.

___2___ 15. I prefer to study alone.

___3___ 16. I can name many different things in the environment such as clouds, rocks, and plant types.

___1___ 17. I like to draw pictures, graphs, or charts to better understand information.

___3___ 18. I have a good memory for names and dates.

___3___ 19. When I hear music, I "get into it" by moving, humming, tapping, or even singing.

___2___ 20. I learn better by asking a lot of questions.

___3___ 21. I enjoy playing competitive sports.

___3___ 22. I communicate very well with other people.

2   23. I know what I want and I set goals to accomplish it.

1   24. I have some interest in herbal remedies and natural medicine.

3   25. I enjoy working puzzles or mazes.

1   26. I am a good storyteller.

2   27. I can easily remember the words and melodies of songs.

2   28. I enjoy solving problems in math and chemistry and working with computer programming problems.

1   29. I usually touch people or pat them on the back when I talk to them.

3   30. I understand my family and friends better than most other people do.

2   31. I don't always talk about my accomplishments with others.

1   32. I would rather work outside around nature than inside around people and equipment.

2   33. I enjoy and learn more when seeing movies, slides, or videos in class.

3   34. I am a very good listener and I enjoy listening to others' stories.

1   35. I need to study with music.

1   36. I enjoy games like Clue, Battleship, chess, and Rubik's Cube.

3   37. I enjoy physical activities such as bicycling, jogging, dancing, snowboarding, skateboarding, or swimming.

3   38. I am good at solving people's problems and conflicts.

3   39. I have to have time alone to think about new information in order to remember it.

1   40. I enjoy sorting and organizing information, objects, and collectibles.

Refer to your score on each individual question. Place that score beside the appropriate question number below. Then, tally each line at the side.

SCORE					TOTAL ACROSS	CODE
1 3	9 2	17 1	25 3	33 2	11	Visual/Spatial
2 2	10 3	18 3	26 1	34 3	15	Verbal/Linguistic
3 2	11 3	19 3	27 2	35 1	11	Musical/Rhythm
4 1	12 2	20 2	28 2	36 1	8	Logic/Math
5 1	13 1	21 3	29 1	37 3	9	Body/Kinesthetic
6 2	14 3	22 3	30 3	38 3	14	Interpersonal
7 3	15 2	23 2	31 2	39 3	12	Intrapersonal
8 2	16 3	24 1	32 1	40 1	8	Naturalistic

MIS TALLY

Multiple Intelligences

Look at the scores on the MIS. What are your top three scores? Write them in the space below.

Top Score _____ 15 _____   Code _Verbal_

Second Score _____ 14 _____   Code _Interpersonal_

Third Score _____ 12 _____   Code _Intrapersonal_

This tally can help you understand where some of your strengths may be. Again, this is not a measure of your worth or capacities, nor is it an indicator of your future successes. Read the following section to better understand multiple intelligences.

A New Way of Looking at Yourself

UNDERSTANDING MULTIPLE INTELLIGENCES

In 1983, Howard Gardner, a Harvard University professor, developed a theory called Multiple Intelligences. In his book *Frames of Mind,* he outlines seven intelligences that he feels are possessed by everyone: visual/spatial, verbal/linguistic, musical/rhythm, logic/math, body/kinesthetic, interpersonal, and intrapersonal. In 1996, he added an eighth intelligence: naturalistic. In short, if you have ever done things that come easily for you, you are probably drawing on one of your intelligences that is well developed. On the other hand, if you have tried to do things that are very difficult to master or understand, you may be dealing with material that calls on one of your less-developed intelligences. If playing the piano by ear comes easily to you, your musical/rhythm intelligence may be very strong. If you have trouble writing or understanding poetry, your verbal/linguistic intelligence may not be as well developed. This does not mean that you will never be able to write poetry; it simply means that you have not fully developed your skills in this area.

THE EIGHT INTELLIGENCES

The "smart" descriptors were adapted from Thomas Armstrong (1994).

Visual/spatial *(picture smart).* Thinks in pictures; knows where things are in the house; loves to create images and work with graphs, charts, pictures, and maps.

Verbal/linguistic *(word smart).* Communicates well through language, likes to write, is good at spelling, great at telling stories, loves to read books.

Musical/rhythm *(music smart).* Loves to sing, hum, and whistle; comprehends music; responds to music immediately; performs music.

Logic/math *(number smart)*. Can easily conceptualize and reason, uses logic, has good problem-solving skills, enjoys math and science.

Body/kinesthetic *(body smart)*. Learns through body sensation, moves around a lot, enjoys work involving the hands, is graced with some athletic ability.

Interpersonal *(people smart)*. Loves to communicate with other people, possesses great leadership skills, has lots of friends, is involved in extracurricular activities.

Intrapersonal *(self-smart)*. Has a deep awareness of own feelings, is very reflective, requires time to be alone, does not get involved with group activities.

Naturalistic *(environment smart)*. Has interest in the environment and in nature; can easily recognize plants, animals, rocks, and cloud formations; may like hiking, camping, and fishing.

Making It Work for You
USING MULTIPLE INTELLIGENCES TO ENHANCE STUDYING AND LEARNING

Below, you will find some helpful tips to assist you in creating a study environment and study habits using your multiple intelligences.

VISUAL/SPATIAL

- Use visuals in your notes such as time lines, charts, graphs, and geometric shapes.
- Work to create a mental or visual picture of the information at hand.
- Use colored markers to make associations or to group items together.
- Use mapping or webbing so that your main points are easily recognized.
- When taking notes, draw pictures in the margins to illustrate the main points.
- Visualize the information in your mind.

VERBAL/LINGUISTIC

- Establish study groups so that you will have the opportunity to talk about the information.
- Using the information you studied, create a story or a skit.
- Read as much information about related areas as possible.
- As you read chapters, outline them in your own words.
- Summarize and recite your notes aloud.

DID YOU KNOW?

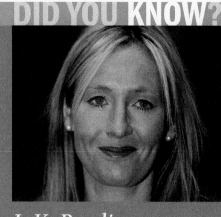

J. K. Rowling

was dismissed from a secretarial job because her boss caught her writing stories on her computer at work. She supported herself and her family on unemployment pay while she wrote the first *Harry Potter*. Today, she continues to write and is a billionaire.

MUSICAL/RHYTHM

- Listen to music while studying (if it does not distract you).
- Write a song or rap about the chapter or information.
- Take short breaks from studying to listen to music.
- Commit the information being studied to the music from your favorite song.

LOGIC/MATH

- Strive to make connections between subjects.
- Don't just memorize the facts; apply them to real-life situations.
- As you study the information, think of problems in society and how this information could solve those problems.
- Create analyzing charts. Draw a line down the center of the page, put the information at hand in the left column and analyze, discuss, relate, and synthesize it in the right column.
- Allow yourself some time to reflect after studying.

BODY/KINESTHETIC

- Don't confine your study area to a desk or a chair; move around, explore, go outside.
- Act out the information.
- Study in a group of people and change groups often.
- Use charts, posters, flash cards, and chalkboards to study.
- When appropriate or possible, build models using the information studied.
- Verbalize the information to others.
- Use games such as chess, Monopoly, Twister, or Clue when studying.
- Trace words as you study them.
- Use repetition to learn facts; write them many times.
- Make study sheets.

INTERPERSONAL

- Study in groups.
- Share the information with other people.
- Teach the information to others.
- Interview outside sources to learn more about the material at hand.
- Have a debate with others about the information.

INTRAPERSONAL

- Study in a quiet area by yourself.
- Allow time for reflection and meditation about the subject matter.
- Study in short time blocks and then spend some time absorbing the information.
- Work at your own pace.

NATURALISTIC

- Study outside whenever possible.
- Relate the information to the effect on the environment whenever possible.
- When given the opportunity to choose your own topics or research projects, choose something related to nature.
- Collect your own study data and resources.
- Organize and label your information.
- Keep separate notebooks on individual topics so that you can add new information to each topic as it becomes available to you.

Understanding Learning Styles Theory

Rita Dunn defines learning styles as "the way in which each learner begins to concentrate on, process, and retain new and difficult information." We must note that there is a difference between a learning *style* and a learning *strategy*. A learning strategy is how you might choose to learn or study, such as by using note cards, flip charts, color slides, or cooperative learning groups. Flip charts and slides are strategies. Learning styles are more sensory. They involve seeing, hearing, and touching.

If you learn best by *seeing* information, you have a more dominant *visual* learning style. If you learn best by *hearing* information, you have a more dominant *auditory* learning style. If you learn best by *touching or doing,* you have a more dominant *tactile* learning style. You may also hear the tactile learning style referred to as kinesthetic or hands-on.

Some of the most successful students have learned to use all three styles. If you were learning how to skateboard, you might learn best by hearing someone talk about the different styles or techniques. Others might learn best by watching a video where someone demonstrates the techniques. Still others would learn best by actually getting on the board and trying it. However, the student who involved all of his or her senses might gain the most. She might listen to the instructor tell about skateboarding, watch the video, and then go do it. Therefore, she would have involved all of her learning styles: visual, auditory, and tactile.

Take time now to complete the assessment on the following page. Then read more about the three learning styles on page 115.

TAKE THE LEAD

The Learning Evaluation and Assessment Directory

Robert M. Sherfield, Ph.D., 1999, 2002, 2005

Directions: Read each statement carefully and thoroughly. After reading the statement, rate your response using the scale below. There are no right or wrong answers. This is not a timed survey. The LEAD is based, in part, on research conducted by Rita Dunn.

3 = Often Applies

2 = Sometimes Applies

1 = Never or Almost Never Applies

_2_ 1. I remember information better if I write it down or draw a picture of it.

_1_ 2. I remember things better when I hear them instead of just reading or seeing them.

_1_ 3. When I get something that has to be assembled, I just start doing it. I don't read the directions.

_2_ 4. If I am taking a test, I can "see" the page of the text or lecture notes where the answer is located.

_3_ 5. I would rather the instructor explain a graph, chart, or diagram than just show it to me.

_1_ 6. When learning new things, I want to "do it" rather than hear about it.

_3_ 7. I would rather the instructor write the information on the board or overhead instead of just lecturing.

_3_ 8. I would rather listen to a book on tape than read it.

_2_ 9. I enjoy making things, putting things together, and working with my hands.

_2_ 10. I am able to quickly conceptualize and visualize information.

_1_ 11. I learn best by hearing words.

_1_ 12. I have been called hyperactive by my parents, spouse, partner, or instructor.

_2_ 13. I have no trouble reading maps, charts, or diagrams.

_3_ 14. I can usually pick up on small sounds like bells, crickets, or frogs, or distant sounds like train whistles.

_1_ 15. I use my hands and gesture a lot when I speak to others.

Refer to your score on each individual question. Place that score beside the appropriate question number below. Then, tally each line at the side.

SCORE					TOTAL ACROSS	CODE
1 _2_	4 _2_	7 _3_	10 _2_	13 _2_	11	Visual
2 _1_	5 _3_	8 _3_	11 _1_	14 _3_	11	Auditory
3 _1_	6 _1_	9 _2_	12 _1_	15 _1_	6	Tactile

Look at the scores on the LEAD. What is your top score? _11_

Here are brief descriptions of the three learning styles:

Visual *(eye smart)*. Thinks in pictures. Enjoys visual instructions, demonstrations, and descriptions; would rather read a text than listen to a lecture; avid note-taker; needs visual references; enjoys using charts, graphs, and pictures.

Auditory *(ear smart)*. Prefers verbal instructions; would rather listen than read; often tapes lectures and listens to them in the car or at home; recites information out loud; enjoys talking, discussing issues, and verbal stimuli; talks out problems.

Tactile *(action smart)*. Prefers hands-on approaches to learning; likes to take notes and uses a great deal of scratch paper; learns best by doing something, by touching it, or manipulating it; learns best while moving or while in action; often does not concentrate well when sitting and reading.

What Can You Learn About Personality?

To begin, take the PAP assessment below.

THE PERSONALITY ASSESSMENT PROFILE (PAP)

Robert M. Sherfield, Ph.D., 1999, 2002, 2005

Directions: Read each statement carefully and thoroughly. After reading the statement, rate your response using the scale below. There are no right or wrong answers. This is not a timed survey. The PAP is based, in part, on the Myers-Briggs Type Indicator® (MBTI) by Katharine Briggs and Isabel Briggs-Myers.

3 = Often Applies

2 = Sometimes Applies

1 = Never or Almost Never Applies

___2___ 1a. I am a very talkative person.

___1___ 1b. I am a more reflective person than a verbal person.

___2___ 2a. I am a very factual and literal person.

___3___ 2b. I look to the future and I can see possibilities.

___3___ 3a. I value truth and justice over tact and emotion.

___3___ 3b. I find it easy to empathize with other people.

___2___ 4a. I am very ordered and efficient.

___2___ 4b. I enjoy having freedom from control.

___3___ 5a. I am a very friendly and social person.

___2___ 5b. I enjoy listening to others more than talking.

(continued)

_3_ 6a. I enjoy being around and working with people who have a great deal of common sense.

_2_ 6b. I enjoy being around and working with people who are dreamers and have a great deal of imagination.

_3_ 7a. One of my motivating forces is to do a job very well.

_3_ 7b. I like to be recognized for, and I am motivated by, my accomplishments and awards.

_1_ 8a. I like to plan out my day before I go to bed.

_1_ 8b. When I get up on a non-school or non-work day, I just like to let the day "plan itself."

_3_ 9a. I like to express my feelings and thoughts.

_2_ 9b. I enjoy a great deal of tranquility and quiet time to myself.

_2_ 10a. I am a very pragmatic and realistic person.

_1_ 10b. I like to create new ideas, methods, or ways of doing things.

_2_ 11a. I make decisions with my brain.

_3_ 11b. I make decisions with my heart.

_2_ 12a. I am a very disciplined and orderly person.

_2_ 12b. I don't make a lot of plans.

_1_ 13a. I like to work with a group of people.

_3_ 13b. I would rather work independently.

_2_ 14a. I learn best if I can see it, touch it, smell it, taste it, or hear it.

_1_ 14b. I learn best by relying on my gut feelings or intuition.

_1_ 15a. I am quick to criticize others.

_2_ 15b. I compliment others very easily and quickly.

_2_ 16a. My life is systematic and organized.

_1_ 16b. I don't really pay attention to deadlines.

_3_ 17a. I can be myself when I am around others.

_3_ 17b. I can be myself when I am alone.

_2_ 18a. I live in the here and now, in the present.

_2_ 18b. I live in the future, planning and dreaming.

_2_ 19a. I think that if someone breaks the rules, the person should be punished.

_1_ 19b. I think that if someone breaks the rules, we should look at the person who broke the rules, examine the rules, and look at the situation at hand before a decision is made.

_3_ 20a. I do my work, then I play.

_1_ 20b. I play, then do my work.

Using the score sheet below, record your score on each individual question. Place that score beside the appropriate question numbers. Then, tally each horizontal line using the right-hand column.

SCORE					TOTAL ACROSS	CODE
1a 2	5a 3	9a 3	13a 1	17a 3	12	**E** Extrovert
1b 1	5b 2	9b 2	13b 3	17b 3	11	**I** Introvert
2a 2	6a 5	10a 2	14a 2	18a 2	11	**S** Sensing
2b 3	6b 2	10b 1	14b 1	18b 2	9	**N** iNtuition
3a 3	7a 3	11a 2	15a 1	19a 2	11	**T** Thinking
3b 3	7b 3	11b 3	15b 2	19b 1	12	**F** Feeling
4a 2	8a 1	12a 2	16a 2	20a 3	10	**J** Judging
4b 2	8b 1	12b 2	16b 1	20b 1	7	**P** Perceiving

Personality Indicator

Look at the scores on your PAP. Is your score higher in the E or I line? Is your score higher in the S or N line? Is your score higher in the T or F line? Is your score higher in the J or P line? Write the code to the side of each section below.

Is your higher score	E or I	Code	12 E
Is your higher score	S or N	Code	S
Is your higher score	T or F	Code	12 F
Is your higher score	J or P	Code	J

UNDERSTANDING PERSONALITY TYPING (TYPOLOGY)

The questions on the PAP helped you discover whether you are extroverted or introverted (E or I), sensing or intuitive (S or N), thinking or feeling (T or F), and judging or perceiving (J or P). These questions were based, in part, on work done by Carl Jung, Katharine Briggs, and Isabel Briggs-Myers. What personality typing can do is to "help us discover what best motivates and energizes each of us as individuals" (Tieger and Tieger, 2001).

Why Personality Matters

Let's take a look at the four major categories of typing. Notice that the stronger your score in one area, the stronger your personality type is for that area. For instance, if you scored 15 on the E (extroversion) questions, this means that you are a strong extrovert. If you scored 15 on the I (introversion) questions, this means that you are a strong introvert. However, if you scored 7 on the E questions and 8 on the I questions, your score indicates that you possess almost the same amount of extroverted and introverted qualities. The same is true for every category on the PAP.

E VERSUS I (EXTROVERSION/INTROVERSION)

This category deals with the way we *interact with others and the world around us.* Extroverts prefer to live in the outside world, drawing their strength from other people. They are outgoing and love interaction. They usually make decisions with others in mind. They enjoy being the center of attention. There are usually few secrets about extroverts. Introverts draw their strength from the inner world. They need to spend time alone to think and ponder. They are usually quiet and make decisions alone.

S VERSUS N (SENSING/INTUITION)

This category deals with the way we *learn and deal with information.* Sensing types gather information through their five senses. They have a hard time believing something if it cannot be seen, touched, smelled, tasted, or heard. They like concrete facts and details. They do not rely on intuition or gut feelings. They usually have a great deal of common sense. Intuitive types are not very detail-oriented. They can see possibilities, and they rely on their gut feelings. Usually, they are very innovative people. They tend to live in the future and often get bored once they have mastered a task.

Yes You Can!
IDEAS FOR SUCCESS

Consider the following tips for making the most of your learning styles, personality type, and dominant intelligence:

- Understand that everyone has a strength and aptitude for some skill or task.

- Improve your weaker learning styles by incorporating at least one aspect of those learning styles into your daily study plans.

- If your personality type clashes with your instructor's personality type, try to make adjustments that enable you to get through the class successfully.

- Strengthen your less dominant intelligences by involving yourself in activities that cause you to use them.

- Adjust your learning style to match your instructor's teaching style if possible.

- Understand that your primary intelligence can help you decide on your life's vocation.

T VERSUS F (THINKING/FEELING)

This category deals with the way we *make decisions.* Thinkers are very logical people. They do not make decisions based on feelings or emotion. They are analytical and sometimes do not take others' values into consideration when making decisions. They can easily identify the flaws of others. They can be seen as insensitive and lacking compassion. Feelers make decisions based on what they feel is right and just. They like to have harmony, and they value others' opinions and feelings. They are usually very tactful people who like to please others. They are very warm people.

J VERSUS P (JUDGING/PERCEIVING)

This category deals with the way we *live*. **Judgers** are very orderly people. They must have a great deal of structure in their lives. They are good at setting goals and sticking to their goals. They are the type of people who would seldom, if ever, play before their work was completed. **Perceivers** are just the opposite. They are less structured and more spontaneous. They do not like time lines. Unlike the judger, they will play before their work is done. They will take every chance to delay a decision or judgment.

With this information, you can make some decisions about your study habits and even your career choices. For instance, if you scored very strong in the extroversion section, it may not serve you well to pursue a career where you would be forced to work alone. It would probably be unwise to try to spend all of your time studying alone. If you are a strong extrovert, you would want to work and study around people.

Making Your Personality Work for You

ENHANCING YOUR LEARNING

Having identified your personality type, use the suggestions on pages 120–121 to enhance studying using your present personality type, while improving your study skills using your less dominant type.

TYPE	CURRENT SUGGESTIONS	IMPROVEMENT
Extrovert	Study with groups of people in cooperative learning teams. Seek help from others. Discuss topics with friends. Establish debate or discussion groups. Vary your study habits; meet in different places with different people. Discuss new ideas and plans with your friends.	Work on listening skills. Be sure to let others contribute to the group. Force yourself to develop solutions and answers before you go to the group. Spend some time reflecting. Let others speak before you share your ideas and suggestions. Work to be more patient. Think before acting or speaking.
Introvert	Study in a quiet place, undisturbed by others. When reading and studying, take time for reflection. Use your time alone to read and study support and auxiliary materials. Set aside large blocks of time for study and reflection.	Get involved in a study group from time to time. Allow others inside your world to offer advice and opinions. Share your opinions and advice with others more often. Seek advice from others. Use mnemonics to increase your memory power. Instead of writing responses or questions, speak aloud to friends and peers.
Sensor	Observe the world around you. Experience the information to the fullest degree; feel it and touch it. Explain to your study group or partner the information in complete detail. Apply the information to something in your life that is currently happening. Create a study schedule and stick to it. If your old study habits are not working, stop and invent new ways of studying. Explore what others are doing.	Try to think about the information in an abstract form. Think "What would happen if . . ." Let your imagination run wild. Think about the information in the future tense. Let your gut feelings take over from time to time. Take more chances with the unknown. Trust your feelings and inspirations. Think beyond reality. Don't oversimplify.
Intuitive	After studying the information or data, let your imagination apply this to something abstract. Describe how the information could be used today, right now, in your life at the moment. Describe how this information could help others. View new information as a challenge. Vary your study habits; don't do the same thing all the time. Rely on your gut feelings.	Work on becoming more detail-oriented. Look at information through the senses. Verify your facts. Think in simple terms. Think about the information in a logical and analytical way. Try to explain new information in relation to the senses.

(continued)

TYPE	CURRENT SUGGESTIONS	IMPROVEMENT
Thinker	Make logical connections between new information and what is already known. Remain focused. Explain the information in detailed terms to a study group. Put things in order. Study with people who do their part for the group.	Try to see information and data in more abstract terms. Look for the "big picture." Develop a passion for acquiring new information. Think before you speak. Strive to be more objective and open.
Feeler	Establish a supportive and open study group. Teach others the information. Continue to be passionate about learning and exploring. Explain the information in a cause/effect scenario. Focus on the "people" factor.	Strive to look at things more logically. Work to stay focused. Praise yourself when others do not. Try to be more organized. Work to stick to policies, rules, and guidelines. Don't give in to opposition just for the sake of harmony. Don't get caught up in the here and now; look ahead.
Judger	Set a schedule and stick to it. Strive to complete projects. Keep your study supplies in one place so that you can locate them easily. Prioritize tasks that need to be completed. Create lists and agendas.	Take your time in making decisions. Complete all tasks. Look at the entire situation before making a judgment. Don't act or make judgments too quickly. Don't beat yourself up if you miss a deadline.
Perceiver	Study in different places with different people. Since you see all sides of issues, share those with your study group for discussion. Obtain as much information as possible so that you can make solid decisions. Create fun and exciting study groups with snacks and maybe music. Be the leader of the study team. Allow yourself a great deal of time for study so that you can take well-deserved breaks.	Become more decisive. Finish one project before you begin another. Don't put off the harder subjects until later; study them first. Learn to set deadlines. Create lists and agendas to help you stay on target. Do your work; then play.

The most important thing to remember about learning styles, multiple intelligences, and personality typology is that, unlike an IQ test, they do not pretend to determine if you are "smart" or not. They simply allow you to look more closely at how you learn, what strengths you have in your innate personality, and what dominant intelligence you have.

Discovering your learning style can greatly enhance your classroom performance. For example, finally understanding that your **learning style** is visual and that your instructor's **teaching style** is totally verbal can answer many questions about why you may have performed poorly in the past. Now, you have the knowledge and the tools to make your learning style work for you, not against you.

what's it ALL ABOUT?

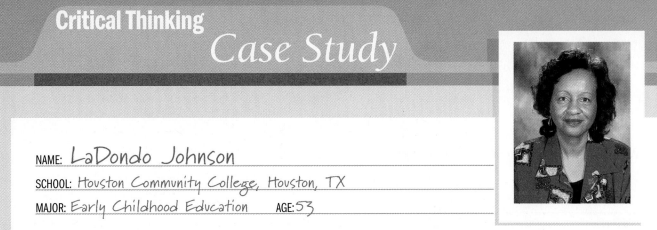

NAME: LaDondo Johnson

SCHOOL: Houston Community College, Houston, TX

MAJOR: Early Childhood Education   AGE: 53

Below is a real-life situation faced by LaDondo. Read the brief case and respond to the questions.

Returning to school at 53 was not an easy decision, but I knew that I wanted to reach my goal of working with children. It has been a dream of mine for many years. I found that my biggest problem in returning to the classroom was learning to listen to the instructor. I continued to wonder why this was such a problem for me, and then I took a Learning Styles Inventory and discovered that my primary learning style is visual. It made perfect sense to me then—my learning style was not matching my instructor's teaching style.

I knew that my instructor was not going to change teaching styles, so I had to learn to adapt and adjust. I began going home after each class and converting my notes onto note cards. By doing this, I was able to make the lecture visual. I would write questions on one side and answers on the other, sometimes drawing examples or using color to help me absorb the information better.

I found that by making the lecture visual, I understood what was being taught and could study the information more effectively. I also discovered that the more I looked at my cards, the more I retained. I discovered that repetition is as important to my learning process as visualization. Discovering both of these has helped me greatly.

Toward the end of the semester, I noticed another thing. I performed in class much better when I was able to interact and be a part of a group. I have always had an outgoing personality, but again, I never thought this would play a part in my education. I found that because of my personality, I love to participate and share and draw from others. I guess my dominant intelligence is interpersonal.

By discovering these things about my learning abilities, I am certain that I will be able to complete this program and reach one of the most important goals in my life.

If LaDondo has a very outgoing personality, what is most likely her personality type according to this chapter? Why did you choose this type?

_____

_____

_____

With LaDondo's outgoing personality, how could she be successful in a class that offered NO interaction or group work?

_____

_____

_____

What role does personality play in academic success?

_____

_____

_____

If LaDondo takes a class that is totally verbal (the instructor does only lecture), what other tips would you offer her to succeed in that type of setting?

_____

_____

_____

How can any student successfully complete a class that centers on his or her LEAST dominant intelligence (for example, how can Jane succeed in math when math is her least dominant intelligence)?

_____

_____

_____

ADVICE TO GO

CORNERSTONES

for learning styles

Get involved in a *variety* of learning and social situations.

Use your less dominant areas more often to *strengthen* them.

Read more about personality typing and learning styles.

Answer inventories and surveys *thoughtfully*.

Remember, learning styles *do not* measure your worth.

Work to *improve* your less dominant areas.

Surround yourself with people who are very different from you.

Try *different ways* of learning and studying.

LEARN

6 Record

LaTonya had been through a very difficult evening. She had received a phone call from home to say that her grandmother was very ill and had been taken to the hospital. LaTonya was very close to her grandmother because she had lived with her since she was a little girl. Her grandmother was the only mother she had ever known. She wondered how she could possibly concentrate in class the following morning before she left to drive home to see her grandmother.

Because this was one of her most difficult classes, LaTonya knew that she must find a way to listen to her instructor and that she must take very careful notes since the midterm exam was coming up in two weeks. LaTonya knew this would be very difficult because she kept thinking of her grandmother. "She's so important to me. What would I do without her?" was the main thought on her mind.

LaTonya knew that she had to find a way to focus on the lecture and to get her mind off her grandmother until the class was over. Then she could drive home and spend time with her grandmother. She remembered studying listening skills, so she reviewed them in her mind. She also thought about her note-taking skills class and decided that she could combine these two skills and be able to get through the class and record the appropriate notes. LaTonya knew that she must listen and not just hear. She knew that she

> *LaTonya was pleased that she had been able to listen and take good notes even though she was facing one of the most difficult times in her life.*

had to listen with a purpose and to take constructive notes. Because she felt distracted, she was extra careful to get the right notebook and to take all her materials. During the drive to class the next morning, she worked on her mental attitude. As she sat in class, her mind was flooded with memories of her life with her grandmother. She could smell the chocolate chip cookies and hear her grandmother's laughter. She could feel her grandmother's gentle kiss on her forehead when she left for school. It was difficult not to cry.

Ability is what you are capable of doing. Motivation determines what you do. Attitude determines how well you do it. —LOU HOLTZ

She heard her instructor beginning his class, so she sat up straight, looked right at the instructor, making eye contact, and focused her mind on class. In order to stay engaged and to keep her mind off her grandmother, she asked a question. She listened for key words to use in her notes. She also made a note to review the PowerPoint presentation the instructor made available on his website and to complete the chapter-end review questions from the text. When the instructor discussed the midterm exam, she listened very carefully, took good notes, and asked more questions.

Finally, the class was over, and LaTonya could begin her trip home to see her grandmother. She made a mental note to translate her notes after she visited her grandmother. She was pleased that she had been able to listen and take good notes even though she was facing one of the most difficult times in her life.

QUESTIONS FOR REFLECTION

Consider responding to these questions online in the Questions for Reflection module of the Companion Website.

1. What is the relationship between successful note taking and listening?

2. Compare LaTonya's situation to a situation you have encountered.

3. Why is translating notes as soon as possible after class important to the note-taking process?

Where are you... AT THIS MOMENT

Before reading this chapter, take a moment and respond to the following 10 questions. Consider each one carefully before answering, and then respond by circling the number in the appropriate box. When you have answered the questions, add your points and find your total score on the feedback chart below.

STATEMENT	STRONGLY DISAGREE	DISAGREE	DON'T KNOW	AGREE	STRONGLY AGREE	SCORE
1. It is more important to focus on what speakers are saying than on how they say it.	1	2	3	(4)	5	4
2. A sign of a good listener is to constantly try to guess what will be said next.	(5)	4	3	2	1	5
3. Listening for key words or phrases is important to the note-taking process.	1	2	3	4	(5)	5
4. Listening and hearing mean exactly the same thing where note taking is concerned.	5	(4)	3	2	1	4
5. I know how to listen for important verbal and nonverbal information and clues when taking notes.	1	2	(3)	4	5	3
6. When listening, it is important to try to relate what I'm hearing to something I already know.	1	2	3	(4)	5	4
7. I find it difficult to take notes and listen to my teacher at the same time.	5	4	3	2	(1)	1
8. When I review my notes, I'm often unsure about the meaning of what I have written.	5	4	3	2	(1)	1
9. I keep my notes from different classes mixed together in the same notebook.	5	(4)	(3)	2	1	4
10. Before I go to class, I prepare mentally to listen and take notes.	1	2	3	(4)	5	4
TOTAL VALUE						35

SUMMARY

43–50   You are exceptional in your ability to focus, process, and understand when you listen. You put effort into comprehending what you listen to and realize that good listeners must actively try to incorporate what they hear into their existing knowledge base.

35–42   You are above average in your skills. You likely have few difficulties knowing what the important ideas are when listening, and you spend time and energy making sure you have heard accurately. You relate what you've heard to ideas and concepts you already know.

26–34   Your listening and note-taking skills are average. You can usually pick out the key ideas in what you hear and can understand them. Refining your listening skills will benefit you in terms of your comprehension and ability to remember and apply what you've heard.

18–25   You have below average listening and note-taking skills. You may be able to remember what you've heard for short periods of time, but you likely have difficulty understanding the meaning of what you've heard. Improving your skills will benefit your studies.

10–17   Your listening and note-taking skills are very limited. You have difficulty picking out the main or important ideas in what you listen to and paying attention when listening. You have to develop these skills to be an effective student in the classroom.

Based on the summary above, what is one goal you would like to achieve related to becoming a better listener and note taker?

Goal _____

_____

Think of three actions you can take that might help you move closer to realizing this goal.

1. _____
2. _____
3. _____

Questions
FOR BUILDING ON YOUR BEST

As you read this chapter, consider the following questions. At the end of the chapter, you should be able to answer all of them. We encourage you to ask a few questions of your own. Consider turning to your classmates or instructors to assist you.

1. What is the difference between listening and hearing?
2. What are the major obstacles to listening? How can I overcome them?
3. What roles do my emotions play in the listening process?
4. How can the L-STAR system help me take better notes?
5. Which class is best suited for the Cornell note-taking system?

What additional questions might you have about listening and note taking?

1. _____
2. _____
3. _____

Listening to people from different cultures, backgrounds, and religions can open many doors.

The Importance of Listening

Listening is one of the most important and useful skills human beings possess. For all animals, listening is a survival skill needed for hunting and obtaining food; for humans, listening is necessary for establishing relationships, growth, survival, knowledge, entertainment, and even health. It is one of our most widely used tools. How much time do you think you spend listening every day? Research suggests that we spend almost 70 percent of our waking time communicating, and 53 percent of that time is spent in listening situations (Adler, Rosenfeld, and Towne, 2001). Effective listening skills can mean the difference between success and failure, A's and F's, relationships and loneliness.

For students, good listening skills are critical. Over the course of your program, you will be given a lot of information in lectures. Cultivating and improving your active listening skills will help you to understand the lecture material, take accurate notes, participate in class discussions, and communicate with your peers.

The Difference Between Listening and Hearing

We usually do not think much about listening until a misunderstanding occurs. You've no doubt been misunderstood or misunderstood someone yourself. Misunderstandings arise because we tend to view listening as an automatic response when it is instead a learned, voluntary activity, like driving a car, painting a picture, or playing the piano. Having ears does not make you a good listener.

After all, having hands does not mean you are capable of painting the *Mona Lisa*. You may be able to paint the *Mona Lisa,* but only with practice and guidance. Listening, too, takes practice and guidance. Becoming an active listener requires practice, time, mistakes, guidance, and active participation.

Hearing, however, is not learned; it is automatic and involuntary. If you are within range of a sound you will probably hear it although you may not be listening to it. Hearing a sound does not guarantee that you know what it is or what made it. Listening actively, though, means making a conscious effort to focus on the sound and to determine what it is.

LISTENING DEFINED

According to Ronald Adler (Adler, Rosenfeld, and Towne, 2001), the drawing of the Chinese verb "to listen" provides a comprehensive and practical definition of listening (see Figure 6.1). To the Chinese, listening involves the ears, the eyes, un-

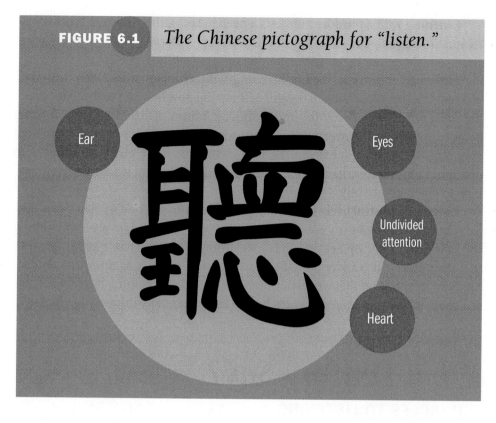

FIGURE 6.1 *The Chinese pictograph for "listen."*

Ear

Eyes

Undivided attention

Heart

divided attention, and the heart. Do you make it a habit to listen with more than your ears? The Chinese view listening as a whole-body experience. People from Western cultures seem to have lost the ability to involve their whole body in the listening process. We tend to use only our ears, and sometimes we don't even use them. At its core, listening is "the ability to hear, understand, analyze, respect, and appropriately respond to the meaning of another person's spoken and nonverbal messages" (Daly and Engleberg, 2002, p. 270). Although this definition involves the word "hear," listening goes far beyond just the physical ability to catch sound waves.

The first step in listening *is* hearing, but true listening involves one's full attention and the ability to filter out distractions, emotional barriers, cultural differences, and religious biases. Listening means that you are making a conscious decision to understand and show reverence for the other person's communication efforts.

Listening needs to be personalized and internalized. To understand listening as a whole-body experience, we can define it on three levels:

1. Listening with a purpose
2. Listening objectively
3. Listening constructively

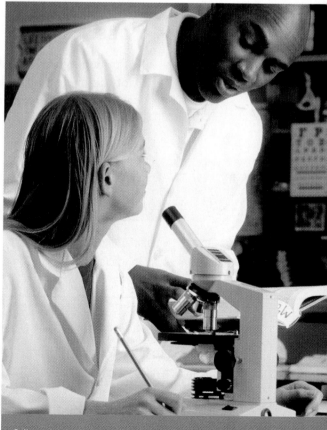

College classes demand active critical listening skills.

Listening with a purpose suggests a need to recognize different types of listening situations—for example, class, worship, entertainment, and relationships. People do not listen the same way in every situation.

Listening objectively means listening with an open mind. You will give yourself few greater gifts than the gift of knowing how to listen without bias and prejudice. This is perhaps the most difficult aspect of listening. If you have been cut off in mid-conversation or mid-sentence by someone who disagreed with you, or if someone has left the room while you were giving your opinion of a situation, you have had the experience of talking to people who do not know how to listen objectively.

Listening constructively means listening with the attitude of "How can this be helpful to my life or my education?" This type of listening involves evaluating the information you are hearing and determining whether it has meaning to your life. Sound easy? It is more difficult than it sounds because, again, we all tend to shut out information that we do not view as immediately helpful or useful. To listen constructively, you need to know how to listen and store information for later.

What Did You Say?

OBSTACLES TO LISTENING

Several major obstacles stand in the way of becoming an effective listener. To begin building active listening skills, you first have to remove some barriers.

OBSTACLE ONE: PREJUDGING

Prejudging means that you automatically shut out what is being said; it is one of the biggest obstacles to active listening. You may prejudge because of the content; the person communicating; or your environment, culture, social status, or attitude.

Tips for Overcoming Prejudging

1. Listen for information that may be valuable to you as a student. Some material may not be pleasant to hear but may be useful to you later on.

2. Listen to the message, not the messenger. If you do not like the speaker, try to go beyond personality and listen to what is being said, without regard to the person saying it. Conversely, you may like the speaker so much that you automatically accept the material or answers without listening objectively to what is being said.

3. Try to remove cultural, racial, gender, social, and environmental barriers. Just because a person is different from you or holds a different point of view does not make that person wrong; and just because a person is like you and holds a similar point of view does not make that person right. Sometimes, you have to cross cultural and environmental barriers to learn new material and see with brighter eyes.

OBSTACLE TWO: TALKING

Not even the best listener in the world can listen while he or she is talking. The next time you are in a conversation with a friend, try speaking while your friend is speaking—then see if you know what your friend said. To become an effective listener, you need to learn the power of silence. Silence gives you the opportunity to think about what is being said before you respond.

Tips for Overcoming the Urge to Talk Too Much

1. Force yourself to be silent at parties, family gatherings, and friendly get-togethers. We're not saying you should be unsociable, but force yourself to be silent for 10 minutes. You'll be surprised at what you hear. You may also be surprised how hard it is to do this. Test yourself.

2. Ask someone a question and then allow that person to answer the question. Too often we ask questions and answer them ourselves. Force yourself to wait until the person has formulated a response. If you ask questions and wait for answers, you will force yourself to listen.

OBSTACLE THREE: BRINGING YOUR EMOTIONS TO THE TABLE

Emotions can form a strong barrier to active listening. Worries, problems, fears, and anger can keep you from listening to the greatest advantage. Have you ever sat in a lecture, and before you knew what was happening your mind was a million miles away because you were angry or worried about something? If you have, you know what it's like to bring your emotions to the table.

Tips for Overcoming Emotions

1. Know how you feel before you begin the listening experience. Take stock of your emotions and feelings ahead of time.

2. Focus on the message; determine how to use the information.

3. Create a positive image about the message you are hearing.

Listening for Key Words, Phrases, and Hints

Learning how to listen for key words, phrases, and hints can help you become an active listener and an effective note taker. For example, if an Auto Mechanics instructor begins a lecture saying, "There are ten basic elements to engine maintenance," jot down the number 10 under the heading "Maintenance" or number your notebook page 1 through 10, leaving space for notes. If at the end of class you listed six elements, you know that you missed a part of the lecture. At this point, you need to ask the instructor some questions.

Here are some key phrases and words to listen for:

- in addition
- most important
- you'll see this again
- for example
- in contrast
- the characteristics of
- on the other hand

- another way
- such as
- therefore
- to illustrate
- in comparison
- the main issue is
- as a result of

- above all
- specifically
- finally
- as stated earlier
- nevertheless
- moreover
- because

WORLD OF WORK

The ability to listen actively is a critical component to being successful in the world of work. As a cast member with Disneyland Resorts, I spend a great deal of my day listening to guests and other cast members. My capacity to completely focus on what the individual is saying is key to my ability to provide outstanding service to all those I work with. My position requires that I do a significant amount of entertaining, and learning to listen in the various environments in which I work has been quite a challenge. I've had to learn how to really hear what people are saying and then translate it into information that can be disseminated to the individuals who must act on the information.

One of the most important things that I learned in college was the importance of actively listening. I noticed in your textbook that the authors use the Chinese character to describe what active listening really involves. I've found that I must give the individual with whom I am speaking my undivided attention and utilize not only my ears but also my eyes and heart to truly understand what they are saying. College helped me to hone my listening skills, but I must constantly strive to become a better listener.

Another thing that I have come to realize is that listening is critical to my relationships with others. Call it

pixie dust, call it magic, or call it a miracle, but your ability to interact and communicate with other people will get you further than almost any other skill that you have. Take every opportunity to learn social skills and graces, learn to communicate with others, and learn the fine art of give and take. Teamwork is the key to success.

Life is about learning, both through higher education and through daily lessons from living. You never know where life is going to lead you. Be open, think beyond the moment, and all your dreams may come true.

QUESTIONS FOR REFLECTION

Consider responding to these questions online in the Questions for Reflection module of the Companion Website.

1. When was there a time in your life when your livelihood depended on your listening abilities like Ms. Rudisill?

2. Why is listening with the eyes, heart, and undivided attention so important to Ms. Rudisill's profession?

3. Why does Ms. Rudisill see teamwork and communication as essential in the workplace?

Maritza E. Rudisill, CMP, Catering and Convention Services Assistant Director, Disneyland Parks and Resorts, Anaheim, CA

Picking up on transition words will help you filter out less important information and thus listen more carefully to what is most important. There are other indicators of important information, too. You will want to listen carefully when the instructor:

Writes something on the board.

Uses an overhead.

Uses computer-aided graphics.

Speaks in a louder tone or changes vocal patterns.

Uses gestures more than usual.

Draws on a flip chart.

Once you have learned how to listen actively, you will reap several key benefits as a student, as an employee, and as a citizen.

Listening When English Is Your Second Language

SUGGESTIONS FOR ESL STUDENTS

For students whose first language is not English, the college classroom can present some uniquely challenging situations. One of the most pressing and important challenges is the ability to listen, translate, understand, and capture the message on paper in a quick and continuous manner. According to Lynn Forkos, Professor and Coordinator of the Conversation Center for International Students at the Community College of Southern Nevada, the following tips can be beneficial:

- Don't be afraid to **stop the instructor** to ask for clarification. Asking questions allows you to take an active part in the listening process. If the instructor doesn't answer your questions sufficiently, be certain to make an appointment to speak with him or her during his or her office hours.

- If you are in a situation where the instructor can't stop or you're watching a movie or video in class, listen for words that you do understand and try to **figure out unfamiliar words in the context** of the sentence.

- **Enhance your vocabulary** by watching and listening to TV programs such as *Dateline, 20/20, Primetime Live, 60 Minutes,* and the evening news. You might also try listening to radio programming such as National Public Radio as you walk or drive.

- Be certain that you **write down everything** that the instructor puts on the board, overhead, or PowerPoint. You may not need every piece of this information, but this technique gives you (and hopefully your study group) the ability to sift through the information outside of class. It gives you a visual history of what the instructor said.

- Finally, if there is a conversation group or club that meets on campus, take the opportunity to join. **By practicing language**, you become more attuned to common words and phrases. If a conversation group is not available, consider starting one of your own.

Good note-taking skills help you do more than simply record what you're taught in class or read in a book so that you can recall it. These skills can also help to reinforce that information so that you actually know it.

Writing It Right

TIPS FOR EFFECTIVE NOTE TAKING

You have already learned several skills you will need to take notes: *First,* you need to cultivate and build your active listening skills. *Second,* you need to overcome obstacles to effective listening, such as prejudging, talking during a discussion, and bringing emotions to the table. *Finally,* you must scan, read, and use your textbook to understand the materials presented. Following are a few more important tips for taking notes.

Attend class. This may sound like stating the obvious, but it is surprising how many college students feel they do not need to go to class. You may be able to copy notes from others, but you may very well miss the meaning behind them. To be an effective note taker, class attendance is crucial; there is no substitute for it.

Come to class prepared. Do you read your assignments nightly? Instructors are amazed at the number of students who come to class and then decide they should have read their homework. Doing your homework—reading your text, handouts, or workbooks or listening to tapes—is one of the most effective ways to become a better note taker. It is always easier to take notes when you have a preliminary understanding of what is being said. As a student, you will find fewer tasks more difficult than trying to take notes on material that you have never seen or heard before. Coming to class prepared means doing your homework and coming to class ready to listen.

Coming to class prepared also means bringing the proper materials for taking notes: your textbook or lab manual, at least two pens, enough sharpened pencils to make it through the lecture, a notebook, and a highlighter. Some students also use a tape recorder. If you choose to use a tape recorder, be sure to get permission from the instructor before recording.

Bring your textbook to class. Although many students think they do not need to bring their textbook to class if they have read the homework, you will find that many instructors repeatedly refer to the text while lecturing. Always bring your textbook to class with you. The instructor may ask you to highlight, underline, or refer to the text in class, and following along in the text as the instructor lectures may also help you organize your notes.

Ask questions and participate in class. Two of the most critical actions you can perform in class are to ask questions and to participate in the class discussion. If you do not understand a concept or theory, ask questions.

Don't leave class without understanding what has happened and assume you'll pick it up on your own. Many instructors use students' questions as a way of teaching and reviewing materials. Your questions and participation will definitely help you, but they could also help others who did not understand something!

There are three common note-taking systems: (1) the **outline** technique; (2) the **Cornell**, or split-page technique (also called the T system); and (3) the **mapping** technique.

You'll Be Seeing Stars

THE L–STAR SYSTEM

One of the most effective ways to take notes begins with the **L-STAR** system.

    L   Listening
    S   Setting It Down
    T   Translating
    A   Analyzing
    R   Remembering

This five-step program will enable you to compile complete, accurate, and visual notes for future reference. Along with improving your note-taking skills, using this system will enhance your ability to participate in class, help other students, study more effectively, and perform well on exams and quizzes.

DID YOU KNOW?

Ludwig van Beethoven

Born in 1770, Beethoven composed many concertos and symphonies, totaling more than 850 pages. At age 32, he began to lose his hearing and fell into deep depression that would haunt him until his death. *While completely deaf* and in poverty, he composed The Ninth Symphony, considered to be his most beautiful and impressive work.

L—LISTENING

One of the best ways to become an effective note taker is to become an active listener. A concrete step you can take toward becoming an active listener in class is to sit near the front of the room where you can hear the instructor and see the board and overheads. Choose a spot that allows you to see the instructor's mouth and facial expressions. If you see that the instructor's face has become animated or expressive, you can bet that you are hearing important information. Write it down. If you sit in the back of the room, you may miss out on these important clues.

S—SETTING IT DOWN

The actual writing of notes can be a difficult task. Some instructors are organized in their delivery of information; others are not. Your listening skills, once again, are going to play an important role in determining what needs to be written down. In most cases, you will not have time to take notes word for word. You will have to be selective about the information you choose to set down. One of the best ways to keep up with the information being presented is to develop a shorthand system of your own. Many of the symbols you use will be universal, but you may use some symbols, pictures, and markings that are uniquely your own.

Some of the more common symbols are:

w/	with	w/o	without
=	equals	≠	does not equal
<	less than	>	greater than
%	percentage	#	number
&	and	ˆ	increase
+	plus or addition	−	minus or subtraction
*	important	etc	and so on
eg	for example	vs	against
esp	especially	"	quote
?	question	. . .	and so on

These symbols can save you valuable time when taking notes. Because you will use them frequently, it might be a good idea to memorize them. As you become more adept at note taking, you will quickly learn how to abbreviate words, phrases, and names.

T—TRANSLATING

One of the most valuable activities you can undertake as a student is to translate your notes immediately after each class. Doing so can save you hours of work when you begin to prepare for exams. Many students feel that this step is not important, or too time-consuming, and leave it out. Don't. Often, students take notes so quickly that they make mistakes or use abbreviations that they may not be able to decipher later. After each class, go to the library or some other quiet place and review your notes. You don't have to do this immediately after class, but before the end of the day, you will need to rewrite and translate your class-room notes. This process gives you the opportunity to put the notes in your own words and to incorporate your text notes into your classroom notes. You can correct spelling, reword key phrases, write out abbreviations, and prepare questions for the next class. Sounds like a lot of work, doesn't it? It is a great deal of work, but if you try this technique for one week, you should see a vast improvement in your comprehension of material. Eventually, you should see an improvement in your grades. Translating your notes helps you to make connections among previous material and will prove a valuable gift to yourself when exam time comes.

A—ANALYZING

This step takes place while you translate your notes from class. When you analyze your notes, you are asking two basic questions: (1) What does this mean? and (2) Why is it important? If you can answer these two questions about your material, you have almost mastered the information. Though some instructors will want you to spit back the exact same information you were given, others will ask you for a more detailed understanding and a synthesis of the material. When you are translating your notes, begin to answer these two questions using your notes, textbook, supplemental materials, and information gathered from outside research. Once again, this process is not simple or quick, but testing your understanding of the material is important. Remember that many lectures are built on past lectures.

R—REMEMBERING

Once you have listened to the lecture, set your notes on paper, and translated and analyzed the material, it is time to study, or remember, the information. Some effective ways to remember information include creating a visual picture, speaking the notes out loud, using mnemonic devices, and finding a study partner.

Yes You Can!
IDEAS FOR SUCCESS

Consider the following tips for improving listening in the classroom:

- Sit near the front of the room.

- Establish eye contact with the instructor.

- Read the text or handout beforehand. Listening is aided greatly when you have advance knowledge of the subject.

- Memorize the *key words* listed previously to help you identify when important information is coming.

- Don't give up—even if the information is difficult and the instructor is hard to understand.

- Enter class with a mind-set of learning. Remember, listening purposefully requires that you know the type of listening situation in which you will be involved and then prepare for that situation.

It's as Simple as A, B, C—1, 2, 3
THE OUTLINE TECHNIQUE

The outline system uses a series of major headings and multiple subheadings formatted in hierarchical order. The outline technique is one of the most commonly used note-taking systems, yet it is also one of the most misused systems. It can be difficult to outline notes in class, especially if your instructor does not follow an outline while lecturing.

When using the outline system, it is best to get all the information from the lecture and afterward to combine your lecture notes and text notes to create an outline. Most instructors would advise against using the outline system of note taking in class, although you may be able to use a modified version. The most important thing to remember is not to get bogged down in a system during class; what is critical is getting the ideas down on paper. You can always go back after class and rearrange your notes as needed.

If you are going to use a modified or informal outline while taking notes in class, you may want to consider grouping information together under a heading as a means of outlining. It is easier to remember information that is logically grouped than to remember information that is scattered across several pages. If your study skills lecture is on listening, you might outline your notes using the headings "The Process of Listening" and "Definitions of Listening" (see Figure 6.2).

FIGURE 6.2 *The outline technique.*

Study Skills 101   Oct. 17
                                                    Wednesday
Topic: Listening

I. The Process of Listening (ROAR)
    A. R = Receiving
        1. W/in range of sound
        2. Hearing the information
    B. O = Organizing & focusing
        1. Choose to listen actively
        2. Observe the origin, direction & intent
    C. A = Assignment
        1. You assign a meaning
        2. May have to hear it more than once
    D. R = Reacting
        I. Our response to what we heard
        2. Reaction can be anything
II. Definitions of Listening (POC)
    A. P = Listening w/ a purpose
    B. O = Listening w/ objectivity
    C. C = Listening constructively

It's a Split Decision

THE CORNELL (MODIFIED CORNELL, SPLIT PAGE, OR T) SYSTEM

The basic principle of the Cornell system, developed by Dr. Walter Pauk of Cornell University, is to split the page into two sections, each section to be used for different information. Section A is used for questions that summarize information found in Section B; Section B is used for the actual notes from class. The blank note-taking page should be divided as shown in Figure 6.3

Sometimes the basic Cornell layout is modified to include a third section at the bottom of the page for additional or summary comments. In such cases the layout is referred to as a "T system" for its resemblance to an upside-down T. To implement the Cornell system, you will want to choose the technique that is most comfortable and beneficial for you; you might use mapping (discussed next) or outlining on a Cornell page (see Figure 6.4).

FIGURE 6.3 — A blank Cornell frame.

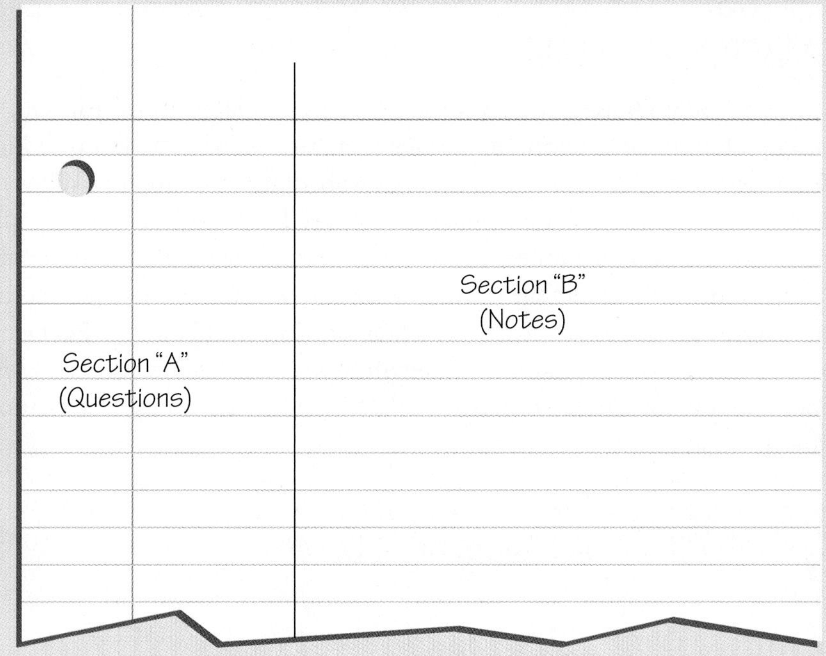

Section "B"
(Notes)

Section "A"
(Questions)

FIGURE 6.4 — Outline using a Cornell frame.

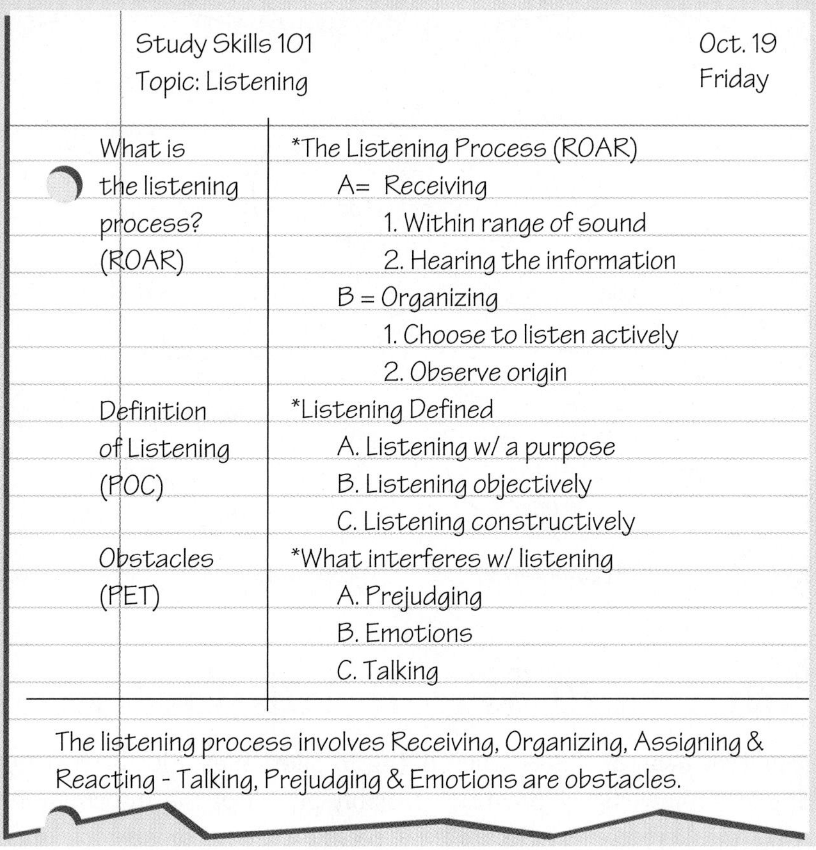

Study Skills 101   Oct. 19
Topic: Listening   Friday

What is the listening process? (ROAR)	*The Listening Process (ROAR)
	   A= Receiving
	     1. Within range of sound
	     2. Hearing the information
	   B = Organizing
	     1. Choose to listen actively
	     2. Observe origin

Definition of Listening (POC)	*Listening Defined
	   A. Listening w/ a purpose
	   B. Listening objectively
	   C. Listening constructively

Obstacles (PET)	*What interferes w/ listening
	   A. Prejudging
	   B. Emotions
	   C. Talking

The listening process involves Receiving, Organizing, Assigning &
Reacting - Talking, Prejudging & Emotions are obstacles.

Going Around in Circles

THE MAPPING SYSTEM

If you are a visual learner, this system may be especially useful for you. The mapping system of note taking generates a picture of information (see Figure 6.5). The mapping system creates a map, or web, of information that allows you to see the relationships among facts or ideas. (See Figure 6.6 for an example of mapping using a Cornell frame.) The most important thing to remember about each note-taking system is that it must work for you. Do not use a system because your friends use it or because you feel that you should use it. Experiment with each system or combination to determine which is best for you. Always remember to keep your notes organized, dated, and neat. Notes that cannot be read are no good to you or to anyone else.

FIGURE 6.5 *The mapping system.*

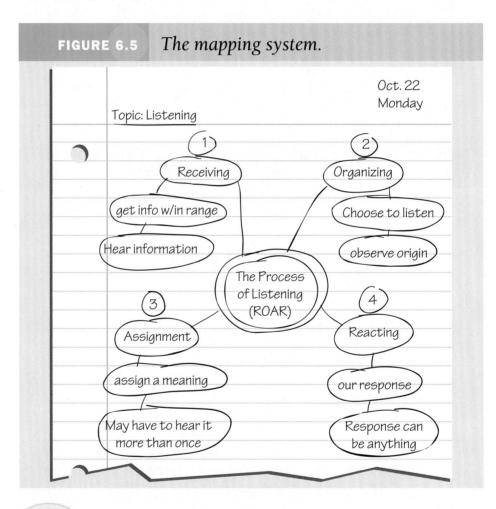

What to Do When You Get Lost

Have you ever been in a classroom trying to take notes and the instructor is speaking so rapidly that you cannot possibly get all of the information? Just when you think you're caught up, you realize that he or she has made an

FIGURE 6.6   *Mapping using a Cornell frame.*

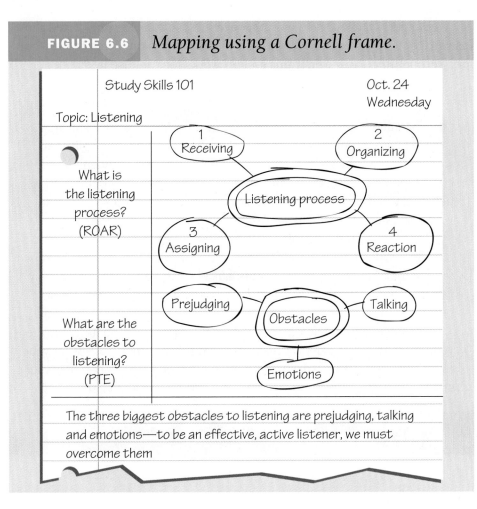

important statement and you missed it. What do you do? How can you handle, or avoid, this difficult note-taking situation? Here are several hints:

- Raise your hand and ask the instructor to repeat the information.
- Ask your instructor to slow down.
- If he or she will do neither, leave a blank space with a question mark at the side margin. You can get this information after class. This can be a difficult task to master. The key is to focus on the information at hand. Focus on what is being said at the exact moment.
- Meet with your instructor during break or immediately after class, or at the earliest time convenient for both of you.
- Form a note-taking group that meets after each class. This serves two purposes: (1) you can discuss and review the lecture, and (2) you will be able to get the notes from one of your note-taking buddies.
- Never lean over and ask questions of another student during the lecture. This will cause them to lose the information as well.
- Rehearse your note-taking skills at home by taking notes from TV news magazines or channels like the History Channel.
- Ask the instructor's permission to use a tape recorder during the lecture. Do not record a lecture without permission.

We suggest that you try to use other avenues, such as the ones listed above, instead of taping your notes. It is a time-consuming task to listen to the lecture for a second time. However, if this system works for you, use it.

Listening is a learned skill that can greatly improve your success as a student, but it is much more than that. Listening is a gift that promotes knowledge, understanding, stronger relationships, and open-mindedness. It is an attribute of the heart that can help you grow personally and professionally. Perhaps most important at this point in your life, listening can help you become a successful student.

Listening also greatly aids in the note-taking process. Note taking is a survival skill. You will rarely take a course in which you do not need to take notes. The ability to take notes quickly, accurately, and effectively can be the difference between succeeding and failing in a course or program.

Becoming good at listening and note taking can contribute greatly to your success as a student. Once you begin to listen with your eyes, your ears, your heart, and undivided attention, you will begin to see how your grades, attitude, relationships, and the world around you change.

what's it ALL ABOUT?

NAME: *Candice Guasco*

SCHOOL: *Empire College, Santa Rosa, CA*

MAJOR: *Medical Assisting Program*   AGE: *20*

To tell you a little about my personal history, I dropped out of high school when I was 15 years old. I had my first child when I was 17, and that experience led me to become interested in nursing. I decided that I wanted to become an RN. At the time, however, I could not find a program that fit my needs. So, I decided to take a high school proficiency exam, and upon passing it, I took a few classes at a junior college in California. A little while later, I learned of the Medical Assisting Program at Empire College and enrolled. Shortly into my program, I had to stop-out for a while due to the birth of my second child.

As I look back, there were several reasons that I left high school, but the overriding reason was that I simply was bored. Most of the classes were lecture and required a great deal of listening. I am the type of person who needs to be more involved and really get into the information and the class. It is hard for me to just sit there and listen.

One of the hardest classes I had to take in the Medical Assisting Program was Anatomy. This is a lecture-intensive class where listening is very important. There is very little opportunity to "get involved" with the information or the class. I found that we needed to know all of the body's organs AND how they functioned and worked with each other. There was so much to learn.

After listening to the lecture and taking notes, I knew that I was going to have to find a way to retain the details. I decided to find someone who knew nothing about anatomy so that I could explain it to another person. I would review my notes, remember what was said in the lecture, and then make up stories so the individual could understand the complex material.

For example, when we studied blood type, I would tell the story of how "Mr. A" could never go into "Mr. B's" neighborhood, because he would get into trouble and cause disaster. By telling these stories and making the information simple, I became familiar with the facts and knew them better. In the classroom I just listened, but on my own time I got involved with the material.

I recently completed my medical assisting degree in the top of my class and even made the dean's list. I now work as a medical assistant with a blood bank in California. By taking action and getting involved in my own learning, I not only got my degree, but also reached my goal of working in the medical field and making a better life for my children.

How can learning to listen help your study skills (such as note taking and test taking)?

What is the most difficult class that you are taking right now?

_____

What exercises or activities can you think of to help you through or "get involved" in this class and become a better listener (for example, Candice told stories)?

_____

_____

When taking notes, how can listening for "key words" help you?

_____

_____

What role does/will effective listening play in your career of choice?

_____

_____

_____

Describe one situation where your poor listening skills caused you trouble. How could better listening skills have helped you during this time?

_____

_____

_____

Why is it important to become the best listener that you can possibly become?

_____

_____

_____

Based on what you know right now, what advice about listening skills would you give a student entering your program?

_____

_____

_____

ADVICE TO GO

CORNERSTONES

for listening and note taking

Evaluate the *content*, not the delivery.

Keep your *emotions* in check when listening.

If it is on the board, overhead, or PowerPoint, *write it down.*

Use *abbreviations* and special notations in your notes.

Sit where you can *see and hear* the instructor.

Listen for *how* something is said.

Listen to the *entire "story"* before making a decision or judgment.

Listen for *major* ideas and *key* words.

Use a *separate* notebook for every class.

RECORD

Listen for what is *not* said.

Keep an *open* mind.

7 Remember

Tyrone walked into Vetinary Tech class beaming. *He was happy, joking, and smiling,* and he spoke to everyone on the way to his seat. He was always a delightful student, *but today he seemed even happier than usual.* Several classmates asked how he could possibly be so up. They could not understand his great attitude because *today was test day.* How could he be happy today of all days? *How could anyone be happy on test day?*

Tyrone told his classmates that *he was happy because he was prepared.* "I'm ready for the world," he said. *"I studied all week and I know this stuff."* Most of his classmates ribbed him and laughed. In the final moments before the test began, all the other students were deeply involved in questioning each other and looking over their notes. Tyrone stood by the window finishing his soda until time was called.

After all was said and done, *Tyrone scored the highest on the exam of all his peers—a 98.* Several students asked him how he did so well. Intrigued by their curiosity, I asked Tyrone to share his secret to successful test taking.

I found his answer extremely useful, *especially in light of his active life:* Tyrone held a part-time job, cared for his elderly grandmother, dated, and worked at the convenience store.

"You have to do it in steps," Tyrone said. *"You can't wait until the night before, even if you have all evening and night."* He explained that he incorporated study time into his schedule several weeks before the test.

If the test was to cover four chapters, he would review two chapters the first week and two chapters the second week. "I have a study room at the library because my house is so full of people. I make an outline of my notes, review my text, answer sample questions in the book, and many times I find someone to quiz me on the material."

Live as if you were to die tomorrow. Learn as if you were to live forever.   —M. K. GANDHI

> *How could he be happy today of all days? How could anyone be happy on test day?*

"Hey, I even got into creating those mnemonics we learned about. It really helped me study the list of cats most commonly registered in the U.S.

"Get this," he began. **"Pemba Boats!** Crazy, isn't it? But it helps me remember this:

- **P**ersian
- **E**xotic
- **M**aine Coon
- **B**irman
- **A**byssinian
- **B**urmese
- **O**riental
- **A**merican Shorthair
- **T**onkinese
- **S**iamese

"See? Pemba Boats is much easier than a list of ten things. You just have to be creative and stay on top of the material every day."

Tyrone's advice to the class was certainly realistic and helpful.

QUESTIONS
FOR REFLECTION

Consider responding to these questions online in the Questions for Reflection module of the Companion Website.

1. How do you usually feel on the day of a test? Why?

2. How can studying in chunks of time benefit you?

3. How can developing test questions as you read, then answering them and studying the answers help you learn the material?

Before reading this chapter, take a moment and respond to the following 10 questions. Consider each one carefully before answering, and then respond by circling the number in the appropriate box. When you have answered the questions, add your points and find your total score on the feedback chart below.

STATEMENT	STRONGLY DISAGREE	DISAGREE	DON'T KNOW	AGREE	STRONGLY AGREE	SCORE
1. I know which environments are best for me when I'm studying.	1	2	3	④	5	4
2. My mind often wanders when I'm trying to study.	5	4	3	②	1	2
3. I often try to visualize or picture what I'm trying to memorize.	1	2	3	④	5	4
4. When I study, I try to think of examples to illustrate the material.	1	2	3	④	5	4
5. I rarely think about how what I'm studying relates to my world or other information that I know.	5	4	③	2	1	3
6. I tend to review information over and over in moderate doses over time rather than "cramming" all at once.	1	2	3	④	5	4
7. I usually only go over my study materials once or twice at most.	5	④	3	2	1	4
8. I try to approach my study times with a positive, upbeat attitude.	1	2	3	④	5	4
9. Memorizing information and understanding it are practically the same thing.	5	4	③	2	1	3
10. I use mnemonics or memory tricks and techniques to help me remember information.	1	2	③	4	5	3
TOTAL VALUE						35

SUMMARY

43–50 You are exceptional in your ability to store and retrieve information. You likely tend to review materials repeatedly, and know that remembering is easier when you can relate materials to things you already know. Your satisfaction at mastering materials further motivates you.

35–42 You are above average in being able to remember information you've studied. You probably tend to study materials several times and know that a key to remembering is understanding. You probably also have some memory tricks up your sleeve, but might benefit from learning a few more.

26–34 Your skills in being able to remember course information are average. You are somewhat aware of how to study materials so that you can later remember them. You may benefit from learning additional memorization strategies and connecting memorization and comprehension of information.

18–25 You have below average skills in knowing how to get information into your memory. You may be minimally aware of when and where to study and probably think that being able to recall information is all that is necessary. You will need to develop strategies to help you remember materials so that you can also understand them.

10–17 Your strategies for getting information into your memory are limited. You likely focus on cramming information into your memory at the last minute and haven't thought much about the factors that help or hurt you in your efforts to memorize material. Significant improvements will need to be made to aid you in your college career.

Based on the summary above, what is one goal you would like to achieve related to studying and memory development?

Goal _____

_____

List three actions you can take that might help you move closer to realizing this goal.

1. _____

2. _____

3. _____

Questions
FOR BUILDING ON YOUR BEST

As you read this chapter, consider the following questions. At the end of the chapter, you should be able to answer all of them. We encourage you to ask a few questions of your own. Consider turning to your classmates or instructors to assist you.

1. How can I study smarter instead of harder?

2. What difference can my study environment really make?

3. What techniques can I use to help my memory develop?

4. Why is it important to make a commitment to understanding the material instead of just memorizing it?

5. How can I transfer information to long-term memory?

What additional questions might you have about studying and memory development?

1. _____

2. _____

3. _____

You may choose a nontraditional study environment, but be sure that you are able to study effectively in it.

Why Study? I Can Fake It

Many students feel that there is no real reason to study. They believe that they can glance at their notes a few moments before a test and fake it. Quite truthfully, some students are able to do this. Some tests and instructors lend themselves to this type of studying technique. More than you may imagine, however, this is not the case. Instructors are usually better known for thorough exams, tricky true–false statements, and multiple choices that would confuse even Einstein. If you want to succeed in your classes here, you must make studying a way of life.

Effective studying requires a great deal of commitment, but learning how to get organized, taking effective notes, reading a textbook, listening in class, developing personalized study skills, and building memory techniques will serve you well in becoming a successful graduate. "Faking it" is now a thing of the past.

The Importance of Your Study Environment

You may wonder why your study place is important. The study environment can determine how well your study time passes. If the room is too hot, too noisy, too dark, or too crowded, your study time may not be productive. In a room that is too hot and dimly lit, you may have a tendency to fall asleep. In a room that is too cold, you may spend time trying to warm yourself. Choose a location that is comfortable for you.

Different students need different study environments. You may study better with a degree of noise in the background, or you may need complete quiet. You have to make this decision. If you always have music in the background while you are studying, try studying in a quiet place one time to see if there is a difference. If you always try to study where it is quiet, try putting soft music in the background to see if it helps you. You may have to try several environments before you find the one that is right for you.

I Forgot to Remember!
UNDERSTANDING MEMORY

There may be times when you feel that your mind is just full. *"I can't remember another thing,"* you might say. That is a total myth. Many researchers and memory experts suggest that we do not come even close to using all of our memory's

WORLD OF WORK

As an inner-city Chicago kid, I was always driven for success. I came from a family of five children and parents with limited education. Although we were far from wealthy, there was an expectation that the children would have two characteristics: *integrity and striving to be our best.*

Because of our financial situation, the opportunity for a college education was always a desire for me, but not a certainty. I was fortunate enough to receive an entry scholarship to Loyola University of Chicago. Frankly, I did not take very good advantage of this opportunity early on in my college career. My performance was not up to expectation. My professors were pretty candid about this, and I knew I needed to refocus. It was at this point that I determined the approach that has influenced the rest of my career:

EDUCATION IS AN OPPORTUNITY AND A PRIVILEGE.

From that time, I attacked every class with interest, curiosity, and a desire to maximize my learning. Upon graduation, this attitude and approach carried over into my work life—no job was too trivial, and every person was one from whom I could learn. As I reflect on those college years, I realize that they were among my most formative ones.

The importance of preparing and "doing one's homework" became very clear to me. Without sounding too "preachy," I would offer the following suggestions on preparation:

- **Be clear on what you want your outcome to be.** It may be getting an A on an exam, mastering a particular subject, or proving to the instructor that you could survive the semester!

- **Determine what you will need to prepare.** Do not wait until you are in the study mode to determine that one of the texts and the two pieces of research that you need are not available. Get the most out of your study time by anticipating what will be needed.

- **Plan your time.** Always begin with scheduling your time. The enemy of preparation is time. The word "cramming" was probably invented for or by students. You are always better served if you can prepare for an exam or write a research paper over time. This allows for review, improvement, and final preparation.

- **Work hard.** It is important to know that there are not any real shortcuts in life. Things earned do come from the sweat of our brow. When you receive those grade reports at the end of the semester, usually you will get what you deserve!

- **Celebrate.** When you have achieved what you set out to do, celebrate. If only for a short time, allow yourself the luxury of having succeeded at a goal.

QUESTIONS FOR REFLECTION

Consider responding to these questions online in the World of Work module of the Companion Website.

1. How have the expectations of others affected your decisions about your program?

2. Have you ever learned from those with whom you work like Mr. Peterson did? Who was the person and what did you learn?

3. Why is it important to celebrate your successes?

Coleman Peterson, Executive Vice President—People Division, Wal-Mart Stores, Inc., Bentonville, AR

Choosing the best study environment can be challenging. The best study place may depend on the different accommodations available to you and may vary with the kinds of studying required. What kind of study environment has worked best for you?

potential. One study in the 1970s concluded that if our brains were fed 10 new items of information every second for the rest of our lives, we would never fill even *half* of our memory's capacity (Texas A&M University). Some researchers suggest that we never forget anything—that the material is simply "covered up" by other material, but it is still in our brain.

So, why is it so hard to remember the formula for drug conversions or the diagnostic chart for an engine or the finer points of a schematic or Ohm's Law? The primary problem is that we never properly filed or stored this information.

What would happen if you typed a letter into the computer and did not give it a file name? When you needed to retrieve that letter, you would not know how to find it. You would have to search through every file until you came across the information you needed. Memory works in much the same way. We have to store it properly if we are to retrieve it easily at a later time. This section will detail how memory works and why it is important to your studying efforts. Next, you will find some basic facts about memory.

- Everyone remembers some information and forgets other information.
- Your senses help you take in information.
- With very little effort, you can remember some information.
- With rehearsal (study), you can remember a great deal of information.
- Without rehearsal or use, information is forgotten.
- Incoming information needs to be filed in the brain if you are to retain it.
- Information stored, or filed, in the brain must have a retrieval method.
- Mnemonic devices, repetition, association, and rehearsal can help you store and retrieve information.

Psychologists have determined that there are three types of memory: sensory memory; short-term, or working, memory; and long-term memory.

Sensory memory. **Sensory memory** stores information gathered from the five senses: taste, touch, smell, hearing, and sight. Sensory memory is usually temporary, lasting about one to three seconds, unless you decide that the information is of ultimate importance to you and make an effort to transfer it to long-term memory. Although your sensory memory bank is *very large,* sensory

Clear your mind of can't.   —SAMUEL JOHNSON

information does not stay with you very long (Woolfolk, 2001). Sensory memory allows countless stimuli to come into your brain, which can be a problem when you are trying to concentrate on a lecture. You need to make a conscious effort to remain focused on the words being spoken and not on competing noise. When you make an effort to concentrate on the information, you are then committing this information to short-term memory.

Short-term memory. **Short-term, or working, memory** holds information for a short amount of time. Your working memory bank can hold a limited amount of information, usually about five to nine separate new facts or pieces of information at once (Woolfolk, 2001). Although it is sometimes frustrating to forget information, it is also useful and necessary to do so. If you never forgot anything, you would not be able to function. Educational psychologist Anita Woolfolk suggests that most of us can hear a new phone number, walk across the room, and dial it without much trouble, but if we heard two or three new numbers, we would not be able to dial them correctly. This is more information than our working memory can handle. If you were asked to give a person's name immediately after being introduced, you would probably be able to do so. If you had met several other new people in the meantime, unless you used some device to transfer the name into long-term memory, you would probably not be able to recall it.

As a student, you would never be able to remember all that your instructor said during a lecture. You have to take steps to help you to remember information. Taking notes, making associations, drawing pictures, and visualizing information are all techniques that can help you to commit information to your long-term memory bank.

Long-term memory. **Long-term memory** stores a lot of information. It is almost like a computer disk. You have to make an effort to put something in your long-term memory, but with effort and memory techniques, such as rehearsal and practice, you can store anything you want to remember there. Long-term memory consists of information that you have heard often, information that you use often, information that you might see often, and information that you have determined necessary. Just as you name a file on a computer disk, you name the files in your long-term memory. Sometimes, you have to wait a moment for the information to come to you. While you are waiting, your brain disk is spinning; if the information you seek is in long-term memory, your brain will eventually find it. You may have to assist your brain in locating the information by using mnemonics and other memory devices.

A
ll things are filled full of signs, and it is a wise person who can learn about one thing from another. —PLOTINUS

This Isn't Your Typical VCR

USING VCR3 TO INCREASE MEMORY POWER

Countless pieces of information are stored in your long-term memory. Some of it is triggered by necessity, some may be triggered by the five senses, and some may be triggered by experiences. The best way to commit information to long-term memory and retrieve it when needed can be expressed by:

V Visualizing
C Concentrating
R Relating
R Repeating
R Reviewing

To **visualize** information, try to create word pictures in your mind as you hear the information. If you are being told about an interior design concept, try to see the design in your mind, or try to paint a mind picture that will help you to remember the information. You may also want to create visual aids as you read or study information.

Concentrating on the information given will help you commit it to long-term memory. Don't let your mind wander. Stay focused. If you find yourself having trouble concentrating, take a small break (two to five minutes).

Relating the information to something that you already know or understand will assist you in filing or storing the information for easy retrieval. Relating the appearance of the African zebra to the American horse can help you remember what the zebra looks like.

Repeating the information out loud to yourself or to a study partner facilitates its transfer to long-term memory. Some people have to hear information many times before they can commit it to long-term memory.

Reviewing the information is another means of repetition. The more you see and use the information, the easier it will be to remember it when the time comes. As you review, try to remember the main points of the information. Walter Pauk, educator and inventor of the Cornell note-taking method, found in a study that people reading a textbook chapter forgot 81 percent of what they had read after 28 days (Pauk, 2001).

What Helps? What Hurts?

ATTENDING TO YOUR MEMORY

For any part of the body, there are things that help you and hurt you. Your memory is no different. Just as your body will begin to fail you without proper attention, exercise, and nutrition, if neglected or mistreated, your memory will do the same. Consider the following things that can help or hinder your memory.

> **MEMORY HELPERS**

- Proper sleep
- Proper nutrition/diet
- Exercise
- Mental exercises such as crossword puzzles, brain teasers, name games
- A positive mind-set
- The proper environment
- Scheduled study breaks
- Repetition and visualization

> **MEMORY HINDRANCES**

- Internal and external distractions
- Alcohol
- Drugs
- Stress
- Closed-mindedness (tuning out things you don't like)
- Inability to distinguish important facts from unimportant facts

With these in mind, try to develop habits that incorporate the "memory helpers" into your life. Eat properly, get enough rest, take study breaks if you feel yourself drifting or getting tired, find the proper place to read and study, keep your mind sharp by reading for pleasure or doing crossword puzzles, and above all, approach your studying with a positive attitude.

KNOWING VERSUS MEMORIZING

Why don't you forget your name? Why don't you forget your address? The answer is that you KNOW that information. You OWN it. It belongs to you. You've used it often enough and repeated it often enough that it is highly unlikely that you will ever forget it. Conversely, why can't you remember the details of Maslow's Hierarchy of Basic Needs or Darwin's Theory of Evolution? Most likely because you memorized it and never "owned" it.

If you think back to what you can and can't remember, memorization plays a great role. Rote memory is when you literally memorize something and days later it is gone. You memorized it because you needed it for something like a test or a discussion, but it was not important enough to you to know it for life.

Knowing something means that you have made a personal commitment to make this information a part of your life. For example, if you needed to remember the name Stephen and his phone number of 925-6813, the likelihood of your remembering this depends on *attitude*. Do you need to recall this information because he is in your study group and you might need to call him, or because he is the caregiver for your infant daughter while you are in class? How badly you need that name and number will determine the commitment level that you make to just *memorizing* it (and maybe forgetting it) or *knowing* it (and making it a part of your life).

Tim McGraw

is a country music sensation. He has recorded almost a dozen albums, has 23 number one hits, and has sold 32 million albums. However, his first series of singles failed so badly that he was told to give up his dream of becoming a country-recording artist, and one producer told him, "You'll never make it."

Think about your study habits for a moment. When you are reading your chapter, listening in class, or studying at home, what is your **commitment level?** How much energy, brain-power, zeal, and fervor do you put into it? Again, it will depend on how you perceive the value of that information.

The difference between **rote memory** and **knowing** (understanding) can make a dramatic and permanent change in every area of your life, certainly in your role as a college student. Rote memory is a task of repeating until you have memorized. Knowing is making a commitment to understanding relationships, making associations, comparing and contrasting, classifying, demonstrating, describing, and applying what you have learned. After you have read a chapter, visualized the information, related it to something you already know, and reviewed it for accuracy, ask yourself a few questions. These questions can help you KNOW the information, thus helping you transfer it to long-term memory and *life-long ownership*.

Questions such as these can help you move from simple memorization to ownership of the material:

- Can I relate x to y?
- Can I illustrate how x does y?
- Can I compare and contrast x to y?
- Can I apply x to y in the real world?
- Can I distinguish x from y?
- Can I define, identify, name, and describe x?
- Can I solve the problem of x?
- Can I modify or rearrange x to make it work with y?
- Can I support the theory of x and y?
- Can I defend my knowledge of x or y?

Ready, Set, Go!
MEMORY AND STUDYING

So far in this chapter, you've found the appropriate study environment. Now it's time to study. That's exciting, isn't it? No? Well, it can be. All it takes is a positive attitude and an open mind, like Tyrone in the opening story. Next, you'll learn about three methods of studying that you can use to put yourself in charge of the material: the SQ3R, mnemonics, and cooperative learning methods. After you've reviewed these methods, you may want to use some combination of them, or you may prefer to use one method exclusively. The only rule for choosing a study plan is that the plan must work for you. You may have to spend a few weeks experimenting with several plans and methods to determine the one with which you are most comfortable. Don't get discouraged if it takes you a while to find what is right for you.

ometimes success is due less to ability and more to zeal. The winner is the person who gives him or herself to his or her work, body and soul. —CHARLES BUXTON

THE SQ3R METHOD

You were introduced to this method in Chapter 4. This method can help you commit material to memory. As a quick review, to use SQ3R, you would:

- **Survey** the chapter: headings, photos, quotes, indentations, bolded words, etc.
- Write **Questions** from headings: use *who, what, when, where, why, how.*
- **Read** the chapter: look up unfamiliar words, highlight important sections, take notes while reading, paraphrase the information.
- **Recite** the information: close the text and determine if you can "tell the story" of the chapter.
- **Review** the chapter: return to the chapter often and look over the information.

MNEMONIC DEVICES

Mnemonic (pronounced ni-**mōn**-ik) devices are memory tricks or techniques that assist you in putting information into your long-term memory and pulling it out when you need it. Tyrone used one about cats in the opening story. I recently gave a test on the basic principles of public speaking. A student asked if she had to know the parts of the communication process in order. When I replied that she should be able to recall them in order, she became nervous and said that she had not learned them in order. Another student overheard the conversation and said, "Some men can read backward fast." The first student asked, "What do you mean by that?" I laughed and said that the mnemonic was great! The student had created a sentence to remember *source, message, channel, receiver, barriers,* and *feedback.* The relationship worked like this:

Some	=	Source
Men	=	Message
Can	=	Channel
Read	=	Receiver
Backward	=	Barriers
Fast	=	Feedback

The first student caught on fast; she could not believe how easy it was to remember the steps in order using this sentence. This is a perfect example of how using memory tricks can help you to retrieve information easily.

The following types of mnemonic devices may help you with your long-term memory.

Jingles/rhymes.   You can make up rhymes, raps, songs, poems, or sayings to assist you in remembering information; for example, "Columbus sailed the ocean blue in fourteen hundred and ninety-two."

As a child, you learned many things through jingles and rhymes. You probably learned your ABC's through a song pattern, as well as your numbers. If you think about it, you can still sing your ABC's, and maybe your numbers through the "Ten Little Indians" song. You could probably sing every word to the opening of *The Brady Bunch* or *Gilligan's Island* because of the continual re-runs on TV. Jingles and rhymes have a strong and lasting impact on our memory—especially when repetition is involved.

Sentences.   You can make up sentences such as "Some men can read backward fast," to help you remember information. Another example is, "Please excuse my dear Aunt Sally," which corresponds to the mathematical operations: **p**arentheses, **e**xponents, **m**ultiplication, **d**ivision, **a**ddition, and **s**ubtraction.

Other sentences in academic areas include:

1. **My Very Elderly Mother Just Saved Us Nine Pennies.** This is a sentence mnemonic for the nine planets in order from the sun: Mercury, Venus, Earth, Mars, Jupiter, Saturn, Uranus, Neptune, Pluto.

2. **Every Good Bird Does Fly** is a sentence mnemonic for the line notes in the treble clef in music.

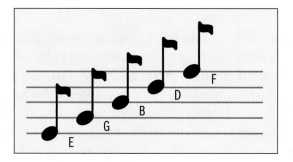

3. **Some Men Help Each Other** is a sentence mnemonic for the Great Lakes from west to east: Superior, Michigan, Huron, Erie, Ontario.

Words.   You can create words. For example, Roy G. Biv may help you to remember the colors of the rainbow: **r**ed, **o**range, **y**ellow, **g**reen, **b**lue, **i**ndigo, and **v**iolet.

Other word mnemonics include:

1. **HOMES** is a word for the Great Lakes in no particular order: Huron, Ontario, Michigan, Erie, Superior.

2. **FACE** is a word mnemonic for the space notes in the treble clef.

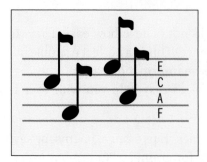

Story lines.   If you find it easier to remember stories than raw information, you may want to process the information into a story that you can easily tell. Weave the data and facts into a creative story that can be easily retrieved from your long-term memory.

Acronyms.   An acronym is a word that is formed from the first letters of other words. You may see re-runs for the famed TV show *M*A*S*H*. This is an acronym for **M**obile **A**rmy **S**urgical **H**ospital. If you scuba dive, you know that *SCUBA* is an acronym for **S**elf-**C**ontained **U**nderwater **B**reathing **A**pparatus. Other common acronyms include:

NASA (**N**ational **A**eronautics and **S**pace **A**dministration)

NASCAR (**N**ational **A**ssociation of **S**tock **C**ar **A**uto **R**acing)

NASDAQ (**N**ational **A**ssociation of **S**ecurities **D**ealers **A**utomated **Q**uotation)

NATO (**N**orth **A**tlantic **T**reaty **O**rganization)

BART (**B**ay **A**rea **R**apid **T**ransit)

Pegging.   The peg system uses association, visualization, and attachment for remembering. With this system, you "attach" what you want to remember to something that is already familiar to you. This is a visual means to remember lists, sequences, and even categories of information. Most peg systems use numbers and rhyming words to correspond, such as:

1 =	sun	6 =	sticks
2 =	shoe	7 =	heaven
3 =	bee	8 =	gate
4 =	shore	9 =	fine
5 =	alive	10 =	pen

To attach information to the number, you visually attach a word (such as *sun, shoe, bee, shore*) to the word you want to remember. For example, if you wanted to remember a shopping list that included ice cream, rice, Ajax, milk, water, and cookies, this might be your plan:

You see **ice cream** melting in the **sun.**

You see **rice** filling a **shoe.**

You see **Ajax** sprinkled on a **bee.**

You see **milk** rushing to the **shore.**

You see **water** keeping you **alive** on a deserted island.

You see **cookies** being offered to you on a **stick** (like a s'more).

You can also "attach" information to a thing or a place. For example, you might place information in the following places: kitchen, hall, bedroom, living room, bathroom, or dining room.

Again, you visually "attach" the information you want to remember to a part of the house (and you should use *your* house, beginning with the door in which you enter). For example, if you were giving a speech on the death penalty, you

Consider the following tips for making the most of your study time and memory development:

- Choose a study environment that is right for YOU.

- Study in blocks of time and don't wait until the last minute to begin studying.

- Make a commitment to KNOW rather than memorize.

- Take short breaks when studying to fight fatigue.

- Use repetition to commit information to long-term memory.

- VISUALIZE the information so that your mind's eye can help you remember it.

- Test your memory and understanding by using Bloom's Taxonomy.

might put the **introduction in the kitchen**, the **transition statement in the hallway**, the **first point in the bedroom**, and the **second point in the living room**. This helps you keep your information organized.

You could "attach" information to parts of a car, such as the steering wheel, the tires, the trunk, the roof, the backseat, the driver's seat, the passenger seat. For example, if you wanted to remember the planets, you could put **Mercury** as the **steering wheel**, **Venus** as the **tire**, **Earth** in the **trunk**, **Mars** on the **roof**, **Jupiter** in the **backseat**, and so forth.

Now that you have your peg system, you can begin to "attach" information to those places and use your visual skills for recall.

COOPERATIVE LEARNING

There is strength in numbers. Many times, groups of people can accomplish what a single individual cannot. This is the idea behind cooperative learning. We form and use groups in our daily lives in situations like work, worship, and hobbies, and we even group our friends together. We develop groups for inspiration, excitement, and reflection, to advance social causes and to grow. Studying in groups can have the same effect. Cooperative learning can benefit you because you have pulled together a group of people who have the same interests and goals as you: to pass the course. Studying and working in groups can help you in ways such as drilling exercises, brainstorming, group sharing, and mapping.

Before we talk about those specific details, we should discuss how to form a study group. The most effective study group will include people with different strengths and weaknesses. It would do little good to involve yourself in an accounting study group with people who are all failing accounting. Here are some tips for forming a cooperative study group:

- Limit the group size to five to seven people.

- Search for students who participate in class.

- Include people who take notes in class.

- Include people who ask questions in class.

- Include people who will work diligently.

- Include people who do their share for the group.

- Invite people who are doing well in a specific area; they may not attend every meeting, but they may be of assistance periodically.

Appoint members of your team to be responsible for the following jobs:

- **Timekeeper.** This person will let the group know when it is time to move on to another topic.

- **Note taker.** This person will keep the notes for the team and will usually assist in getting them copied for everyone in the group.
- **Facilitator.** This person will lead the group and keep the group on task during the meeting.

When the group is formed, you can engage in several different activities to learn, share, and reinforce information.

- **Questioning.** With this technique, group members bring several questions to the session. These may be predicted exam questions, questions about methods or formulas, or questions that the member was not able to answer individually.
- **Comparing.** The study group is a good place to compare notes taken in class or from the text. If you are having problems understanding a concept in your notes, maybe someone in the group can assist you. It is also a good time to compare your notes for accuracy and missing lecture information.
- **Drilling.** This technique assists you with long-term memory development. Repetition is an important step in transferring information to long-term memory. Have a group member drill the other members on facts, details, solutions, and dates. A verbal review of the information will help you and other members retain the information.
- **Brainstorming.** During each session, members can use this technique to predict exam questions, review information, and develop topic ideas for research, projects, future study sessions, and papers.
- **Sharing.** The study group is a time when you can give and receive. At the beginning or end of each session, students in the group can share the most important aspect of the lecture or readings. This will assist other members in identifying main points and issues pertaining to the lecture.
- **Mapping.** This technique can be used in a variety of ways. It is similar to the mapping system discussed in the note-taking chapter. On a board or large sheet of paper, let one member write a word, an idea, or a concept in the center. The next student will add information, thus creating a map or diagram of information and related facts. This can help the group make connections and associations and assist members in identifying where gaps in knowledge exist.

Studying with Small Children in the House

For many college students, finding a place or time to study is the hardest part of studying. Some students live at home with younger siblings; some students have children of their own. If you have young children in the home, you may find the following hints helpful when it comes time to study.

Study at school.   Your schedule may have you running from work to school directly to home. Try to squeeze in even as little as half an hour at school for studying, perhaps immediately before or after class. A half hour of pure study time can prove more valuable than five hours at home with constant interruptions.

Create crafts and hobbies.   Your children need to be occupied while you study. It may help if you have crafts and hobbies available that they can do while you are involved with studying. Choose projects your children can do by themselves, without your help. Depending on their ages, children could make masks from paper plates, color, do pipe cleaner art or papier-mâché, use modeling clay or dough, or build a block city. Explain to your children that you are studying and that they can use this time to be creative; when everyone is finished, you'll share what you've done with each other.

Study with your children.   One of the best ways to instill the value of education in your children is to let them see you participating in your own education. Set aside one or two hours per night when you and your children study. You may be able to study in one place, or you may have separate study areas. If your children know that you are studying and you have explained to them how you value your education, you are killing two birds with one stone: you are able to study, and you are providing a positive role model as your children study with you and watch you.

Rent movies or let your children watch TV.   Research has shown that viewing a limited amount of educational television, such as *Sesame Street, Reading Rainbow,* or *Barney and Friends,* can be beneficial for children. If you do not like what is on television, you might consider renting or purchasing age-appropriate educational videos for your children. This could keep them busy while you study, and it could help them learn as well.

Invite your children's friends over.   What?! That's right. A child who has a friend to play or study with may create less of a distraction for you. Chances are your children would rather be occupied with someone their own age, and you will gain valuable study time.

Hire a sitter or exchange sitting services with another student. Arrange to have a sitter come to your house a couple of times a week. If you have a classmate who also has children at home, you might take turns watching the children for each other. You could each take the children for one day a week, or devise any schedule that suits you both best. Or you could study together, and let your children play together while you study, alternating homes.

Talk to the financial aid office.   In some instances, there will be grants or aid to assist you in finding affordable day care for your child. Studying at any time is hard work. It is even harder when you have to attend to a partner, children, family responsibilities, work, and a social life as well. You will have to be creative in order to complete your degree. You are going to have to do things and make sacrifices that you never thought possible. But if you explore the options, plan ahead, and ask questions of other students with children and with responsibilities outside the classroom, you can and will succeed.

What Do You Mean the Test Is Tomorrow?

STUDYING IN A CRUNCH

Let's be straight up front. No study skills textbook will ever advise you to cram. It is simply a dangerous and often futile exercise in desperation. You'll never read the words, *"Don't waste your time studying, CRAM the night before."*

Cramming is just the opposite of what this whole chapter is about—*knowing* versus memorizing. Cramming will never help you know; it can only help you memorize a few things for storage in short-term memory. You may spend several hours cramming, and shortly after the test, the information is gone, evaporated, vanished!

There may be times when time runs out and the only option is to cram. If you find yourself in this spot, consider the following tips and suggestions for cramming. These probably won't get you an A, but they may help you with a few questions.

Depressurize.   Just tell yourself up front what you are doing. Don't pretend that cramming is going to save you. Let yourself realize that you are memorizing material for short-term gain and that you won't be able to keep it all. With this admission, your stress will diminish.

Ditch the blame game.   You know you're at fault, so accept that and move on. Sitting around bemoaning your fate will not help. Just tell yourself, "I messed up this time; I won't let it happen again."

Know what.   When cramming, it is important to know what you're cramming for. If you're cramming for a multiple-choice test, you'll need different types of information than for an essay test. Know what type of test it is for which you are studying.

Read it quick.   Think about **H2 FLIB.** This is a mnemonic for: read the **headings**, **highlight** the important words, read the **first sentence** of every paragraph, read the **last sentence** of every paragraph, read the **indented** and **boxed** material. This can help you get through the chapter when pinched for time.

Make connections.   As you are reading, quickly determine if any of the information has a connection with something else you know. Is there a comparison or contrast? Is there a relationship of any kind? Is there a cause and effect in motion? Can you pinpoint an example to clarify the information? These questions can help you with retention.

Use your syllabus or study guide.   If your instructor lists questions that you should know (mastery questions) in the syllabus, or if he or she gave you a study sheet, this is the place to start. Answer those questions. If you don't have either, look to see if the text gives study questions at the end of the chapter. Try to answer the questions using the text *and* your lecture notes.

See it.   Visualizing the information through mapping, diagrams, photos, drawings, and outlines can help you commit this information to short-term memory.

Repeat! repeat! repeat!   Repetition is the key to committing information to memory. After you read information from the text or lecture notes, repeat it time and time again. When you think you've got it, write it down, then repeat it again.

Choose wisely.   If you're cramming, you can't do it all. Make wise choices about which material you plan to study. This can be driven by your study sheet, your lecture notes, or questions in your syllabus (if they are listed). One of the most important things about cramming is that this information is going to leave you. Don't rely on it for the next test or the final. You will need to go back and re-learn (truly understand) this information to commit it to long-term memory. Good luck!

Just as reading is a learned skill, so is memory development. You can improve your memory, but it will take practice, patience, and persistence. By making the decision that "this information is important to me and my life," you've won the battle; for when you make that decision, your studying becomes easier.

Making a commitment to *truly understand* and know the material instead of just memorizing it can help you establish a knowledge base that you never imagined. It can help you retain information that otherwise would have been lost. It can help you amass a powerful vocabulary, and it can help you pull information from one class to another for papers, speeches, reports, and discussions.

Your memory needs constant care and attention. If you provide the proper rest, nutrition, and exercise, it will carry you through your program (and beyond) with flying colors.

what's it ALL ABOUT?

NAME: Damion Saunders

SCHOOL: Western Career College, Sacramento, CA

MAJOR: Veterinary Technician   AGE: 29

Below is a real-life situation faced by Damion. Read the brief case and respond to the questions.

After completing high school, I worked a few jobs and tried out a few schools, but ultimately, I began working full-time to support my family. Over the years, the cost of living grew higher and higher in California and I realized that I could not support my family on the wages I was earning. I was very interested in veterinary work and decided to pursue a career as a veterinary technician. Today, I have completed my entire course of study and now I am beginning my 200-hour externship.

It may sound like it was all easy and that I just slid through the program. Nothing could be further from the truth. Having been out of school for 10 years, it was a major adjustment to be in class four or five hours a day and then have to come home and study for another three or four hours every night. I found that my old study techniques were not working well, and I had to find a new way to study and learn.

The wake-up call that I got was on a Critical Care exam. This should have been easy for me since I was already working in a vet's office. I thought I knew the material and did not study as much as I should have. I failed the test, and most of my classmates did, too. It was at that point that I realized this was serious business and that the only way to truly learn the material was to get involved with it, read it, study it, and basically live it.

A lot of my classmates thought they studied enough, too. I heard many excuses, but it all came down to the fact that we were not prepared. I began re-reading and highlighting important phrases and topics. I made flash cards and bookmarkers to help me. I got together with classmates and formed a study group, but most importantly, I ASKED FOR HELP. The doctors in the office where I worked helped me with the things I did not understand, and so did my instructors. Basically, I built a great supporting cast to help me. When you're paying thousands of dollars for a degree or certificate, you need to ask for help instead of making excuses.

Today, I serve as a mentor for incoming students and I help them understand the importance of studying and asking for help before the material becomes overwhelming.

Who is your "supporting cast"? (In other words, who are the people you can turn to when you need academic help?)

_____

_____

_____

How would you go about forming your own study group if one did not exist?

_____

_____

_____

What study techniques do you think you need to improve and how are you going to improve them?

_____

_____

_____

What changes will you have to make to your study environment to make sure you are successful?

_____

_____

_____

There are several memory techniques mentioned in the chapter; which one do you think will help you most? Why?

_____

_____

_____

What role does time management play in effective studying?

_____

_____

_____

for effective studying

Review your classroom and textbook notes.

Use the SQ3R method when studying texts.

Study your *hardest* material *first*.

Take breaks every half hour.

Study in a *brightly lit* area.

Have a *healthy snack*.

Use *mnemonic* devices.

Overlearn the material.

Set *rules* for studying.

Turn the *heat down*.

REMEMBER

8 Assess

Marchia could tell that something was wrong with her friend and classmate, Ellen. Ellen had been quiet and distant for the past two days. That morning during lab, Marchia asked Ellen if there was something bothering her. Ellen confided that the first test in her nursing class was in one week and that if she failed the test, *she would be asked to leave the nursing program.*

Marchia tried to tell Ellen that she had plenty of time to study the material and prepare for the test. Ellen replied that she was not worried so much about knowing the material, *but that she was worried because she was a poor test taker.* "I can know it from beginning to end," Ellen said, "but when she puts that test in front of me, *I can't even remember my name!* What am I going to do? *This test is going to determine the rest of my life.*"

Marchia explained to Ellen that she had suffered through the same type of anxiety and fear in high school until her math teacher taught the class how to take a test and how to reduce test anxiety. *"It's just a skill, Ellen, like driving a car or typing a research paper. You can learn how to take tests if you're really serious."* Ellen asked if Marchia could give her some hints about test taking.

As lab ended, Marchia told Ellen that they could begin working for an hour every morning and an hour every evening to learn how to take exams and to reduce anxiety.

The week of the test rolled around, and *Ellen was confident that she knew the material that she was to be tested on.* She still had a degree of anxiety, *but she had learned how to be in control of her emotions during a test.* She had also learned how to prepare herself physically for the exam. She

The splendid achievements of the intellect, like the soul, are everlasting. —UNKNOWN

went to bed early the night before the exam. On exam day, she got up early, ate a healthy breakfast, had a brief review session, packed all the supplies needed for the exam, and *headed to class early so that she could relax a little* before the instructor arrived.

> *". . . when she puts that test in front of me, I can't even remember my name."*

When the exam was passed out, *Ellen could feel herself getting somewhat anxious,* but she quickly put things into perspective. She sat back and took several deep breaths, listened carefully to the instructor's instructions, read all the test instructions before beginning, *told herself silently that she was going to ace the exam,* and started.

After one hour and five minutes, time was called. Ellen put her pencil down, leaned back in her chair, took a deep breath, rubbed her aching finger, and cracked the biggest smile of her life. Marchia had been right. The strategies worked. *Ellen was going to be a nurse.*

QUESTIONS
FOR REFLECTION

Consider responding to these questions online in the Questions for Reflection module of the Companion Website.

1. What role do you think your attitude (positive or negative) plays in your preparation and execution of exams?

2. What can you do to better prepare physically for an exam?

3. What can you do to better prepare mentally for an exam?

Before reading this chapter, take a moment and respond to the following 10 questions. Consider each one carefully before answering, and then respond by circling the number in the appropriate box. When you have answered the questions, add your points and find your total score on the feedback chart below.

STATEMENT	STRONGLY DISAGREE	DISAGREE	DON'T KNOW	AGREE	STRONGLY AGREE	SCORE
1. I get anxious when taking a test.	5	4	3	2	1	
2. My mind often blanks out during tests.	5	4	3	2	1	
3. I remember the information I've studied after finishing a test.	1	2	3	4	5	
4. I feel a lack of confidence when taking a test.	5	4	3	2	1	
5. I know how to physically prepare myself to take a test.	1	2	3	4	5	
6. I know test-taking strategies for different kinds of test questions (such as multiple choice vs. essay questions).	1	2	3	4	5	
7. I usually have very little idea about what will be on a test before I take it.	5	4	3	2	1	
8. I skip past the directions on the tests that I take.	5	4	3	2	1	
9. I am often tempted not to come to school on days when tests are scheduled.	5	4	3	2	1	
10. When taking a test, it is best to answer the questions you know first and come back to the others later.	1	2	3	4	5	
TOTAL VALUE						

SUMMARY

43–50   You are exceptional in your test preparation and test-taking skills. You know how to prepare yourself mentally and physically for a test, and have a sense of confidence about your test-taking performances. You likely get satisfaction at being able to rise to the challenge of tests.

35–42   You are above average in preparing for and performing on tests. You likely have a good idea about what information will be on the tests and how to approach different types of questions. Adjustments in your strategies might help you perform even better on tests.

26–34   Your skills in preparing for and taking tests are average. You are somewhat aware of how to study for different types of tests, and your test anxieties are manageable. You would benefit from improvement in test preparation strategies to be able to really show what you know.

18–25   You have below average skills in preparing for and taking tests. Your level of test anxiety is likely making matters worse. You need to learn how to anticipate what your tests may look like and how to prepare for them effectively.

10–17   Your skills in preparing for and taking tests are very limited. You likely have very little idea of what to expect on the tests that you take and don't know how to study for different types of test questions. Further, your test anxieties are likely preventing you from doing your best. Significant improvements have to be made to help you be a successful test taker.

Based on the summary above, what is one goal you would like to achieve related to test taking?

Goal _____

_____

List three actions you can take that might help you move closer to realizing this goal.

1. _____
2. _____
3. _____

Questions
FOR BUILDING ON YOUR BEST

As you read this chapter, consider the following questions. At the end of the chapter, you should be able to answer all of them. You are encouraged to ask a few questions of your own. Consider asking your classmates or instructors to assist you.

1. How can I recognize symptoms of extreme test anxiety?
2. How can I determine my personal test-anxiety level?
3. How can I develop strategies for controlling my test anxiety?
4. Which strategies can I apply to taking true–false tests?
5. Which strategies can I use for taking multiple-choice tests?

What additional questions do you have about testing and test anxiety?

1. _____
2. _____
3. _____

How do you really feel about tests? Successful students realize that testing is necessary and even useful, that it has several positive purposes. Testing provides motivation for learning, offers feedback to the student and to the instructor, and determines mastery of material.

Successful people accept testing as a fact of life. You have to be tested to drive a car; to continue in school; to join the armed services; to become a teacher, a lawyer, a doctor, or a nurse; and often to be promoted at work. To pretend that testing is not always going to be a part of your life is to deny yourself many opportunities. Testing now prepares you for the world of work.

You may dread tests for a variety of reasons and may be afraid of the test itself and the questions it may pose. Test anxiety can be overcome, however, and this chapter presents several ways you can become a more confident test taker and get started on the path to success. Remember, too, some test anxiety is normal and can help you do your best!

Controlling Test Anxiety

Some students have physical reactions to testing, including nausea, headaches, and blackouts. Such physical reactions may be a result of being underprepared or not knowing how to take an exam. You reduce anxiety when you are in control of the situation, and you gain control by convincing yourself that you will be successful. If you honestly tell yourself that you have done everything possible to prepare for a test, then the results are going to be positive. Tests are a "mind game" and you can win!

It is important to realize that a test is not an indication of who you are as a person or a mark of your worth as a human being. Not everyone can be good at all things. You will have areas of strength and of weakness. You will spare yourself a great deal of anxiety and frustration if you understand from the start that you may not score 100 on every test. If you expect absolute perfection on everything, you are setting yourself up to fail. Think positively, prepare well, and do your best, but also be prepared to receive less than a perfect score on occasion.

PREDICTING EXAM QUESTIONS

You can also reduce test anxiety by trying to predict what types of test questions the instructor will give. Instructors frequently give clues ahead of time about what they will be asking and what types of questions will be given. Several classes before the test is scheduled, find out from your instructor what type of test you can expect. Some questions you might ask are:

1. What type of questions will be on the test?
2. How long is the test?
3. Is there a time limit on the test?
4. Will there be any special instructions, such as use pen only or use a number 2 pencil?
5. Is there a study sheet?

Most test anxiety can be reduced by studying, predicting questions, reviewing, and relaxing.

6. Will there be a review session?

7. What is the grade value of the test?

Asking these simple questions will help you know what type of test will be administered, how you should prepare for it, and what supplies you will need. You will want to begin predicting questions early. Listen to the instructor intently. Instructors use cue phrases, such as, "You will see this again," and "If I were to ask you this question on the test." Pay close attention to what is written on the board, what questions are asked in class, and what areas the instructor seems to be concentrating on more than others. You will begin to get a feel for what types of questions the instructor might ask on the test.

It may also be beneficial for you to keep a running page of test questions that you have predicted. As you read through a chapter, ask yourself many questions at the end of each section. When it is time to study for the test, you may have already predicted many of the questions your instructor will ask.

Save all quizzes and exams that you are allowed to keep. These are a wonderful resource for studying for the next exam or for predicting questions for the course final.

Helpful Reminders for Reducing Test Anxiety

- Approach the test with an "I can" attitude.

- Prepare yourself emotionally for the test, control your self-talk, and be positive.

- Remind yourself that you studied and that you know the material.

- Overlearn the material—you can't study too much.

- Chew gum or eat hard candy during the test if allowed; it may help you relax.

- Go to bed early. Do not pull an all-nighter before the test.

- Eat a healthy meal before the test.

- Arrive early for the test (at least 15 minutes early).

- Sit back, relax, breathe, and clear your mind if you become nervous.

- Come to the test with everything you need: pencils, calculator, and other supplies.

- Read over the entire test first; read all the directions; highlight the directions.

- Listen to the instructor before the test begins.

- Keep an eye on the clock.

- Answer what you know first, the questions that are easiest for you.

- Check your answers, but remember, your first response is usually correct.

- Find out about the test before it is given; ask the instructor what types of questions will be on the test.

- Find out exactly what the test will cover ahead of time.

- Ask the instructor for a study sheet; you may not get one, but it does not hurt to ask!

- Know the rules of the test and of the instructor.

- Attend the review session if one is offered.

- Know what grade value the test holds.

- Ask about extra credit or bonus questions on the test.

- When you get the test, jot down any mnemonic you might have developed on the back or at the top of a page.

- Never look at another student's test or let anyone see your test.

WORLD OF WORK

As a teacher I always share with my students that in most circumstances, one academic event generally is not going to shape their entire academic career. I base this piece of advice on personal experience as well as on what I've seen happen to others through my years. First as a student, then as a teacher, and now as the online coordinator for our program, I've continued to see others experience similar situations and successfully fulfill their academic and career goals.

As a student I was pursuing an associate's degree in Liberal Arts at a community college where I was very serious about my studies, but I also had to work to support myself. I remember during one particular semester while working in a pizzeria I had to work very late the night before an early-morning class. I arrived at class and noticed that all of my classmates were looking very focused. I glanced at my class syllabus and realized that I had forgotten that an exam was scheduled for that morning. My first reaction was to panic.

I decided that I needed to take stock of what I had learned from coming to class every day and to try to relax. After all, wasn't life just a series of test? Hadn't last night at work been a test? I had spent the entire night working with customers who were constantly quizzing me about their pizza orders and about how long their order was going to take. I was also expected to deal with small crises that came up at work as well as at home. My entire life was a walking, breathing test. Therefore, I just needed to take a breath and remember what had been taught in class since the last quiz. I was grateful at this time that I had attended class regularly and taken notes. I was also thankful that I had reviewed my notes whenever I had a few minutes of extra time during work or other short periods of time throughout my day.

Several years have gone by since I had to take that quiz, but the interesting thing about that day that I've continued to remember is not the grade on the quiz but the fact that I made it through the quiz successfully. In fact, I made it through my schooling because of this "can do" attitude. A few simple practices I learned from my time in college continue to help me with my work today. I find that if I show up for meetings, appointments, and training sessions; if I take notes about what I understand and ask questions about what I don't understand; and if I review the notes I take during short periods of time tucked in between my very busy schedule, I continue to experience success.

I found as a student then and as a teacher now that I usually don't have large blocks of time to spend on a single task. I'm much better off spending smaller blocks of time reviewing notes and preparing for meetings or other events during the time I have rather than waiting for large blocks of time that never seem to happen. In fact, I find it very useful to carry my information around on smaller note cards.

Now, as a teacher, I always make it a priority to discuss with my classes the one instance that can impact their academic and career life—academic misconduct. It is critically important for everyone to understand what is considered academic misconduct by your teacher and your institution. A poor decision to look on another person's exam or to have a tutor do your homework could cost you the grade on the project or quiz you cheated on, the grade for the class you cheated in, as well as possible suspension from your institution. In some instances students in the United States on a student visa have actually lost their visa because of a poor academic misconduct decision. I have always wanted my students to understand the importance their decisions have on their overall academic career. If they understand this, then perhaps their decisions will be wise ones.

Consider responding to these questions online in the World of Work module of the Companion Website.

1. Ms. Weizmann experienced success in reducing her test anxiety by using some specific techniques. What techniques have you developed to help you avoid test anxiety?

2. Ms. Weizmann found that she was able to study in smaller blocks of time and that she could use note cards to carry information with her wherever she went. What practices have you developed to help you study "on the go"?

3. What can you do to increase your awareness of your institution's academic integrity code?

Mary Weizmann, *Online Coordinator,* General Education, Florida Metropolitan University, Tampa, FL

Three Types of Responses to Test Questions

Almost every test question will elicit one of three types of responses from you as the test taker:

- Quick-time response
- Lag-time response
- No response

Your response is a *quick-time response* when you read a question and know the answer immediately. You may need to read only one key word in the test question to know the correct response. Even if you have a quick-time response, however, always read the entire question before answering. The question may be worded in such a way that the correct response is not what you originally expected. By reading the entire question before answering, you can avoid losing points to careless error.

You have a *lag-time response* when you read a question and the answer does not come to you immediately. You may have to read the question several times or even move on to another question before you think of the correct response. Information in another question will sometimes trigger the response you need. Don't get nervous if you have a lag-time response. Once you've begun to answer other questions, you usually begin to remember more, and the response may come to you. You do not have to answer questions in order on most tests.

No response is the least desirable situation when you are taking a test. You may read a question two or three times and still have no response. At this point, you should move on to another question to try to find some related information. When this happens, you have some options:

1. Leave this question until the very end of the test.
2. Make an intelligent guess.
3. Try to eliminate all unreasonable answers.
4. Watch for modifiers within the question.
5. See if one question answers another.
6. Look for hints throughout the test.
7. Don't panic . . . simply move on.

Test-Taking Strategies and Hints for Success

The most common types of questions are:

- Matching
- True–false
- Multiple-choice
- Short answer
- Essay

Before you read about the strategies for answering these different types of questions, think about this: There is no substitute for studying! You can know all the tips, but if you have not studied, they will be of little help to you.

STRATEGIES FOR MATCHING QUESTIONS

Matching questions frequently involve knowledge of people, dates, places, or vocabulary. When answering matching questions, you should:

- Read the directions carefully.
- Read each column before you answer.
- Determine whether there is an equal number of items in each column.
- Match what you know first.
- Cross off information that is already used.
- Use the process of elimination for answers you might not know.
- Look for logical clues.
- Use the longer statement as a question; use the shorter statement as an answer.
- Answer all the questions.

What's Sleep Got to Do with It?

You've heard the old saying, "You are what you eat." This may be true, but many sleep experts would say, "You are how you sleep." Sleep deprivation is one of the leading causes of poor productivity and academic performance, workplace and auto accidents, lack of concentration, diminished immune systems, decreased metabolism, cardiovascular problems, and even poor communication efforts.

The National Traffic Safety Administration estimates that 100,000 crashes each year are the result of sleepy drivers. These crashes cause nearly 1,600 deaths, 71,000 injuries, and $12.5 billion in property loss and diminished activity (*Hidden Menace*, 2003).

Mark Rosekind, Ph. D., an expert on fatigue and performance issues and a member of the board of directors for the National Sleep Foundation, states, "Without sufficient sleep it is more difficult to concentrate, make careful decisions, and follow instructions; we are more likely to make mistakes or errors, and are more prone to being impatient and lethargic. Our attention, memory, and reaction time are all affected" (Cardinal, 2003).

According to the National Sleep Foundation, the following symptoms can signal inadequate sleep:

- Dozing off while engaged in an activity such as reading, watching TV, sitting in meetings, or sitting in traffic.

- Slowed thinking and reacting.

- Difficulty listening to what is said or understanding directions.

- Difficulty remembering or retaining information.

- Frequent errors or mistakes.

- Narrowing of attention, missing important changes in a situation.

- Depression or negative mood.

- Impatience or being quick to anger.

- Frequent blinking, difficulty focusing eyes, or heavy eyelids.

Indeed, lack of sleep can decrease your ability to study, recall information, and perform well on tests and assignments. This can be especially true during midterm and final exam periods. Those late or all-night cram sessions can actually be more detrimental to your academic success than helpful. By including your study sessions in your time-management plan, you can avoid having to spend your sleep time studying.

Different people need different amounts of sleep within a 24-hour period. Some people absolutely need 8–10 hours of sleep, while others can function well on 4–6 hours. If you are not sleeping enough to rest and revive your body, you will experience sleep deprivation.

Researchers suggest that missing as little as 2 hours of sleep for *one* night can take as long as 6 days to recover—if it is recovered at all (Moss, 1990). It is generally estimated that 8–9 hours of *good, solid, restful* sleep per night can decrease your chances of sleep deprivation.

Below, you will find some helpful hints for getting a good night's rest:

- Avoid alcohol and caffeine (yes, alcohol is a depressant, but it interrupts both REM and slow-wave sleep, and caffeine can stay in your system for as long as 12 hours).

- Exercise during the day (but not within four hours of your sleep time).

- Regulate the temperature in your bedroom to a comfortable setting for you.

- Wind down before trying to sleep. Complete all tasks at least one hour prior to your bedtime. This gives you time to relax and prepare for rest.

- Avoid taking naps during the day.

- Have a set bedtime and try to stick to it.

- Take a warm bath before bedtime.

- Go to bed only when you are tired. If you are not asleep within 15–30 minutes, get up and do something restful like reading or listening to soft music.

- Use relaxation techniques such as visualization and mind travel.

- Avoid taking sleeping aids. This can cause more long-term problems than sleep deprivation.

Sample Test #1: Matching

Directions: Match the information in column A with the correct information in column B. Use uppercase letters.

LISTENING SKILLS

A

____ They can be long or short, social, academic, religious, or financial

____ A step in the change process

____ Studying cooperatively

____ Your "true self"

____ Listening with an open mind

B

A. Child within

B. Objectivity

C. Letting go

D. Group or teamwork

E. Goals

STRATEGIES FOR TRUE–FALSE QUESTIONS

True–false tests ask if a statement is true or not. True–false questions can be some of the most challenging questions you will encounter on tests. Some students like them; some hate them. There is a 50/50 chance of answering correctly, but you can use the following strategies to increase your odds on true–false tests:

- Read each statement carefully.
- Watch for key words in each statement, for example, negatives.
- Read each statement for double negatives, such as "not untruthful."
- Pay attention to words that may indicate that a statement is true, such as "some," "few," "many," and "often."
- Pay attention to words that may indicate that a statement is false, such as "never," "all," "every," and "only."
- Remember that if any part of a statement is false, the entire statement is false.
- Answer every question unless there is a penalty for guessing.

Y ou are fast becoming what you are going to be.   —ANONYMOUS

Sample Test #2: True–False

Directions: Place "T" for true or "F" for false beside each statement.

NOTE-TAKING SKILLS

1. _____ Note taking creates a history of your course content.

2. _____ "Most importantly" is not a key phrase.

3. _____ You should always write down everything the instructor says.

4. _____ You should never ask questions in class.

5. _____ The L-STAR system is a way of studying.

6. _____ W/O is not a piece of shorthand.

7. _____ You should use 4-by-6-inch paper to take classroom notes.

8. _____ The outline technique is best used with lecture notes.

9. _____ The Cornell method should never be used with textbook notes.

10. _____ The mapping system is done with a series of circles.

STRATEGIES FOR MULTIPLE-CHOICE QUESTIONS

Many instructors give multiple-choice tests because they are easy to grade and provide quick, precise responses. A multiple-choice question asks you to choose from among usually two to five answers to complete a sentence. Some strategies for increasing your success in answering multiple-choice questions are the following:

- Read the question and try to answer it before you read the answers provided.

- Look for similar answers; one of them is usually the correct response.

- Recognize that answers containing extreme modifiers, such as *always, every,* and *never,* are usually wrong.

- Cross off answers that you know are incorrect.

- Read all the options before selecting your answer. Even if you believe that A is the correct response, read them all.

- Recognize that when the answers are all numbers, the highest and lowest numbers are usually incorrect.

- Recognize that a joke is usually wrong.

- Understand that the most inclusive answer is often correct.

- Understand that the longest answer is often correct.

- If you cannot answer a question, move on to the next one and continue through the test; another question may trigger the answer you missed.

- Make an educated guess if you must.

- Answer every question unless there is a penalty for guessing.

Sample Test #3: Multiple Choice

Directions: Read each statement and select the best response from the answers given below.

STUDY SKILLS

1. When reading your text, you should have

    A. an open mind.

    B. a dictionary.

    C. a highlighter.

    D. all of the above.

2. There are three types of memory; they are:

    A. short-term, sensory, computer.

    B. computer, long-term, perfect.

    C. perfect, short-term, long-term.

    D. sensory, short-term, long-term.

3. To be an effective priority manager, you have to:

    A. be very structured and organized.

    B. be very unstructured and disorganized.

    C. be mildly structured and organized.

    D. be sometimes a little of both.

    E. know what type of person you are and work from that point.

STRATEGIES FOR SHORT-ANSWER QUESTIONS

Short-answer questions, also called fill-in-the-blanks, ask you to supply the answer yourself, not to select it from a list. Although "short answer" sounds easy, these questions are often very difficult. Short-answer questions require you to draw from your long-term memory. The following hints can help you answer this type of question successfully:

- Read each question and be sure that you know what is being asked.
- Be brief in your response.
- Give the same number of answers as there are blanks; for example, _____ and _____ would require two answers.
- Never assume that the length of the blank has anything to do with the length of the answer.
- Remember that your initial response is usually correct.
- Pay close attention to the word immediately preceding the blank; if the word is "an," give a response that begins with a vowel (a, e, i, o, u).

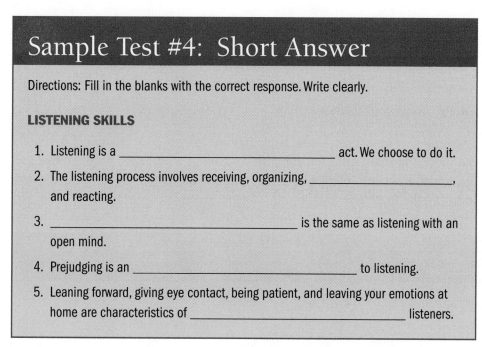

Sample Test #4: Short Answer

Directions: Fill in the blanks with the correct response. Write clearly.

LISTENING SKILLS

1. Listening is a _____ act. We choose to do it.

2. The listening process involves receiving, organizing, _____, and reacting.

3. _____ is the same as listening with an open mind.

4. Prejudging is an _____ to listening.

5. Leaning forward, giving eye contact, being patient, and leaving your emotions at home are characteristics of _____ listeners.

- Look for key words in the sentence that may trigger a response.
- Answer all the questions.

STRATEGIES FOR ESSAY QUESTIONS

Most students look at essay questions with dismay because they take more time. Yet essay tests can be among the easiest tests to take because they give you a chance to show what you really know. An essay question requires you to supply the information. If you have studied, you will find that once you begin to answer an essay question, your answer will flow easily. Some tips for answering essay questions are the following:

- More is not always better; sometimes more is just more. Try to be as concise and informative as possible. An instructor would rather see one page of excellent material than five pages of fluff.
- Pay close attention to the action word used in the question and respond with the appropriate type of answer. Key words used in questions include the following:

discuss	illustrate	enumerate	describe
compare	define	relate	list
contrast	summarize	analyze	explain
trace	evaluate	critique	interpret
diagram	argue	justify	prove

- Write a thesis statement for each answer.
- Outline your thoughts before you begin to write.
- Watch your spelling, grammar, and punctuation.
- Use details, such as times, dates, places, and proper names, where appropriate.

- Be sure to answer all parts of the question; some discussion questions have more than one part.
- Summarize your main ideas toward the end of your answer.
- Write neatly.
- Proofread your answer.

Learning how to take a test and learning how to reduce your anxiety are two of the most important gifts you can give yourself as a student. Although tips and hints may help you, don't forget that there is no substitute for studying and knowing the material.

Sample Test #5: Essay

Directions: Answer each question completely. Use a separate paper if you wish.

STUDY SKILLS

1. Identify and discuss two examples of mnemonics.

_____

_____

_____

2. Discuss why it is important to use the SQ3R method.

_____

_____

_____

3. Justify your chosen notebook and study system.

_____

_____

_____

4. Compare an effective study environment with an ineffective study environment.

_____

_____

_____

Academic and Personal Integrity

MAKING THE RIGHT DECISIONS

As a student, you will be faced with temptations that require you to make hard choices. You have probably already been forced to make decisions based on ethics. Do I cheat and make a higher grade so I can compete with top students? Will cheating help me earn higher grades so I get a better job? Do I copy this paper from the Internet? Who will know? No one said specifically that copying from the Internet is wrong. Why shouldn't I do this if everybody else is copying? What if I just copy someone's homework and not cheat on a test? What if I lie to the instructor and say I was sick so I can get more time for a test for which I am not prepared? What if someone looks on my paper during a test; I'm not cheating, am I? These are all ethical questions that require you to use your personal integrity to make the right decision.

Integrity is purely and simply doing what is right. It's about understanding who you are as a person and making decisions about what is right and wrong according to your personal code of ethics. What will you do when nobody knows but you? It is also making decisions about what is right and wrong according to your institution's standards. As a college student, you will see many people do things that you think are not right. You have to decide what is right for you and follow your values no matter what others may be doing. Just because "everyone is doing it" doesn't make it right, and certainly it doesn't make it right for you.

Your continuing education experience should refine your character and hopefully help you assess and evaluate your value system. You will no doubt find some of your views and values changing over the next few years. One of your challenges is to ensure that you are improving your character rather than compromising who you are and hope to become. You are building yourself today for the long haul—not for a few short years!

LISTEN TO YOUR CONSCIENCE

What does your conscience tell you? If it nags at you about an action you are about to take, don't do it! Making ethical decisions can be as simple as listening to your conscience. If you have a nagging, recurring feeling that what you are doing is not right, it probably isn't. If you can't sleep at night because you have done something that you cannot respect, chances are you need to reflect on your decisions. Real integrity is doing the right thing when nobody knows but you, or refraining when you could probably get away with copying a test question or committing an infraction of the rules. Your personal code of ethics is based on your value system, the standards and ideals that you use to make tough decisions.

DID YOU KNOW?

Rolihlahla (Nelson) Mandela

was raised in deep poverty. Throughout his life, he suffered abuse and discrimination. He was asked to leave college because of his beliefs and protests. He endured a 5-year trial for treason and later spent 27 years in prison. He was released in 1990. In 1994, at the age of 76, he became the first black president of South Africa.

IDEAS FOR SUCCESS

Consider the following tips for taking tests and relieving test anxiety:

- Prepare carefully, thoroughly, and continuously in order to prevent test anxiety.

- Pay close attention to the instructor in order to predict the types of questions that may be included on an exam.

- If the instructor offers study sessions, attend and ask questions if you do not understand any part of the review.

- Use the suggestions in this chapter to respond to a variety of test questions.

- Review your institution's student handbook and become familiar with the code of ethics that has been endorsed by your faculty, students, and administrators.

- Be sure you understand exactly what constitutes plagiarism, including using information found on the Internet.

- Establish an exemplary code of personal ethics and academic integrity so that, above all else, you can respect yourself and earn the respect of others.

Even if you cheat and don't get caught, you lose. You lose respect for yourself, your self-esteem is likely to decline, and you cheat yourself of the knowledge for which you are paying. You also lose because you damage your character and the person you hope to become. Cheating can cause you to feel guilty and stressed because you are afraid that someone might find out.

Eventually, cheating will become a crutch that you lean on in order to pass and make good grades, and it will become easy to decide to cheat instead of working and earning your grades. The habit of cheating is likely to carry over into the workplace if you have embraced it as a way of life in college. Gradually, day by day, you are building the person you want to become. Ultimately, the person who is harmed the most by cheating is the one who does it. In some shape or fashion, cheating will always come back to haunt you. You, personally, will pay the price.

Academic integrity says a lot about who you are and what you believe in. Following a code of ethics is important for another reason as well. If you are honest, work hard, and do your own work, you will most likely get a good education. Your future depends on what you are learning today!

WHAT DO YOU NEED TO KNOW ABOUT ACADEMIC MISCONDUCT?

It is important to know what constitutes dishonesty in an academic setting. The following is a list of offenses that most institutions consider academic misconduct.

- Looking on another person's test paper for answers.

- Giving another student answers on tests, homework, or lab projects.

- Using any kind of "cheat sheets" on a test or project.

- Using a computer, calculator, dictionary, or notes when not approved.

- Discussing exam questions with students who are taking the same class at another time.

- Plagiarism or using the words or works of others without giving proper credit. This includes the Internet!

- Stealing another student's class notes.

- Using an annotated instructor's edition of a text.

- Having tutors do your homework for you.

- Submitting the same paper for more than one class during any semester.
- Copying files from a lab computer or borrowing someone else's disk with the work on it.
- Bribing a student for answers or academic work such as papers or projects.
- Buying or acquiring papers from individuals or the Internet.
- Assisting others with dishonest acts.
- Lying about reasons you missed a test or a class.

Change occurs, progress is made, and difficulties resolved if people merely do the right thing, and rarely do people **not know** what the right thing is. —FATHER HESSBURG

Learning to deal with test anxiety and to get your fears under control early in your program can lead to greater success as you move through your education. With the right kinds of practice, you can become much more adept at test taking and can greatly reduce your stress.

Another important part of this chapter dealt with academic and personal integrity. You can't control anyone's behavior other than your own. Your challenge is to focus on developing excellent test-taking abilities and study habits while earning the best grades you can. When you have done this, you can look in the mirror and be proud of the person you see without having to be ashamed of your character or having to worry about being caught cheating. You are building your character for the long haul—not just a few short years.

what's it ALL ABOUT?

NAME: Oscar Bowser, Jr.

SCHOOL: Midlands Technical College, Columbia, SC

MAJOR: Nursing   AGE: 52

Below is a real-life situation faced by Oscar. Read the brief case and respond to the questions.

I am a former Marine, an ex–New York state public safety officer, an ex–correctional officer, and a certified rescue scuba diver. Over the course of my life, there have been very few things that I have feared and not conquered. It may seem strange, but I was afraid of math.

My goal is to become a professional registered nurse, and math is a major part of that curriculum. When I began career college, I would avoid registering for any math course or I would register and withdraw at some point during the course to avoid my anxiety of math. Numerous times, I've taken math exams without having read or studied the chapter; therefore, I could not comprehend the directions.

Finally, it dawned on me that the cause of my math anxiety, or any anxiety in general, is simply this: "the lack of knowing." You don't have anxiety when driving a car because you know how by repetition. You don't have anxiety walking through your home at night without lights on because you have familiarized yourself with the environment. Due to this discovery, I have eliminated my anxiety. To study for my math exams, I use the following techniques: reading, writing, reciting, repeating, and memorizing.

In addition, I have learned that to conquer anything in life you must practice self-motivation, self-determination, and self-discipline. This semester, my grades in math thus far are 95, 105, 89, and 100! Nursing degree, here I come!

How can a positive attitude like Oscar's affect your classroom performance?

_____

_____

_____

Do you think Oscar is correct in his explanation of what causes anxiety? Why or why not?

_____

_____

_____

What role does self-discipline play in reducing test anxiety?

_____

_____

_____

How can reducing test anxiety help you perform better?

_____

_____

_____

What concrete methods do you plan to employ to reduce your testing anxiety?

_____

_____

_____

How do you plan to improve your self-discipline and self-determination to help with your test-taking strategies?

_____

_____

_____

Where can you go at your institution to learn more about controlling test anxiety, learning to take tests more effectively, and studying for tests in general?

_____

_____

_____

ADVICE TO GO
CORNERSTONES

for test taking

Maintain your personal *integrity.*

Never use drugs or alcohol to get through a test.

Read over the entire test *before* beginning.

Check punctuation, spelling, and grammar.

Write your *name* on every test page.

Ignore the pace of your classmates.

Ask questions of the instructor.

Answer *all* questions.

Watch *time* limits.

Think *positively.*

Write *clearly.*

ASSESS

9 Think

"O K," Todd thought to himself. *"You just need to sit down for a minute and think. Think. Think."*

Todd is a Pharmacy Tech student in his third quarter at Heartland Medical and Technical Institute. His dream of working in a pharmacy seems to be slipping further and further away. He has done well in most of his classes before this quarter. He aced his courses in Mathematical Conversions, Food and Drug Administration Oversight, Medical Ordering, Controlled Substance Law, and even Pharmacy and Federal Law. Now, however, he is enrolled in Pediatric Dosage Calculation and Oral and Intravenous Drug Calculations. He has the same instructor for both classes. He is also taking two other classes with two different instructors.

As Instructor McAllen covers the material in the conversion classes, most of the class is struggling to keep up. *This material is new to them and it is hard.* The classes involve math and science and logic and problem solving and psychology. Todd has never encountered anything like this before.

He decides to speak with Mr. McAllen after class, but Mr. McAllen tells Todd that he will have to speak to him during his office hours. Todd tells Mr. McAllen that he has to go to work in the afternoon and cannot come during Mr. McAllen's office hours. Instructor McAllen simply replies, *"Then that's a problem, isn't it?"*

As the quarter progresses, Todd struggles with the material. These two classes are the hardest he has taken, and to make matters even worse, he had missed a few days at the beginning of the quarter due to illness. He has also taken a new part-time job in the late afternoon to help support his family. *The*

stress is taking its toll on him and his grades. He notices himself being short and rude to his wife and impatient with his children. He is not doing his best at his new part-time job, he is not getting along very well with his instructor, and now, *his grades are falling day by day.* He scores a D on a test in Pediatric Drug Calculation and a C— on a test in Oral Drug Calculation.

Todd knows that something has to change. "Think," he says to himself. "Think about what you are going to do. *Think about how you're going to fix this."*

Later that day, Todd decides to take a break from school and family and work just to try to figure out what has gone wrong. He usually goes to a nearby sandwich shop to grab lunch before the last class of the day, but today, he decides to simply *go to the library, find a quiet corner,* and try to *piece together a plan* to put his life and career back on track.

"OK," he thinks. "List all of the things that are not going well in my life. That's where I'll start." His list includes:

- Poor relationship with my calculations instructor
- Rude to my wife
- Impatient with my children
- Not enough time in the day to get it all done
- A new part-time job
- Two very hard and demanding classes
- Some bad grades in two classes
- Still not feeling well

"There it is," he surmises. "That is my life and it is not pretty." He sits back in his chair and knows that he has to make some hard choices if he is going to *pass his classes, keep his family,* and *reach his ultimate goal.*

"Now, what do I do with this information?" Todd remembers a class he took in his first quarter that dealt with problem solving and decision making. "A plan," he thinks to himself. *"I need to develop a problem-solving plan."* At that moment, Todd remembers that he has to find the root of the problem—*the thing* that is causing all of this to happen.

After thinking about the issues and what is going on in his life, Todd determines that the real problem is not his intellectual ability, his love for his wife and children, or even his part-time job. The real problem is that there are *not enough hours in the day.*

"I don't have enough time and that is stressing me out," he says to himself. "I haven't sat down with my wife and worked out a time-management plan in over eight months, and my old plan is not working now."

"So what do I do now?" he questions. He remembers that his instructor in the first quarter taught them how to analyze a problem and look at all of the options and then make a decision. Todd *begins to list all of his options* and what they mean to his life and his goals. His chart looks like the one to the right.

By listing all that is wrong and all of the options to correct the root of the problem, *Todd begins to see* that he can actually make this work. He begins to see that by giving himself enough time to think about the problem, he might very well save his marriage, his grades, and his career.

By using critical thinking, Todd is able to rationally develop some options to help him solve his problem. This is just one of the many everyday uses of learning how to become a more critical thinker.

QUESTIONS FOR REFLECTION

Consider responding to these questions online in the Questions for Reflection module of the Companion Website.

1. Do you think that Todd's problems are common with today's students? Why or why not?

2. What is the relationship between time management and critical thinking?

3. How can you use critical thinking to solve a problem in your life?

Quit my part-time job	Not really an option because we need the money to pay the bills and get food and gas. I could, however, ask my boss to schedule me for a later shift if possible.
Get less sleep	No. I'm already running on five hours of sleep a night. Getting less sleep will only make the stress worse.
Spend less time with my family	No. My family is the most important thing in my life and they are the reason I'm in this program. If I lose my family, then this is not worth it.
Spend less time studying	No. If I spend less time studying then things are not going to get any better. I'll flunk out of the program and never be able to provide for my family.
Delegate and ask for help	Possible. If I sit down with my family and talk to them and ask them to take on a few of my chores, I'll have more time. After all, this is not forever—just a little while longer.
Form a lunch-time study group	Yes. I can ask around and see if anyone is interested in doing this. We can bring our lunch and study together for an hour between classes. This gives me another hour of study time and frees me up a little more at home.

Where are you . . . AT THIS MOMENT

Before reading this chapter, take a moment and respond to the following 10 questions. Consider each one carefully before answering, and then respond by circling the number in the appropriate box. When you have answered the questions, add your points and find your total score on the feedback chart below.

STATEMENT	STRONGLY DISAGREE	DISAGREE	DON'T KNOW	AGREE	STRONGLY AGREE	SCORE
1. I tend to trust the information I get from the TV and newspaper without analyzing it.	5	(4)	3	2	1	
2. It is difficult for me to approach a topic with an open mind once I have already come to a conclusion about it.	5	4	3	2	1	
3. I question the "facts" that I get from others.	1	2	3	4	5	
4. I am easily persuaded by information that sounds rational.	5	4	3	2	1	
5. The ability to think critically is really only of use in school.	5	4	3	2	1	
6. When I'm trying to understand another person's point of view, my emotions or opinions get in the way.	5	4	3	2	1	
7. Information I get from TV, magazines, or newspapers doesn't need to be questioned or challenged.	5	4	3	2	1	
8. When I'm trying to solve a problem, I rely on the "try something and see" approach, rather than devising a plan.	5	4	3	2	1	
9. I possess the courage and tolerance for the risk taking it takes to be creative in problem solving and thinking.	1	2	3	4	5	
10. I know how to tell if a statement is a fact or an opinion.	1	2	3	4	5	
TOTAL VALUE						

SUMMARY

43–50 You have exceptional critical-thinking skills. You likely make it a habit to question and analyze most information that you come across. You probably incorporate creative and flexible thinking in your analyses.

35–42 You have above average critical-thinking skills. You know that it is important to distinguish real facts from statements that just sound like facts. You are also probably good at analyzing information from an open-minded, neutral perspective.

26–34 You are average in your critical-thinking and reasoning skills. You are likely able to distinguish fact from opinion and sometimes stop to question the information that you've been exposed to. You would benefit from refined critical-thinking strategies.

18–25 You have below average skills in critically analyzing information. You need to learn how to better separate fact from propaganda. You likely also need to improve your ability to eliminate your emotional reactions to information while analyzing it.

10–17 Your critical-thinking skills are limited. You have difficulty keeping an open mind, are easily influenced by opinions, and need to sharpen your ability to separate facts from things that sound like facts. You must explore these issues to be successful in school and the outside world.

Based on the summary above, what is one goal you would like to achieve related to critical and creative thinking?

Goal _____

_____

List three actions you can take that might help you move closer to realizing this goal.

1. _____
2. _____
3. _____

Questions
FOR BUILDING ON YOUR BEST

As you read this chapter, consider the following questions. At the end of the chapter, you should be able to answer all of them. We encourage you to ask a few questions of your own. Consider asking your classmates or professors to assist you.

1. Why is critical thinking important to my life?
2. How can critical thinking help me become a better student?
3. What steps can I take to become a more critical and creative thinker?
4. Why is problem solving important to my life?
5. When will I ever need to use critical thinking in the "real world"?

What additional questions might you have about thinking more critically and creatively?

1. _____
2. _____
3. _____

Almost any profession you choose to go into will require the ability to think through problems, make decisions, and apply other critical-thinking skills.

Thinking About Thinking

Understanding why and how we formulate thoughts and ideas is the main objective of this chapter. This chapter is about believing and disbelieving, seeking, uncovering, debunking myths, proving the impossible possible. It is about proof, logic, evidence, and developing ideas and opinions based on hard-core facts or credible research. This chapter is about seeking truth and expanding your mind to unimaginable limits. This chapter is about the fundamental aspect of becoming an educated citizen; it is about human thought and reasoning.

What Is It Anyway?

A WORKING DEFINITION OF CRITICAL THINKING

Suppose your best friend asked you why you favored (or did not favor) the death penalty. What would your answer be? If you are FOR the death penalty, would you say that it is justified, warranted, necessary, or reasonable? If you are AGAINST the death penalty, would you say that it is murder, inhumane, cruel, unjustifiable, unneeded, reprehensible, or vindictive?

For those of you who are *for* the death penalty, let's say that you hold the death penalty as *justified*. For those of you who are *against* the death penalty, let's say that you hold the death penalty as *vindictive*.

Before you go any further, explain to your friend just what *justified* (or *vindictive*) means. Make him or her understand it. Make him or her understand your reason for using that word. Can you do it? You know what you mean, but can you make your friend understand your position? Can you explain in great detail what the word is and how it applies to capital punishment? Can you define the word? Can you explain what it implies? Can you give examples of the word as related to the death penalty?

This technique, as explained by Peter Facione (1998), is the best way to define critical thinking. Critical thinking is what you are doing with that word *right now*. It is searching, plotting, making associations, explaining, analyzing, probing for multiple angles, justifying, scrutinizing, making decisions, solving problems, and investigating. *It is literally thinking about something from many angles.* Another way to define critical thinking is to consider people who use critical thinking in their daily lives:

- The lawyer who found the loophole to free his client.
- The doctor who searched deeply enough, ordered the correct tests, and found the cancer that was missed by three other physicians.
- The computer repair technician who found the one tiny circuit problem in your computer.
- The auto repair person who found the faulty wiring in your car through several diagnostic tests.

- The medical office assistant who re-organized the billing procedure and saved the office $10,000 per year.
- The teacher who finally found a way to teach Johnny to read with pictures.
- The homemaker who discovered a way to reduce the household debt each month.
- The marketing expert who developed the winning campaign for Mountain Dew.
- The student who discovered that reading the material before class made listening easier.

These people and their discoveries define critical thinking better than any definition we could provide here. Critical thinking is about making informed, enlightened, educated, open-minded decisions in college, in relationships, in finances, and in life in general.

When Will I Ever Use It?
THE IMPORTANCE OF CRITICAL THINKING

Have you ever made a decision that turned out to be a mistake? Have you ever said to yourself, "If only I could go back . . . "? Have you ever regretted actions you took toward a person or situation? Have you ever planned an event or function that went off flawlessly? Have you ever had to make a hard, painful decision that turned out to be "the best decision of your life"? If the answer to any of these questions is yes, you might be able to trace the consequences back to your thought process at the time of the decision. Let's face it, sometimes good and bad things happen out of luck. More often than not, however, the events in our lives are driven by the thought processes involved.

Critical thinking can serve us in many areas as students and citizens in society. As a student, critical thinking can help you focus on issues; gather relevant, accurate information; remember facts; organize thoughts logically; analyze questions and problems; and manage your priorities. It can assist in your problem-solving skills and help you control your emotions so that you can make rational judgments. It can help you determine the accuracy of printed and spoken words. It can help you detect bias and determine the point of arguments and persuasion.

A Plan for Critical Thinking
MAKING IT WORK FOR YOU

As you begin to build and expand your critical-thinking skills, consider the steps involved. Critical-thinking skill development involves

- restraining emotions
- looking at things differently

WORLD OF WORK

As students who will soon be entering the world of work in your chosen career, you need to know that many situations you will face will be vastly different from the past. Diversity is a frequently discussed issue and impacts every aspect of the workplace, from employment practices to promotion, from leadership and management styles to employee relations, from domestic relationships to global interaction, and from product creation to marketing. I can tell you without reservation that learning to celebrate and appreciate diversity is an absolute must for success in your career.

As an African American with more than 35 years' experience in the automotive industry, I have experienced some "not too pleasant" people along the way; however, I have learned to stay focused on my career goals and to be absolutely sure that I am being fair and consistent in my own workplace habits where diversity is concerned. I am responsible for my actions. I can't do anything about other people's personal prejudices and biases whether based on race, religion, gender, national origin, or sexual orientation, but I can be sure that I give every person a fair chance and judge them on their character and performance. This is where emotional restraint and problem solving come into play.

As a corporate executive for the world's largest manufacturer, I have had unlimited opportunities to interact with people from diverse backgrounds—from the White House to a remote Habitat building site in Poland. I, therefore, had to adjust in order to form solid relationships with people who are different from me. My personal reward is accepting those differences and learning to appreciate people for who they are and for what they can contribute to the betterment of my job, my company, my country, and the world. Learning to be open-minded about other cultures took a great deal of critical and creative thinking.

About 10 years ago, I was vice president for corporate communications at Saturn Corporation, a wholly owned subsidiary of General Motors, located in Spring Hill, Tennessee. My primary responsibility was to protect and enhance the image and reputation of the company. That meant taking into consideration many factors that might impact our diverse customer base, especially in Japan.

I have taken those **"best practices"** from Saturn to my current position at GMAC, one of the largest financial service organizations in the world. It is my responsibility to ensure that our advertising, promotion, communication, and public relation efforts send the right messages to our worldwide audience. I must constantly analyze information and separate fact from opinion—another quality of critical thinking.

GMAC is part of an even larger organization, General Motors Corporation, with nearly 380,000 employees selling vehicles and services in 200 countries around the world. Working in such a global organization, I cannot and will not act in a manner that could have a negative impact on my career or the image and reputation of my company. I encourage you to open your minds and hearts. You will be richly rewarded in your career and in your personal development. The ability to think critically will help you achieve this goal.

QUESTIONS FOR REFLECTION

Consider responding to these questions online in the World of Work module of the Companion Website.

1. Why do you think Mr. Farmer has been so successful in his career?

2. What kinds of prejudices do you think Mr. Farmer has experienced?

3. What can you learn from Mr. Farmer that you can apply to your own life and later at work?

James E. Farmer, Vice President, Merchandising, Advertising, and Communications, General Motors (GMAC), Detroit, MI

- analyzing information
- asking questions
- solving problems
- distinguishing fact from opinion

The remainder of this chapter will detail, through explanation, exploration, and exercises, how to build a critical-thinking plan for your academic and personal success.

STEP ONE: RESTRAINING EMOTIONS

Did James Earl Ray really kill Martin Luther King Jr.? Is there life on other planets? Should Eminem's music be banned from music stores? Should the drinking age be lowered to 18? Should 16-year-olds be allowed to drive a car? Should hate crime laws be abolished? What emotions are you feeling right now? Did you immediately formulate answers to these questions in your mind? Are your emotions driving your thinking process?

Emotions play a vital role in our lives. They help us feel compassion, help others, and reach out in times of need, and they help us relate to others. Emotions, on the other hand, can cause some problems in your critical-thinking process. You do not have to eliminate emotions from your thoughts, but it is crucial that you know when your emotions are clouding an issue.

Consider the following topics:

- Should drugs and prostitution be legalized?
- Can the theories of evolution and creationism coexist?
- Is affirmative action reverse discrimination?
- Should terminally ill patients have the right to state-assisted and/or privately assisted suicide?

As you read these topics, did you immediately form an opinion? Did old arguments surface? Did you feel your emotions coming into play as you thought about the questions? If you had an immediate answer, it is likely that you allowed some past judgments, opinions, and emotions to enter the decision-making process, unless you have just done a comprehensive, unbiased study of one of these issues. As you discussed these in class or with your friends, how did you feel? Did you become angry? Did you find yourself groping for words? Did you find it hard to explain why you held the opinion that you voiced? If so, these are warning signs that you are allowing your emotions to drive your decisions. If we allow our emotions to run rampant (not using restraint) and fail to use research, logic, and evidence (expansive thinking), we cannot examine the issues critically or have a logical discussion regarding the statements.

Candid discussions, and sometimes brutal honesty, are useful and necessary when you are addressing complex or difficult issues. However, be careful not to let emotions take over your objectivity.

If you feel that your emotions caused you to be less than objective, you might consider the following tips when you are faced with an emotional decision:

- Listen to all sides of the argument or statement before you make a decision or form an opinion.
- Make a conscious effort to identify which emotions are causing you to lose objectivity.
- Do not let your emotions withdraw you or turn you off from the situation.
- Don't let yourself become engaged in "I'm right, you're wrong" situations.
- Work to understand why others feel their side is valid.
- Physiological reactions to emotions, such as increased heart rate and blood pressure and an increase in adrenaline flow, should be recognized as an emotional checklist. If you begin to experience these reactions, relax, take a deep breath, and concentrate on being open-minded.
- Control your negative self-talk or inner voice toward the other person(s) or situation.
- Determine whether your emotions are irrational.

In the space provided below, develop a step-by-step plan to evaluate one of the controversial topics listed previously. You do not have to answer the question; your task is to devise a plan to address the topic critically without emotional interference. For example: Do violent TV programs and movies cause violent crime? Before you answer yes or no, your first step might be to define violent TV/movies. A second step might be to define violent crime. A third step might be to research the connection between the two. A fourth step might be to evaluate the research objectively, asking the following questions: (1) From where does the research originate: the TV or movie industry, a parental guidance group, or a completely independent agency? (2) How old is the research? (3) For how long a period was the research conducted? This type of questioning does not allow your emotions to rule the outcome.

Select a topic and devise a plan for critical analysis.

Statement _____

_____

Step 1. _____

_____

Step 2. _____

_____

Step 3. _____

_____

Step 4. _____

_____

Step 5. _____

_____

STEP TWO: LOOKING AT THINGS DIFFERENTLY

Critical thinking involves looking at an issue from many different angles. It encourages you to dig deeper than you have before; get below the surface; struggle, experiment, and expand. It asks you to look at something from an entirely different angle so that you might develop new insights and understand more about the problem, situation, or question. Thinking on a higher level involves looking at something that you may have never seen before or something that you may have seen many times, and trying to think about it more critically than before.

As you begin to look "with different eyes," take a moment to complete the activities below. They are provided to encourage you to look at simple, common situations in a new light. Remember, these exercises do not measure intelligence. Review the following example of a "brain teaser" and solve the remaining teasers. You will need to break down a few barriers in thought and look at them from a new angle to get them all.

BRAIN TEASERS

Examples:

4 W on a C	4 Wheels on a Car
13 O C	13 Original Colonies

1. SW and the 7 D — Snow White and the 7 dwarfs
2. I H a D by MLK — I had a Dream by Martin Luther King
3. 2 P's in a P — 2 peas in a pod
4. HDD (TMRUTC)
5. 3 S to a T
6. 100 P in a D — 100 pennies in a Dollar
7. T no PLH
8. 4 Q in a G — 4 quarts in a gallon
9. I a SWAA
10. 50 S in TU

How did you do? Was it hard to look at the situation backward? Most of us are not used to that. As you continue to build your critical-thinking skills, look at the design at the right. You will find nine dots. Your mission is to connect all nine dots with four straight lines without removing your pencil or pen from the paper. Do not retrace your lines. Can you do it?

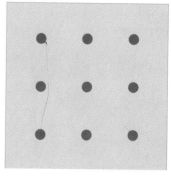

Finally, as you begin to think beyond the obvious, examine the penny. You will see the front and back sides of the penny. Pretend that the world has ended and all traces of civilization are gone. Someone from another planet, who speaks our language, has come to earth and the only thing left from our civilization is one penny. List the things that could be assumed about our civilization from this one small penny. You should find at least 10.

Although these activities may seem somewhat trivial, they are provided to help you begin to think about and consider information from a different angle. This is a major step in becoming a critical thinker: looking beyond the obvious, thinking outside the box, examining details, and exploring possibilities.

STEP THREE: ANALYZING INFORMATION

Critical thinking goes further than thinking on a different or higher level or using emotional restraint; it also involves analyzing information. To analyze, you break a topic, statement, or problem into parts to understand it more clearly. This is a simple, yet crucial, step in critical thinking. An easy way to analyze is to create a chart of the information using right- and left-hand columns. Consider the example in the box that examines the death penalty.

As you can see, a question properly analyzed prevents you from simply answering the question with a bland and poor answer such as, "It's good," or "It's bad." It can also prevent you from becoming too emotional since you must rely on facts to support your answer. An analysis forces you to ask *why* it is good or bad, right or wrong, proper or improper.

This method can also be used to formulate new information on a subject as Todd did in the opening story. If you read a chapter or an article, hear a conversation, or are faced with a problem, you can analyze it by first writing a question that needs to be answered. Then create a chart in which you provide brief, pointed answers to the question in Column A and more detailed explanations in Column B (see the example below). You may have to use more than one source of information to answer the questions you posed.

Example

Why should the death penalty be abolished?

COLUMN A	COLUMN B
It is barbaric.	The United States is the last industrialized nation in the world to use capital punishment. We are in the company of the Congo, Iran, and China.
It is racist.	More African Americans and Hispanics are put to death than Caucasians. The proportion of African American and Hispanic inmates on death row is greater than their porportion of the general population.
It is expensive.	It costs over $3 million to put a person to death, while it costs slightly more than $500,000 to imprison him or her for 40 years.

Now, it's your turn. Analyze the following question: *How can you write an effective cover letter?* Hint: The answer can be found in Chapter 10.

Use the chart on the following page to analyze this question.

COLUMN A (ANSWER)   **COLUMN B (EXPLANATION)**

_____   _____
_____   _____
_____   _____
_____   _____
_____   _____
_____   _____
_____   _____
_____   _____
_____   _____
_____   _____
_____   _____

STEP FOUR: ASKING QUESTIONS

You've asked questions all of your life. As a child, you asked your parents, "What's that?" a million times. You probably asked them, "Why do I have to do this?" In later years, you've asked questions of your friends, teachers, strangers, store clerks, and significant others. Questioning is not new to you, but it may be a new technique for exploring, developing, and acquiring new knowledge. Curiosity may have killed the cat, but it was a smart cat when it died! Your curiosity is one of the most important traits you possess. It helps you grow and learn, and it may sometimes cause you to be uncomfortable. That's OK. This section is provided to assist you in learning how to ask questions to promote knowledge, solve problems, foster strong relationships, and critically analyze difficult situations.

Let's start with a simple questioning exercise. If you were asked to write a paper dealing with assisted suicide or hybrid cars, or homeland security, what questions would you want to have answered? Take some time to think about the issue. Write down at least five questions on one of these topics.

My five questions are:

1. _____

2. _____

3. _____

4. _____

5. _____

Questioning also involves going beyond the obvious. Examine the following advertisement. The car dealership has provided some information, but it

is not enough to make an educated decision. What other questions would you ask to make sure that you are getting a good deal?

1. _____

2. _____

3. _____

4. _____

5. _____

Asking questions can be fun in many situations. They help us gain insight where we may have limited knowledge. They can also challenge us to look at issues from many different angles. Answering properly posed questions can help us expand our knowledge base.

STEP FIVE: SOLVING PROBLEMS

You face problems every day; some are larger and more difficult than others. You may have transportation problems. You may have child care problems. You may have academic problems or interpersonal problems. Many people don't know how to solve problems at school, home, or work. They simply let the problem go unaddressed until it is too late to reach an amiable solution. There are many ways to address and solve problems. In this section, we will discuss how to identify and narrow the problem, research and develop alternatives, evaluate the alternatives, and solve the problem.

It is important to remember that every problem does have a solution, but the solution may not be what we wanted. It is also imperative to remember the words of Mary Hatwood Futrell, President of the NEA. She states that "finding the right answer is important, of course. But more important is developing the ability to see that problems have multiple solutions, that getting from X to Y demands basic skills and mental agility, imagination, persistence, and patience."

Identify and narrow the problem. Put your problem in writing. When doing this, be sure to jot down all aspects of the problem, such as why it is a problem, whom it affects, and what type of problem it is. Examine the following situation: You have just failed two tests this week and you are dreadfully behind on your work. Now, that's a problem . . . or is it? If you examine and reflect on the problem, you begin to realize that because of your nighttime job, you always get to class late, you are tired and irritable when you get there, and you never have time to study. So, the real problem is not that you can't do the work; the problem is that your job is interfering with your study time. Now that you have identified and narrowed the problem, you can begin to work toward a solution.

Research and develop alternatives. A valuable method of gathering ideas, formulating questions, and solving problems is brainstorming. To brainstorm, gather a group of people and ask them to let ideas flow. A brainstorming session allows all thoughts to be heard without any fear of ridicule. You can brainstorm any matter, almost anywhere. You may want to set some guidelines for your sessions to make them more productive.

- Identify the topic, problem, or statement to be discussed.
- Set a time limit for the entire brainstorming session.
- Write all ideas on a board or flip chart.
- Let everyone speak.
- Don't criticize people for their remarks.
- Concentrate on the issue; let all of your ideas flow.
- Suspend judgment until all ideas are produced or the time is up.
- If you're using the session to generate questions rather than solutions, each participant should pose questions rather than make statements.

When solving a problem, it is helpful to look at all possible alternatives and decide on the best one. Sometimes there is one right answer, but often you'll have to settle for the best answer.

Using the problem of "my nighttime job is causing me to not have enough time for sleep or study," jot down the first few alternatives that come to mind. Don't worry about content, clarity, or quality. Just let your mind flow. Verbalize these ideas when the class brainstorms this problem.

Evaluate the alternatives. Some of your ideas or your classmates' ideas may not be logical in solving the problem. After careful study and deliberation, without emotional interference, analyze the ideas and determine if they are appropriate or inappropriate for the solution. To analyze, create Columns A and B. Write the idea in Column A and a comment in Column B. Example:

A (IDEA)	B (COMMENTS)
Quit the job.	Very hard to do. I need the money for tuition and car.
Cut my hours at work.	Will ask my boss.
Find a new job.	Hard to do because of the job market—but will look into it.
Get a student loan.	Visit financial aid office tomorrow.
Quit school.	No—it is my only chance for a promotion.

With your comments in Column B, you can now begin to eliminate some of the alternatives that are inappropriate at this time.

Solve the problem. Now that you have a few strong alternatives, you have some work to do. You will need to talk to your

DID YOU KNOW?

Lance Armstrong

In 1997, Lance Armstrong was sponsored by the French racing team, Cofidis. When the company learned of his testicular cancer, they fired him and even refused to pay him his remaining salary and medical bills. He successfully fought his cancer and went on to win SEVEN *Tour de France* races and is ranked as the number one cyclist in the world.

Put into action the following tips for critical thinking:

- Don't let your emotions cloud the truth about a situation or problem.

- Keep an open mind about people and don't stereotype them.

- Remember that negative attitudes about people, places, and situations can get in the way of critical thinking.

- If you have difficulty thinking through a situation, use the analysis technique with an A and B column.

- Be certain to listen to all sides of the argument before making up your mind.

- Try to stay away from the "I'm right, you're wrong" mentality.

- When faced with a new situation, try to look at it differently, as you did with the penny exercise.

- Don't just accept information as real or factual. Do your homework.

boss, go to the financial aid office, and possibly begin to search for a new job with flexible hours. After you have researched each alternative, you will be able to make a decision based on solid information and facts.

STEP SIX: DISTINGUISHING FACT FROM OPINION

One of the most important aspects of critical thinking is the ability to distinguish fact from opinion. In many situations—real life, TV, radio, friendly conversations, and the professional arena—opinions surface more often than facts. Reread the previous sentence. This is an example of an opinion cloaked as a fact. There is no research supporting this opinion. It sounds as if it could be true, but without evidence and proof, it is just an opinion. A fact is something that can be proven, something that can be objectively verified. An opinion is a statement that is held to be true, but one that has no objective proof. *Statements that cannot be proved should always be treated as opinion.* Statements that offer valid proof and verification from credible, reliable sources can be treated as factual. When trying to distinguish between fact and opinion, you should take the following guidelines into consideration:

- If you are in doubt, ask questions and listen for solid proof and documentation to support the statement.

- Listen for what is not said in a statement.

- Don't be led astray by those you assume are trustworthy and loyal.

- Don't be turned off by those you fear or consider untruthful.

- Do your own homework on the issue. Read, research, and question.

- If you are unsure about the credibility of the source or information, treat the statement as opinion.

Examine the following statements. Before you glance at the answers on the following page, indicate if you think each statement is a fact or an opinion.

Gone with the Wind is a movie.	Fact	Opinion
Gone with the Wind is a movie made in 1939.	Fact	Opinion
Gone with the Wind is the best movie ever made.	Fact	Opinion
Tom Hanks is an actor.	Fact	Opinion
There is a "heaven" and a "hell."	Fact	Opinion
Some people believe in a "heaven" and a "hell."	Fact	Opinion
Lincoln was the best president to ever head the United States.	Fact	Opinion

STATEMENT	ANSWER	EVIDENCE
Gone With the Wind is a movie.	Fact	This can be proven by watching the movie and by reading movie reviews.
Gone With the Wind is a movie made in 1939.	Fact	This can be verified by many movie sources and by the Motion Picture Association of America.
Gone With the Wind is the best movie ever made.	Opinion	This is only the opinion of some critics and could never be proven.
Tom Hanks is an actor.	Fact	This can be proven by viewing his movies and verifying his two Academy Awards® for acting.
There is a "heaven" and a "hell."	Opinion	As controversial as this answer is, the existence of heaven and hell has never been scientifically proven. Both are opinions of various religions.
Some people believe in a "heaven" and a "hell."	Fact	This can be verified by many books and articles and by simply taking a poll of people you know.
Lincoln was the best president to ever head the United States.	Opinion	This is only an opinion that can be disputed by many people. This cannot be proven.

Critical thinking requires a great deal of commitment on your part. Critical thinking is not easy for everyone, but with practice, dedication, and an understanding of the need, everyone can improve his or her thinking skills.

Critical thinking can affect the way you live your life, from relationships to purchasing a new car, from solving family problems to investing money, from taking the appropriate classes for graduation to getting a promotion at work.

Critical thinking is truly the hallmark of an educated person. It is the hallmark of character and integrity, and it is the hallmark of successful students. Let it be yours.

what's it ALL ABOUT?

NAME: Steve Rodriguez

SCHOOL: College of Southern Nevada, Las Vegas, NV

MAJOR: Architectural Drafting /   AGE: 39
     Interior Design

I completed high school 20 years ago at the top of my class. I attended a magnet school for architectural drafting and even designed two homes that were later built in southern Nevada. I began college immediately after high school and majored in Architecture. Due to family and personal issues, I had to drop out after my first year.

I worked a series of jobs from stocking a grocery store to working at a coffee stand to taking bets at a race and sports book in one of the major casinos. Nothing brought me pleasure, and before I knew it, 20 years had passed.

One day at work after talking to a coworker, it hit me that I had to make some major changes in my life, but I simply did not know how to do it. I had been muddling along for so long and now I needed to get back on track and follow my dream—but how?

A friend suggested that I write down my ultimate goal and then map out a way to get there.

The ultimate goal was easy, but the map for getting there was not. I did not even know how to think about the steps. I did not know how to critically analyze my current situation and plot a course for success. I had no idea that critical thinking would play a role in my career.

The only thing I knew to do was to enroll in school and try to start again. Later, I learned about obtaining my previous transcripts, having them evaluated, determining the classes I needed to take from the school's catalog, and how to plan the classes for my degree. I thought the hard part was over. Now, after four semesters in my program, I am faced with narrowing or even changing my major. I found that I really enjoy the aspect of design more than drafting. Once again, planning, researching, plotting, and critical thinking have made their way into my life and into my career decisions.

What role did critical thinking play in your decision to return to school?

_____

_____

_____

What role did critical thinking play in your decision to major in your selected program?

_____

_____

_____

What advice would you give Steve right now about deciding on his direction in either design or drafting?

_____

_____

_____

What role might critical thinking play in your current classes?

_____

_____

_____

What role might critical thinking play in your future profession?

_____

_____

_____

What role does critical thinking play in your everyday life?

_____

_____

_____

What is the most difficult decision you have ever had to make and how did you arrive at the decision?

_____

_____

_____

What role did critical thinking play in making that decision?

_____

_____

_____

ADVICE TO GO

CORNERSTONES

for critical thinking

Use only *credible* and *reliable* sources.

Distinguish *fact* from *opinion*.

Be *flexible* in your thinking.

Use emotional *restraint*.

Avoid generalizations.

Avoid *stereotyping*.

Strive for *objectivity*.

Reserve judgment.

Do *not* assume.

Ask questions.

Seek *truth*.

THINK

10 Prosper

Kelly finally has her "dream" career. For years, she had aspirations of working in an emergency room. She thought that she would love the action and intensity of the work, and she was right. When Kelly began her training, she thought she would like to become an LPN. After one quarter in her program, *she discovered that she really wanted to be an RN.* After shadowing in a few hospitals, she learned something pretty shocking about herself: Not only did she *want* to be a nurse, she *wanted to work* in the psychiatric treatment emergency room of the hospital. Today, after two years in her profession, she has the respect and trust of most every person in the hospital. Even many of the doctors rely on Kelly's advice and experience when administering treatment.

You might ask, "Why is Kelly so successful in her profession?" The answer is quite simple, yet highly complex. The day that Kelly enrolled in her program at Varsity Medical Institute, she decided that it was time that she became a nurse not only on paper, but also in *spirit, mind, body, and soul.* She understood what so many people fail to grasp—a piece of paper does not make one a nurse or a hygienist or a veterinary technician or a graphic designer or a legal assistant. To *become something,* one must begin to act and think as if he or she is already there. Kelly understood that if she was to be a successful psychiatric nurse, she had to begin acting, thinking, and breathing like a psychiatric nurse right now. She understood that no degree or certificate could make her successful.

Kelly also understood one more important thing about her profession, and indeed, every profession. She understood the meaning of trust—earning it and giving it. The doctors and other nurses with whom Kelly worked had many opportunities to see and judge Kelly on the job. They knew that she was honest, caring, conscientious, and most of all, reliable. She worked hard every day to prove that she was at Memorial Hospital because she *wanted to be there*—not because she *had to be there.* She never understimated the power and importance of her work, and she proved this with every patient, with every colleague, and with every day. She was not *given* trust, she *earned* it.

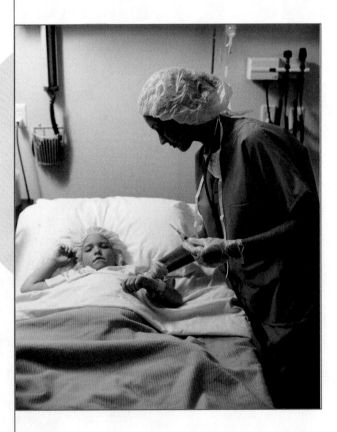

> *Kelly never underestimated the power and importance of her work. She earned trust.*

Trust is confidence in a person's word, action, or motivation appropriately based on repeated observation of his or her past behavior in various situations. Trust, however, isn't all or nothing; it is a line with many tiny stops along the way from "no confidence" to "great confidence" in a person's word, behavior, and motivation. People, just like Kelly and *YOU, earn* a spot somewhere along that line every day.

As you enter the world of work, your attitude, professionalism, and trustworthiness are going to be major factors in your success. Along with these traits, your gusto and passion will be just as important. Working daily with no passion and zest turns a career into an ordinary job. With them, your career can become a source of joy, energy, and satisfaction.

QUESTIONS
FOR REFLECTION

Consider responding to these questions online in the Questions for Reflection module of the Companion Website.

1. What attitudes might you have to change to become as passionate about your future career as Kelly was about hers?

2. When have you witnessed someone who was not professional in his or her career? How did it affect you and your life?

3. When has your trust been misplaced in the past? How did it make you feel to trust someone and then have them betray you? How does this affect your willingness to trust people now?

The best index to a person's character is (a) how he or she treats people who can't do him or her any good, and (b) how he or she treats people who can't fight back. —ABIGAIL VAN BUREN ("DEAR ABBY")

Before reading this chapter, take a moment and respond to the following 10 questions. Consider each one carefully before answering, and then respond using the legend below. When you have answered the questions, add your points and find your total score on the feedback chart below.

STATEMENT	STRONGLY DISAGREE	DISAGREE	DON'T KNOW	AGREE	STRONGLY AGREE	SCORE
1. I have written a resume in the past and understand how to do it correctly.	1	2	3	4	5	
2. Being professional at work is not really that important to me or my profession.	5	4	3	2	1	
3. I consider it very important to be able to get along with others in the workplace.	1	2	3	4	5	
4. I understand the key components of a cover letter and can write one effectively.	1	2	3	4	5	
5. Ethics is not really that important in my chosen field of study.	5	4	3	2	1	
6. My cover letter is a very important part of my resume package.	1	2	3	4	5	
7. I would never discuss money on the first interview unless the employer brought it up.	1	2	3	4	5	
8. In the grand scheme of things, it is not really important to know the workings of a formal table setting.	5	4	3	2	1	
9. What I wear to work does not really matter as long as I'm comfortable.	5	4	3	2	1	
10. I think it is good to research a company before I go on my interview.	1	2	3	4	5	
TOTAL VALUE						

SUMMARY

43–50 You are exceptional in your ability to write a cover letter and resume. You know how to dress for an interview and conduct yourself in a professional manner. You know the importance of getting along with others and learning to work with difficult people. You also know the importance of etiquette in a professional setting.

35–42 Your resume and cover letter–writing skills and interviewing skills are above average. You likely know how to conduct yourself in a professional manner and how to proceed with an interview. You know the importance of professional presence and first impressions.

26–34 Your resume and cover letter–writing skills and interviewing skills are likely average. You probably realize how important professionalism and first impressions are in the workplace. You most likely would do well in an interview.

18–25 Your resume and cover letter–writing skills and interviewing skills are below average, but can be improved with practice and patience. You will need to learn strategies for improving your resume/cover letter–writing and interviewing skills. Your attitude about professional presence will improve as you learn more about the world of work.

10–17 Your resume writing and interviewing skills are weak. You will need to read and talk to others more about workplace politics, difficult people, and professionalism on the job. You will need to study different models for resume and cover letter writing.

Based on the summary above, what is one goal you would like to achieve related to making positive change in your life?

Goal _____

_____

Think of three actions you can take that might help you move closer to realizing this goal.

1. _____
2. _____
3. _____

Questions
FOR BUILDING ON YOUR BEST

As you read this chapter, consider the following questions. At the end of the chapter, you should be able to answer all of them. We also encourage you to ask a few questions of your own. Consider turning to your classmates or instructors to assist you.

1. What is the importance of professional etiquette?
2. Why is it important for me to know how to write a resume?
3. What role does professionalism play in one's overall success?
4. How can I improve my ability to work with difficult people?
5. Why are ethics important in the workplace?

What additional questions might you have about preparing for success in the world of work?

1. _____
2. _____
3. _____

Your Future Is So Bright, You Might Have to Wear Shades

THE COMING JOB BOOM

The job market is crazy—up one day and down another. Some years people are losing jobs all around you, whereas in other years employers are begging for employees and willing to pay high salaries. Thanks to the coming retirement of aging baby boomers, the job market is predicted to be outstanding for you and your fellow classmates for years to come. There are 76 million baby boomers and only 46 million Gen Xers to take their places, says Eisenberg (2002). As the population ages, certain industries are desperately seeking qualified employees.

Hospitals need more health care professionals, and many pay starting bonuses to attract applicants. Pharmacies are paying high salaries to attract new graduates. According to Eisenberg, we also need more electricians, plumbers, and contractors. Engineers and accountants are in great demand. The service industry in this country is exploding with great demand for excellent managers in hospitality, retail, information management, computer-aided design, and the entertainment industry.

Graduates who have the right skills, work attitudes, and habits will be in the driver's seat. All of this is very good news for you. A good job should be there waiting for you. However, having a well-paying, high-profile "perfect" job may not bring you the happiness or peace you are seeking. As you begin to think more about your career and what you really want, you need to include time to think about you as a person—your qualities and what uniqueness you can bring to the table.

As you begin your journey, you will begin to discover that one of the daily challenges is having personal and professional lives that are parallel. That is to say, quite simply, there should be a match between your personal value and goal system and that of your employer and company. Oftentimes, people find themselves torn between the two. Will you go against what you value for a hefty raise? Will you relinquish your own goals and dreams for the sake of advancement in a company? Are you strong enough in your morals to stand up and say, "This is wrong," or "I can't do that"?

These are questions and challenges you will face in the years to come. Our advice is to determine who you are, establish the things for which you stand, and develop an overriding, ongoing philosophy of life; then you will be in a better position to make judgments about your future.

In the space below, list at least three things that you would NOT alter about your values, morals, and goals for the sake of money or advancement.

Employers are looking for people who excel as team members.

1. _____

2. _____

3. _____

went into the woods because I wished to live deliberately, to front only the
if I could not learn what it had to teach, and not, when I came to die, dis

—HENRY DAVID THOREAU

It Can Be Shaky Ground, But You Will Make It

DEFINING AND REFINING YOURSELF IN TODAY'S "WORKQUAKE"

People holding degrees and certificates are a dime a dozen. This does not mean, however, that *you* are a dime a dozen. Herein lies the challenge. How do you distinguish yourself from the countless job seekers out there? What are you going to do that sets you apart from your competition? What do you have to offer that no one else can possibly offer to an employer? Below, we will discuss some of the talents and qualities that are becoming increasingly rare, yet constantly sought after, in today's "workquake." By understanding more about these qualities, you can put yourself miles ahead of the competition.

WRITING, SPEAKING, AND LISTENING SKILLS

As you have read through this book, you may have thought that we were beating a dead horse. Over and over again, in almost every chapter, we have offered some type of advice, suggestion, or tip for becoming a more effective communicator in written, verbal, and nonverbal forms. We did so because these are constantly listed as top skills needed for success—in ANY profession. We do so because so few people actually possess these qualities. If you want to put yourself ahead of the competition, then attend every class, every seminar, every meeting, and every function where you can learn more about effective writing, speaking, and listening skills.

A STRONG WORK ETHIC

For more than 30 years, my (Robert Sherfield's) father worked in the textile industry in South Carolina. During my entire life, I only remember him missing two days of work—when his father died. I watched him work when he was sick, tired, and drained. But that was the way he was raised: you take a job, you commit to that job, and you report to that job when you are supposed to do so. Biased though I may be by my father's work ethic, I would wager that there are not many people who maintain his position on work—and that may be good.

Most medical and scientific research suggests that working while sick and working under immense stress can be detrimental to your overall health.

Contrary to popular belief, most employers don't want you to work yourself to death. In today's environment, however, they do want to make sure they are getting every penny's worth they pay you. Our suggestion is to develop a strong work ethic that is healthy for you and your employer. Working yourself into sickness or even death will not serve anyone in the long run.

LOYALTY AND TRUSTWORTHINESS

Today, competition is extremely strong among companies vying for the same customers. In some instances, you may have to sign a legal document that forbids you from discussing or sharing your work with anyone. Some industries also ask for a non-compete clause. If you leave Company X or Hospital Y, this clause prohibits you from working with Company Z or Hospital C—and sometimes in the same industry—for six months to one year. Maybe even longer.

In this light, loyalty to your employer is a highly regarded trait. However, one's loyalty cannot be measured by a resume or determined by a simple interview. Proving that you have loyalty and are trustworthy comes over time as we saw with Kelly in the opening story. It may take years to establish these characteristics with your company and within your industry, but be warned, it only takes seconds to destroy what took years to create.

TEAMWORK

Employers are looking for people who not only understand the details of teamwork, but who excel as team members. There is a humorous cartoon figure who says, "Teamwork is a bunch of people doing what I say!" Unfortunately, many people think this IS teamwork. A true team has shared responsibilities, shared purposes, shared goals, shared visions, and most important, shared accountability.

Team players understand that successful and efficient teamwork involves listening, respecting, and supporting each other; lifting one another up in times of trouble; working together to resolve conflicts quickly; making each other look good; and ultimately, bringing your personal best to the table every time you meet. Strive to be a team player; you will quickly reap the benefits.

PROFESSIONALISM

This term varies from workplace to workplace. What is professional for one office or setting may be totally inappropriate for another. This includes everything from language usage to dress to personal grooming to conduct to your overall demeanor. Unlike loyalty and trustworthiness, professionalism *can be* judged before a potential employer ever meets you. Most interviewers can establish the level of your professionalism by your resume and cover letter. Some will even judge the quality of paper on which your resume is printed. We have never actually met a person who lost a job over a watermark being turned the wrong way on your cover letter, but it certainly says something about your professionalism to many who will interview you.

CONFIDENCE AND DECISION-MAKING ABILITIES

There is a difference between confidence and the ability to make decisions, and being "cocky." Confidence comes from experiences and calculated risk taking. Employers are looking for people who are not afraid to make hard decisions and for individuals who have confidence in their abilities. When you meet with the person interviewing you, move away from saying (and believing) "I'm a nurse," or "I'm an accountant," or "I'm a computer networking engineer." Instead, move toward discussing your overall qualities. Steer the conversation to your general and specific abilities and characteristics.

PRIORITY MANAGEMENT SKILLS

Today, maybe more than any other time in mankind's history, we are faced with more and more to do and what seems like less and less time in which to do it. Your success depends on how well you manage your priorities both personally and professionally. Priority management not only involves getting today's work accomplished, it also involves the ability to plan for the future.

You should contribute all that you can to your career and employer, but you must also take time to enjoy your life, your family, your friends, and your relationships.

THE ABILITY TO CHANGE AND GROW

A decade ago, few people could have predicted that there would be full-time, well-paid positions called Webmasters. Now, many companies employ webmasters. This is a perfect example of how changes in technology drive changes in business, health professions, and industry. If you are unable or unwilling to change and grow, thousands of your peers can, and will. Our advice is to keep abreast of trends and technology pertaining to your field. Attend conferences, read professional literature, take classes, and have open discussions with colleagues and mentors regarding the issues surrounding your company and industry.

CRITICAL-THINKING SKILLS

Not only do employers want associates who can make decisions and proceed with confidence, they also demand that you be able to think your way through problems and challenges. Employers are looking for people who can distinguish fact from opinion; identify fallacies; analyze, synthesize, and determine the value of a piece of information; think beyond the obvious and see things from varying angles; and arrive at sound solutions.

MULTITASKING

A recent newspaper cartoon suggested that you are too busy if you are multitasking in the shower. This may be true, but in keeping pace with today's workforce, this is another essential task: the ability to do more than one thing at a time—and the ability to do them all very well. If you have not had much experience in multitasking, we suggest that you begin slowly. Don't take on too many things at one time. As you understand more about working on and completing several tasks at a time, you can expand your abilities in this arena.

HUMAN RELATION SKILLS

We saved this one for last, certainly not because it is least important, but because this quality is an overriding characteristic of everything listed previously. Employers are looking for individuals who have "people skills." This concept goes so much further than being a team player; it goes to the heart of many workplaces. It touches on your most basic nature, and it draws from your most inner self.

The ability to get along with grouchy, cranky, mean, disagreeable, burned-out colleagues is, indeed, a rare quality. But don't be mistaken, there are those who do this, and do it well. Peak performers, or those at the "top of their game," have learned that this world is made up of many types of people and there is never going to be a time when one of those cranky, grumpy people is not in our midst. More about this topic is discussed later in this chapter.

Workin' 9 to 5 . . . Or Not!

THE JOB SEARCH PLAN

You've got it all together—education, experience, and a strong sense of your moral and value system. What do you do now? Where do you go to put all of this to work? How do you find the job of your dreams?

The first thing you need to know about searching for a job is this: Getting a job—the right job—is hard work! Regardless of your status in school, now is the time to begin your job search. If you are in the last quarter or module of your program, your job search should be a top priority.

In order to assist you in developing your job search plan and eventually finding the job and career that suit you, consider the following:

- Examining your interests
- Evaluating your qualifications
- Focusing your employer search
- Developing the job/career search

EXAMINE YOUR INTERESTS

What do you want to do . . . specifically? Yes, you majored in Graphic Design, but what do you really want to do with these skills? Advertising? Journalism? Magazine layout? Textbook design?

Where do you want to live? What kind of organization appeals to you? Are salary and benefits the prime factors driving your choice? Do you mind relocating and continuing to relocate? Do you want to travel or are you a homebody?

Do you need the company of colleagues or would you work best with a computer and an Internet link at home? Before you start the search and draft your resume, think about what will make you happy.

A thorough career search includes all of the following components:

- Developing a career objective (If you cannot write an objective, you are not ready to begin the search process for a specific job.)
- Writing an effective resume or assembling an outstanding portfolio
- Developing extraordinary interviewing skills
- Researching organizations to learn more about them to determine if they are right for you

EVALUATE YOUR QUALIFICATIONS

Employers want to know what you have to offer them. What are your assets, your strengths and weaknesses, your work experience? Have you managed other people? What have you learned from extracurricular activities and part-time jobs? Do you write well? Are you excellent with computers? Do you speak a language fluently? Are you good at working with other people?

Once you have evaluated your interests and your qualifications, you can write your resume and assemble your portfolio if one is required. While you are writing your resume, you also should be narrowing the list of companies and positions to which you want to apply.

Have some business cards printed or print them yourself. Most stationery and copy companies have cards you can make yourself. Choose a card that is professional and classic. Avoid colorful, flashy business cards, especially when you are looking for a job. Business cards will make you *look more professional.*

Inappropriate personal card for business use.

More appropriate personal card for business use.

FOCUS YOUR EMPLOYER SEARCH

Once you have defined what you want to do and have evaluated your qualifications realistically, narrow your search to those companies that are at the top of your list. The three areas you need to consider are:

- Geographic location
- Organization focus
- Job focus

DEVELOP THE JOB/CAREER SEARCH

The first thing you must realize is that a degree or certificate doesn't guarantee you a job. An excellent grade point average (GPA) accompanied by a solid work history and demonstrated leadership skills will make you more desirable as a candidate, but this does not guarantee you a job either. In all honesty, sometimes landing a job is simply being in the right place at the right time, knowing the right people, having a special skill, or simply beginning at entry level and working your way up. To give you more exposure, consider the following places to begin your job search:

Career center

Internships or cooperative work experiences

WORLD OF WORK

I have been a veterinarian for more than 15 years. In that time, I have never once dreaded going to work in the morning. This is because I see every day as a new adventure. I love my job and don't think of it as work. I think of it as something that keeps my mind occupied: an occupation, not a job.

It is unusual for a graduate's first job to be the one that becomes a lifelong career. Unfortunately, life is not that simple. Usually, you will find a company that suits you at first and you work there a while, and then you move on for whatever reason. But if you are wise, whether you like your colleagues or not, you will open your mind and your eyes and learn every lesson possible from them. That is the first piece of advice that I would offer as you begin your career; learn something from your colleagues and peers every day! Learn from their mistakes and shortcomings, and from their successes and positive points. Use the time in your early jobs to learn, to grow, and to develop a vision. Save these lessons; write them down and file them away so that later, you will be able to draw from your experiences with that company and the people there.

The second piece of advice that I would offer is to fight the dragon of becoming jaded. There is no worse thing than thinking that you know it all; for when you start believing that you do know it all, you stop learning and growing. In my profession we call this continuing education. I go to symposia, which feature lectures from the most prominent professors from the most prestigious universities in the nation, and this keeps my mind open to change. I've learned you never know it all. A great part of this lesson in my profession is listening to my client's description of their pet's illnesses. If I fail to listen, I fail!

These two pieces of advice helped me beyond measure as I opened my own veterinary hospital. Learning from others and keeping my ears open help me maintain interest in my profession. If you lose interest in, and passion for, your profession, it becomes drudgery, and then you get up in the morning dreading your career.

QUESTIONS FOR REFLECTION

Consider responding to these questions online in the World of Work module of the Companion Website.

1. Why do you think that Dr. Schwartz enjoys his profession so much?

2. Why do you think that it is hurtful to you and your career if you become jaded?

3. Who is a person in your life from whom you have learned a great deal? How has this helped you get to where you are today?

Dr. Martin Schwartz, Veterinarian, Park La Brea Veterinarian Care, Los Angeles, CA

Employment agencies

Newspapers and classified ads

Professional journals

Professional headhunters

Instructors in your field of interest

Developing your own network (friends, family, coworkers, etc.)

You might also consider a combination of all of the above.

Tell Me Everything . . . In Two Pages or Less

CREATING YOUR COVER LETTER AND RESUME

The most important part of the job search process is the preparation that must be done prior to starting the interview process. Two key elements of this preparation are your cover letter and resume. Both are key components in your career search. A carefully crafted letter and resume communicate your past history (skills and experience) that makes you the ideal candidate for their position. It is the first marketing piece and in many cases must stand alone when a recruiter is determining whether or not to interview you.

Just as a well-designed and worded letter and resume can be a wonderful first step, a poorly designed and worded letter and resume can doom you to failure before you ever leave your house. Although there no single way to develop your career resume, and formats may vary from discipline to discipline, there are many books, pamphlets, and websites that can assist you.

DESIGNING A COVER LETTER THAT WORKS

Whenever you send your resume to a company, whether it is in response to a posted advertisement or requested, you must send a cover letter with it. Cover letters are extremely important; in fact, most recruiters say that they read four times as many cover letters as they do resumes because if the cover letter does not "strike a chord" then they never look past it to the resume.

Unfortunately, writing a cover letter is almost as dreaded as writing a resume, and for this reason many people make the mistake of using a "canned" cover letter to accompany all of their resumes. Using the same cover letter regardless of the situation is the quickest way for you to ensure that your resume will never be considered.

The resume gets your foot in the door; the interview gets the job—but job search comes before everything else. If you match your interests and qualifications to a few select positions, write a good resume, and prepare for an interview, you will usually have success. —PAT MOODY

Both your resume and cover letter should be typed and printed on the same type and color of fine-quality paper. Cheap paper and poor-quality printing send the message that you don't care. This is not the place to pinch pennies; buy a good-quality paper stock (100 percent cotton if possible) and make sure that the print quality of your printer is excellent. Your placement office or career center may provide computers and printers for your use.

Step one. A good cover letter should be *personally addressed and job specific*. If at all possible, address your letter to a specific person. Avoid at all cost the dreaded "Dear Sir or Madam" or "To Whom It May Concern." In most cases a phone call to the company will provide the name of the person, their title, and their address. Always verify spelling, even with common names.

Step two. Once your letter is correctly addressed, your first paragraph should be an "attention grabber" and it should answer the question "Why am I writing?" Susan Britton Whitcomb, author of *Resume Magic* (2003), calls this "the carrot." This simply means that your opening has an interesting fact, an appeal, or maybe even a quote—something that makes the reader (hopefully, your future employer) read further.

Step three. Your second paragraph should clearly state why you are qualified for the position you are seeking. Use your cover letter to high-light those areas of your experience that specifically qualify you for the job. Your cover letter is not the time to list all of your qualifications but to indicate the two or three components that most qualify you for the position. You may also include specific attributes that may not be on your resume.

Step four. Your final paragraph should address the question of "Where do we go from here?" Do not be ambiguous here by saying something trite like "I hope to hear from you in the near future," or "If you have any questions please do not hesitate to call me." Be proactive by stating that you will be following up with a phone call to discuss your resume in more detail with them. Make sure that once you have told them that you are going to call that you actually do call. (See the sample cover letter in Figure 10.1 on page 236.)

DIFFERENT TYPES OF RESUMES

There are different types of resumes, but primarily they can be classified as chronological, functional, narrative, or combination. A **chronological resume** organizes education and work experience in a chronological manner; a **functional resume** organizes your work and experience around specific skills and duties. A **narrative resume** provides a discussion that expands information in the major categories of the resume. A **combination resume** generally combines elements of the chronological format with the functional format. You must determine which type of resume best profiles your education, skills, and experience. This may be based on the wording of the job ad.

YOUR PERSONAL RESUME

When choosing your personal resume format, you need to take into careful consideration the field in which you wish to be employed as well as the company with whom you are interviewing. The "one-size-fits-all" ideology does not work with resumes. The personal computer enables you to customize your resume to meet the needs of the individual employer. As you design your personal resume, keep in mind the types of employers you anticipate interviewing with; generally they will fit into a couple of broad categories, thus necessitating only a couple of different resumes.

As you begin to develop your resume, make sure to allow plenty of time to develop it. Plan to enlist several qualified proofreaders to check your work. We cannot stress strongly enough the need for your resume to be perfect. A simple typo or misuse of grammar can disqualify you from the job of your dreams. Don't allow a lack of attention to detail to stand between you and your future career. The ad to which Benjamin is applying appears below. (Figure 10.2 on page 237 shows a sample resume.)

NOW HIRING

A schedule you'll like . . .
. . . a place you'll love!

Grace Care Group is expanding and we are seeking individuals who are dedicated, responsible, and caring to provide exceptional care to our patients. We have the following openings and each carries a $2500 sign-on bonus.

- Phlebotomist
- LPN's
- Medical Assistant
- Respiratory Therapist Aide
- Occupational Therapist
- Pathology Transcriptionist

Contact us at 702.555.1234 or GraceCG@online.com

FIGURE 10.1 *Sample cover letter.*

Benjamin Shaw

1234 Lake Shadow Drive, Maple City, PA 12345   (724) 555-1212 • benj@online.com

Janet Pixler, RN, CNA   September 12, 2006
Director of Placement and Advancement
123 Sizemore Street, Suite 444
Philadelphia, PA 12345

Dear Ms. Pixler,

Seven years ago, my mother was under the treatment of two incredible nurses at Grace Care in Philadelphia. My family and I agree that the care she was given was extraordinary. When I saw your ad in today's *Philadelphia Carrier,* I was extremely pleased to know that I now have the qualifications to be a part of the Grace Care team.

Next month, I will receive my Occupational Associate's Degree from Victory Health Institute as a Medical Assistant. As my resume will indicate, I was fortunate to do my internship at Mercy Family Care Practice in Harrisburg.

As a part of my degree from Victory, I received all A's in the following classes:

- Management Communications
- Microsoft Office Professional (including Excel and Access)
- Business Communication I, II, III
- Anatomy and Physiology I, II, III
- Medical Assisting
- Clinical Assisting
- Medical Office Procedures I, II, III, IV
- Medical Insurance Coding I, II, III
- Principles of Pharmacology

This, along with my past certificate in Medical Transcription and my immense respect for your organization, makes me the perfect candidate for your position.

I have detailed all of my experience on the enclosed resume. I will call you on Friday of next week to discuss my training, career goals, and qualifications that I could bring to Grace Care Group. In the meantime, should you need to contact me, please feel free to do so at the number above.

Sincerely,

Ben Shaw

Benjamin Shaw

FIGURE 10.2 *Sample resume.*

Benjamin Shaw

1234 Lake Shadow Drive, Maple City, PA 12345   (724) 555-1212 • benj@online.com

OBJECTIVE   To obtain a position that will allow me to use my skills and training as a Medical
Assistant, my compassion for people, and my desire to make a difference in an
open, caring health care environment.

PROFESSIONAL PREPARATION

- Occupational Associates Degree—Medical Assistant
  Victory Health Institute, Harrisburg, PA
  May 2006
- Certificate of Completion—Medical Transcription
  Philadelphia Technical Institute
  September 2000
- Vocational High School Diploma—Health Studies
  Philadelphia Vocational High School
  August 1997

SKILLS

Bilingual (English/Spanish)	Data Protection
Claims Reimbursement	Client Relations
Highly Organized	Problem-Solving Skills
Motivated, Self-Starter	Leadership
Priority Management	Office Applications
Team Building Experience	Delegating
Strategic Planning	Budget Management

PROFESSIONAL EXPERIENCE

- **Medical Assistant Intern**   *January 5, 2006–May 1, 2006*
  Mercy Family Care Practice

- **Medical Transcriptionist**   *December 2000–December 2004*
  The Office of Brenda Wilson, MD

- **Ward Orderly**   *February 1997–November 2000*
  Wallace Hospital

- **Administrative Assistant**   *August 1995–January 1997*
  Ellen Sagger Nursing Care Facility

REFERENCES   Available upon request

If You Can't Say Anything Nice . . .

HOW TO SOLICIT LETTERS OF REFERENCE

There are five steps to soliciting letters of reference.

Step one. Select three to five people to serve as references. As you are determining whom to select, choose people who are very familiar with your work ability. Current and former employers with whom you have experienced a good working relationship are excellent sources of references. Teachers are also an excellent source. If you do not have anyone who falls into these two categories, consider asking friends of your family who are respected members of the community. As you consider possible reference sources, be sure to choose individuals who are responsible and timely in their reply to your request. References are a reflection of you, and if the reference sources do not respond in the appropriate manner, they will cast a shadow on your credibility.

Step two. Request permission from your reference sources. During your conversation with them, discuss your career goals and aspirations. Give them a copy of your resume and cover letter. Ask them to critique them for you and make any necessary changes.

Step three. Obtain all necessary contact information from them: name, job title, business address, e-mail address, phone number, and fax number.

Step four. Send thank-you letters to those who agree to serve as references for you. Stay in contact with them throughout your job search. Giving them updates and a periodic thank-you in the form of a card, an e-mail, or a phone call is very appropriate. At the end of your job search, a small token of your appreciation may be appropriate.

Step five. Develop a typed list of all references—including contact information—and carry it with you to all interviews.

So, Tell Us a Little About Yourself

PREPARING FOR THE INTERVIEW

Finding the right job is hard work! You may have several interviews before you find the job you want, and you will probably spend many hours preparing for these interviews. In the beginning it is advisable for you to go to all interviews even if you know you don't want the job. The more you interview, the more confident and comfortable you should become. The interview is the determining factor in getting a job and must be taken seriously. While an outstanding resume is important, it will not secure the job for you. The resume gets the interview; the interview gets the job!

Most people fail to get the job they really want, fail not because they are not qualified but because they failed in the interview. And most failure occurs in the interview because they aren't prepared.
—DAVID W. CRAWLEY JR.

FIRST STEPS

Just as you prepared for exams, you will need to prepare for the interview. If you have done a careful job search, you have information on the company that wants to interview you. If not, the first thing you must do after you schedule an interview is to research the company. Interviewers are usually impressed if you know something about the company and are able to talk about it and ask intelligent questions. If you go to an interview knowing nothing about the company, you are not likely to get the job.

Later in this chapter, we discuss "professional presence" and the importance of dress, grooming, posture, and body language. The interview is an important time to put the tips to work. You need to look your best because your appearance will impact your performance. If you look like a professional, you are much more likely to perform at your peak.

You should take several copies of your resume (and a typed reference sheet) with you. Though one person typically conducts interviews, some employers designate several people. Place your resumes and your job search information on the company in a portfolio or nice folder. Using your company research, make a list of questions that you want to ask the interviewer. Never attend an interview without asking questions yourself. You are interviewing them just as they are interviewing you. Interviewers are much more impressed if they think you have researched the company and if you have questions to ask.

Remember this cardinal rule of interviewing before you arrive: Interviewers are not interested in what the company can do for you; they are interested in what you can do for the company. Therefore, you must present your case on why you want to work for the company and the contributions you are prepared to make.

If you take someone with you to the interview, he or she should wait outside the building. Under no circumstances should you take anyone inside with you.

THE FIRST IMPRESSION

A good rule is to be nice to everyone. While you are waiting for the interviewer to call you, observe the atmosphere in the building and the attitude of the people. You can usually expect the interviewer to come to the reception area and greet you, or the receptionist may take you into the interviewer's office. As soon as the interviewer sees you, he or she begins to make a decision. Research shows that you have just seven seconds to make the right first impression. You literally send out verbal and nonverbal signals that determine how others see you. The interviewer may not realize this, but you need to be aware of how important the first few seconds are to your success. In the first few seconds, the interviewer performs a quick eye sweep and takes in your attire, your grooming, your posture, and your smile.

Are you confident?

Do you appear to be comfortable in this environment?

Are you glad to be there?

Are you sincere?

Are you impeccably groomed and dressed?

Are you warm and friendly?

You should extend your hand and give the interviewer a firm handshake, looking him or her in the eye while offering a warm and pleasant greeting. Now, the interviewer has more information.

e such a person and live such a life that if every person were as you and every life as yours, the earth would be paradise.   —PHILLIP BROOKS

Interviewers will often say to you, "Tell me about yourself." They are not looking for your life history as much as they are gathering background information on you and observing how well you can present details. As you converse with the interviewer, sit up straight and establish eye contact.

QUESTIONS YOU CAN ANTICIPATE

When the interviewer has gone through the first few minutes, he or she will begin asking additional questions. Some questions you can anticipate follow:

Why are you interested in this company and in the position?

When did you decide on a career in _____?

Tell me about your extracurricular activities.

What are your strengths?

What are your weaknesses?

Do you have a geographic preference? Why?

Are you willing to relocate?

Do you have job experience in _____?

What can you do for the company?

What other companies are you interviewing with?

Tell me about a difficult problem you have had and how you solved it.

Tell me about a time when you worked under stress.

What kind of accomplishment gives you the greatest satisfaction?

What are your long- and short-range goals?

Where do you see yourself in five years?

What one word best describes you?

How do you deal with difficult people?

Describe one goal you have set over the past six months and how you went about accomplishing it.

What is the biggest mistake you ever made? What did you learn from it?

QUESTIONS YOU MIGHT ASK THE INTERVIEWER

You should feel free to ask the interviewer an occasional question during the interview, but the interviewer should lead the majority of the first part of the interview. At the close of the interview, you may be asked if you have any questions. If not, you should say, "I have a few questions if you don't mind." Asking questions of the interviewer is impressive and indicates to them that you are interviewing them as well. Some typical questions follow:

How would you describe a typical day in this position?

What kind of training can I anticipate?

To whom would I report?

Will I have an opportunity to meet some of my coworkers?

Would you describe the training program?

When will my first job performance evaluation take place?

Why do you enjoy working for XYZ?

A Picture Paints a Thousand Words

PROFESSIONAL PRESENCE

Several years ago, John Malloy, an image guru, made this statement: "As much as one-third of your success depends on what you wear." In Malloy's opinion, your appearance, image, and presence contribute greatly to your overall success in your career.

DEVELOPING A SENSE OF WHAT IS BEST FOR YOU (WOMEN)

Maybe your roommate wears bright colors and has long, bleached-blonde hair. Because she seems confident and popular, you have tried to emulate her style, but you never have felt comfortable. You have to do what is right for you.

As a professional in the workplace, you want to look the part. You may be required to wear a uniform, but if you are not, you don't necessarily want to wear clothes that make you stand out; rather, your goal is to always look good. People should expect you to present a consistent and an outstanding image. If you stand out, you need to be sure it is for the right reasons. Consider the following tips for interviewing and workplace apparel and grooming:

- Wear classic business suits in dark colors and stylish but reasonable heels.
- Wear jewelry that is classy and professional.

- Acquire purses and belts that are made of leather.
- Wear well-tailored blouses.
- Avoid fussy prints, frilly lace, and sexy garments.
- Avoid shocking bright colors and large prints.
- Make sure your hair is well groomed, clean, and shiny; avoid excessively long hair.
- Take good care of your nails; avoid bright nail polish.
- Make sure your makeup is conservative and neat.
- Wear hose that coordinate with your outfit; avoid patterned hose, colored hose, and white hose.

DECIDING WHAT IS BEST FOR YOU (MEN)

One of the best ways for a man to stand out is by dressing in an impeccable manner. The average male does not generally give a great deal of attention to his appearance, so when a man does it right, he gets noticed. Women have many more choices than men—and many more ways of making bad decisions. Any man who wants to become a sharp dresser can do so if he is willing to work at it.

If you are going into a profession that does not require a uniform or insists that you wear a suit, consider this: The best time for men to buy suits is right after Christmas and the Fourth of July. Most nice men's stores put their suits on sale twice a year. Look for warehouse sales; they often will provide excellent bargains if you know how to shop for them.

Consider the following tips:

Any man who wants to become a sharp dresser can do so with a little work.

- Have at least two interviewing suits: navy and charcoal gray. Once you own these two colors, you can expand your wardrobe.
- Avoid black because it is an overpowering color; likewise, avoid pastels and anything that even remotely suggests wild patterns or colors.
- If you must interview in clothing other than a suit, wear a blazer and pants that match, and be sure they are immaculately pressed and clean.
- Acquire several dress shirts, including white and light blue.
- For interviewing purposes, consider only one shirt color—white— and it must be starched and immaculate.
- Wear dress shirts that have long sleeves, no matter what the temperature is.
- Wear black socks with navy or gray clothing. They should not show your bare leg if you cross your legs.
- Never, never, never wear white socks with a business suit. Argyles are also a no-no!
- Wear ties that are stylish and buy them with careful consideration.
- Make sure no earrings, tattoos, or any other distinguishing distractions show that can set you apart. Even though you may see earrings and tattoos on the interviewer, the best advice for you is still to maintain the proper dress.

Interviewing While You Eat

DINING ETIQUETTE

In this brief space we cannot discuss everything you need to know about personal and professional etiquette. How you conduct yourself "out in public" at a dinner table, however, can be as important as your experiences, your education, and what you wear. Recently at the Academy Awards®, Jamie Fox (Best Actor winner for *Ray*) spoke of his grandmother and how she pushed him to become a person of character and dignity. She would, in his words, "slap him upside the head" when he did something wrong and say to him, "Act like you are somebody. Act like you've been somewhere!" Finer words were never spoken.

You probably know the basics: Chew with your mouth closed, keep your elbows off the table, pass food to the right, cut your meat only one piece at a time, butter only one small piece of bread at a time, and so forth. The finer points of etiquette need to be studied, however, if you want to be taken seriously. Read a good etiquette book and take it to heart. Research shows that only about 12 percent of new hires are skilled in the social graces. This may be the difference in great success or failure. Excellent manners will set you apart early in your career. Although it may seem trivial, never underestimate the power of gracefulness.

If you are taken to a nice restaurant as part of your interview, order something that is easy to eat (NOT spaghetti or ribs) and not the most expensive thing on the menu. Figure 10.3 shows a diagram of a formal table setting. Study it carefully so

---

FIGURE 10.3 *A formal place setting.*

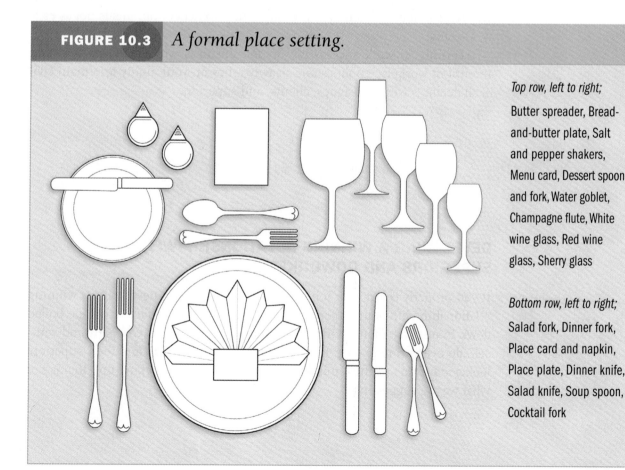

Top row, left to right;

Butter spreader, Bread-and-butter plate, Salt and pepper shakers, Menu card, Dessert spoon and fork, Water goblet, Champagne flute, White wine glass, Red wine glass, Sherry glass

Bottom row, left to right;

Salad fork, Dinner fork, Place card and napkin, Place plate, Dinner knife, Salad knife, Soup spoon, Cocktail fork

you will know what to do if you are dining at a formal restaurant. Start at the outer utensils and use the appropriate fork with each course. A good rule to help you remember what bread plate and glasses are yours is solids on the left, liquids on the right. If you get confused, look and see what others are doing.

If you leave the table, place your napkin on your chair. When you finish your meal and are leaving the table, fold your napkin loosely and place it back on the table. NEVER stack your plates, and don't push them away from you. This is the job of the host or server.

There is much to learn in developing professional presence. You will probably make some mistakes. Learn from them and keep working until you are comfortable in any setting.

Have You Lost That Lovin' Feelin'?
WORKPLACE POLITICS AND CIVILITY

As you enter the workforce you will become part of a group, unless you plan to open your own business where you are the sole operator, that is. This group will consist of coworkers with whom you will spend many hours. You have come together for the sole purpose of fulfilling the goals and objectives of the company that has hired you. Although you probably will not be instrumental in selecting these coworkers, you must nonetheless function in a productive manner with all those in the company, or you will fail at your job. As you may have already experienced in jobs you have held throughout your schooling, this is not as easy as it seems.

Learning to work successfully in the business world involves a certain amount of workplace politics and heavily relies on your ability to remain civil in all dealings with colleagues, clients, and superiors.

Y ou don't turn integrity on and off. To have integrity you must be like the guy who uses a butter knife when nobody is around.   —WALLACE CARR

DEVELOPING A WINNING RELATIONSHIP WITH YOUR SUPERIORS AND COWORKERS

If you properly select your job and your company, then developing a winning relationship with your superiors is relatively simple; in fact, it can be boiled down to one statement. Within the ethical confines of the company and yourself, do everything in your power to make your superiors and their superiors look good. Don't confuse this with "brownnosing" or "sucking up"; that is not what we are suggesting.

We are suggesting that you work very hard to fulfill the goals and objectives set forth by your boss and by the company. If you do this, you can go a long way toward working well with your boss. Some other helpful hints include:

- Remember that establishing a good relationship takes time. Spend time studying your superiors' work habits. Interview him or her about what they expect of you.

- Keep your superiors informed; nothing causes more problems than a boss who thinks you are not keeping him/her informed.

- Always follow up meetings with a written record of what you believe was said in the meeting. This can easily be done by providing your boss with minutes of your meetings.

- *NEVER, NEVER, NEVER* discuss your superiors with colleagues at work; it *ALWAYS* gets back to them.

- Keep your bosses' confidences by not sharing information unless specifically directed to.

- Always follow up on assignments once they are completed to ensure that they meet your company's specifications.

ETHICS IN THE BUSINESS WORLD

Theoretically, if everyone working for the same company shares common goals ensuring that the company is productive and successful, people should have absolutely no problem getting along. Unfortunately some large stumbling blocks must be overcome to see that this happens. First and foremost, the company's goals and objectives must be in sync with your personal goals and objectives. Before you accept a position with a company, study the company's philosophy. Do they treat their employees the way you want to be treated? Do they treat their customers they way you would like to treat your customers? Are their business ethics in harmony with your own? Although we have preached this in all of our career courses and workshops, graduates continue to select positions based on the salary and not on the company's ideology. Students who follow this path may soon find themselves disenfranchised from their company because the actions they must take on the part of their company are in opposition to their own personal ethics and beliefs. If this becomes a routine occurrence, one of two things will happen: They are forced to leave the company or they compromise their own code of ethics, thus becoming that which they hate—and a cycle of dissatisfaction and despair follows until they are able to correct the problem.

DID YOU KNOW?

Tina Turner

During their rough and abusive marriage, Tina Turner was repeatedly beaten and raped by her husband, Ike. During their divorce hearings, she had to defend the right to keep her name. She went on to record many number one hits such as "Private Dancer" and "What's Love Got to Do with It." She has won many Grammy® awards for her work.

Dana May Casperson, in her book *Power Etiquette: What You Don't Know Can Kill Your Career* (1999) gives 13 hints for demonstrating your ethics in the workplace:

- Do not participate in gossip.
- Be courteous and respectful to superiors and to subordinates.
- Be positive and pleasant.
- Accept constructive criticism.
- Maintain personal dignity.
- Make an effort to preserve the dignity of another.
- Keep confidences and maintain confidentiality.
- Show your concern for others.
- Give credit to those deserving.
- Be honest.
- Keep your word.
- Encourage and help others to do their best.
- Make practical and constructive suggestions for improvement.

AVOIDING THE RUMOR MILL

Letitia Baldridge (1985), in her *New Complete Guide to Executive Manners,* states: "Never go to bed at night wondering if you were a conversational gun in the slandering of a person's character or the endangerment of his/her future." Avoid, at all cost, becoming a part of the rumor mill. We know this sounds like an easy thing to do, but in reality, it is human nature to want to be "in the know." Unfortunately, to do this you must engage in gossip, and a gossip is never trusted. One of the quickest ways to lose your credibility is to be seen keeping company with the corporate "busy body."

Yes You Can!
IDEAS FOR SUCCESS

Consider the following tips for resolving conflict and moving on.

- If someone verbally attacks you, let it go and move on. You don't have to stoop to their level of foul play.
- Strive to solve an issue rather than have to "be right" about it.
- Once you've had a conflict with someone, work to forget it and get along with that person.
- Understand that conflicts in any relationship can be viewed as positive growth opportunities.
- When in a conflict, try never to blame or verbally attack the other person, but rather look at every side and spend your energy working toward a solution.
- When in a conflict, try to talk through the issue with the other person.
- When in a conflict, try to feel empathy for the other person and put yourself in his or her shoes.
- When in a conflict, do not manipulate the other person.
- When in a conflict, strive to never attack the person; concentrate only on his or her actions.
- Understand that kindness and civility will solve more conflicts than anger and cruelty—always—every day—period!

Conflict Is Inevitable

HOW DO YOU DEAL WITH IT?

Because we are so very different on many levels, sometimes relationships with others "go bad." Call it human nature, call it pride, call it anger, or call it ignorance, few people, if any, go through life without some degree of conflict. If relationships with friends, family, lovers, coworkers, and people of diverse backgrounds are important to you, you should learn how to recognize the signs of conflict and how to avoid unhealthy conflict when you can. When conflict can't be avoided, learning how to manage it can be beneficial to any relationship—and your future.

You may experience conflict in a classroom when another student takes issue with your opinions and continues to harass you about your ideas after class. You could be placed on a team where conflicts arise among the members. A major conflict could erupt in the parking lot if someone thoughtlessly pulls into a parking space that you have been waiting for. You could even experience conflict with a faculty member because you intensely disagree with the grade he or she assigned you on a project. Conflict can occur in any relationship, whether it is with your parents, girlfriend, or boyfriend, best friend, roommate, classmate, spouse or partner, children, or a total stranger. Remember, YOU are the one in control. You can break the cycle. You are the solution.

According to the *Chronicle of Higher Education,* for the past 10-plus years, students across the nation have stated that their number one reason for attending college was to "get a better job to make more money." There is nothing wrong with this at all. Money can help you do many wonderful things. Although this chapter deals with the techniques for becoming gainfully employed, such as being professional, writing resumes and cover letters, interviewing, and workplace policies in general, we hope that we have also planted the seed that not all of life is about work—or money. Life can be about helping others, giving, finding joy, learning to grow, and writing a history of which you can be proud. We wish you the very best of luck in your education, your job pursuit, and well beyond. Be kind to yourself and the world, in turn, will be kind to you.

what's it ALL ABOUT?

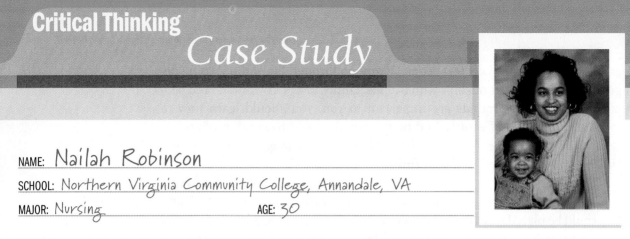

NAME: Nailah Robinson

SCHOOL: Northern Virginia Community College, Annandale, VA

MAJOR: Nursing   AGE: 30

Below is a real-life situation faced by Nailah. Read the brief case and respond to the questions.

I started college right out of high school, but because of my restlessness, lack of a major, and desire to be out in the world, I left college and moved to California. I worked in various jobs such as cosmetology and food service for many years.

I began college again in California to become a teacher. I quickly realized, however, that going back to college after being in the workforce was not very easy. You get used to a full-time salary and have full-time responsibilities, and those things stopped me once again.

About two years ago I had my first child, and during my stay in the hospital, I met the most wonderful nurse. She spent time with me and talked to me about my hopes and dreams, and it was in my conversations with her that I finally realized my place in this world. My grandmother used to say, "Sometimes, we can't see any further than where we are." That had been true with me, but my nurse helped me see down the road.

I knew that I wanted to be able to support and provide for my son, so I shadowed a nurse to make sure that my dream wasn't a nightmare. After my shadowing experience I began college at NOVA, and just last week I passed the entrance exam and was accepted into the nursing program. My dream is to work with at-risk, low-income children and give them the same care that my nurse gave me.

How can adversity affect your career decisions and your persistence?

_____

_____

_____

Nailah spent 10 years away from college. Where do you hope to be 10 years from now?

_____

_____

_____

How can other people (like Nailah's nurse) affect one's entire life perspective?

_____

_____

_____

Has anyone ever touched your life like Nailah's nurse touched hers? Who? What "gift" did they give to you?

_____

_____

_____

If the answer to the question above was no, do you feel that you have ever touched anyone's life in this way? Why or why not? How can your current major help you help others?

_____

_____

_____

ADVICE TO GO

CORNERSTONES

for success in the world of work . . . and beyond

Do all that you can to *ready* yourself for coming opportunities.

Strive for *perfection* with your cover letter and resume.

Commit yourself to be *loyal* and *trustworthy*.

Identify and *memorize* your assets.

Learn to *promote* yourself in an interview.

Strive to *develop* a strong work ethic.

Work to *perfect* your professional presence and dress.

Find references who *know* your qualities.

Above all, never compromise your *ethics* and *values* for money.

PROSPER

Glossary

Academic freedom   Professors in institutions of higher education are allowed to conduct research and to teach that research, regardless of controversial issues or subject matter. Academic freedom allows the professor the right to teach certain materials that might not have been allowed in high school.

Academic integrity   You have read, fully understand, and adhere to the policies, codes, and moral values of your institution. It implies that you will not cheat, plagiarize, or be unfair in your academic, social, cultural, or civic work.

Accreditation   Most high schools and colleges in the United States are accredited by a regional agency. This agency is responsible for ensuring that a minimum set of standards are held at all institutions that are members in the accreditation agency. The Southern Association of Colleges and Schools is one example of an accreditation agency.

Adding   Adding a class during registration periods or during the first week of classes means that you will be taking an additional class in your schedule.

Administration   The administration of a college is usually made up of nonteaching personnel who handle all of the administrative aspects of the college. The administration is headed by the president and vice presidents. The structure of the administration at each college varies.

Advising   To make sure that you will know what classes to take and in which order, you will be assigned an academic advisor—most often a faculty member in your discipline or major—when you arrive on campus. This advisor will usually be with you during your entire degree. She is responsible for guiding you through your academic work at the college.

African American Studies   This curriculum deals with the major contributions by African Americans in art, literature, history, medicine, sciences, and architecture. Many colleges offer majors and minors in African American Studies.

AIDS   This acronym stands for Acquired Immune Deficiency Syndrome, a disease that is transmitted sexually, intravenously, or from mother to child. Currently, no known cure for AIDS exists, but several medications, such as AZT and protease inhibitors, help to slow the deterioration of the immune system.

Alumna, alumni, alumnus   These terms are used to describe students who hold degrees from a college. The term *alumna* refers to a woman, *alumnus* refers to a man, and *alumni* refers to multiple women or men. The term *alumni* is used most often.

Anti-Semitism   Discrimination against people of Jewish or Arabic descent.

Articulation   An articulation agreement is a signed document between two or more institutions guaranteeing that the courses taken at one college will transfer to another college. For example, if Oak College has an articulation agreement with Maple College, it means that the course work taken at Oak College will be accepted toward a degree at Maple College.

Associate degree   The associate degree is a two-year degree that usually prepares the student to enter the workforce with a specific skill or trade. It is also offered to students as the first two years of their bachelor's, or four-year degree. Not all colleges offer the associate degree.

Attendance   Each college has an attendance policy, such as "a student can miss no more than 10 percent of the total class hours or he will receive an F for the course." This policy is followed strictly by some professors and more leniently by others. You should always know the attendance policy of each professor with whom you are studying.

Auditing   Most colleges offer the choice either to enroll in a course or to audit a course. If you enroll in a course, you pay the entire fee, attend classes, take exams, and receive credit. If you audit a course, the fee is usually lower, you do not take exams, and you do not receive credit. Course auditing is usually done by people who are having trouble in a subject or by those who want to gain more knowledge about a particular subject. Some colleges charge full price for auditing a course.

Baccalaureate   The baccalaureate degree, more commonly called the bachelor's degree, is a four-year degree in a specific field. Although this degree can be completed in as few as three years or as many as six-plus years, traditionally the amount of academic work required is four years. This degree prepares students for such careers as teaching, social work, engineering, fine arts, and journalism, to name a few. Graduate work is also available in these fields.

Bankruptcy   Bankruptcy is when a person must file legal papers through a lawyer to declare that she cannot pay her bills. Filing bankruptcy destroys one's credit history, and it takes 10 years for the bankruptcy to disappear from one's credit report.

Binge drinking   Binge drinking is defined as having five or more alcoholic beverages at one sitting.

Blackboard   Blackboard is a delivery platform for distance education courses taken over the web. Several platforms exist, including WebCT and Course Compass.

Board of Trustees   The Board of Trustees is the governing body of the college. For state schools, the board is appointed by government officials (usually the governor) of each state. The board hires the president and must approve any curriculum changes to degree programs. The board also sets policy for the college.

Campus   The campus is the physical plant of the university or college. The term refers to all buildings, fields, arenas, auditoriums, and other properties owned by the college.

Campus police   Each college and university has a campus police office or a security office. You will need to locate this office once you arrive on campus so that, in case of emergency, you will be able to find it quickly. Campus security can assist you with problems ranging from physical danger to car trouble.

Carrel This is a booth or small room located in the library. You can reserve a carrel for use throughout the semester or on a weekly basis. Many times, the carrel is large enough for only one person. Never leave any personal belongings or important academic materials in the carrel because they may be stolen.

Case study A case study is a story based on real-life events. Cases are written with open-ended conclusions and somewhat vague details to allow the reader to critically examine the story and develop logical solutions to resolve issues.

Catalog The college catalog is a book issued to you at the beginning of your college career. This book is one of the most important tools that you will use in developing your schedule and completing your degree. The catalog is a legally binding document stating what your degree requirements are for the duration of your study. You will need to obtain and keep the catalog of the year in which you entered college.

Certificate A certificate program is a series of courses, usually one year in length, designed to educate and train an individual in a certain area, such as welding, automotive repair, medical transcription, tool and die, early childhood, physical therapy assistance, or fashion merchandising. While these programs are certified and detailed, they are not degrees. Often, associate and bachelor's degrees are offered in these areas as well.

CLEP The College Level Examination Program, or CLEP, is designed to allow students to "test" out of a course. CLEP exams are nationally normalized and often are more extensive than a course in the same area. If you CLEP a course, it means that you do not have to take the course in which you passed the CLEP exam. Some colleges have limits on the number of hours that can be earned by CLEP.

Club drugs Club drugs are drugs taken at raves, parties, or dance clubs. Some of the most common club drugs are GHB (gamma hydroxybutyrate), Ecstasy, roofies, and meth.

Cognate A cognate is a course (or set of courses) taken outside of your major. Some colleges call this a minor. For instance, if you are majoring in English, you may wish to take a cognate in history or drama. Cognates are usually chosen in a field close to the major. It would be unlikely for a student to major in English and take a cognate in pharmacy.

Communications College curricula often state that a student must have nine hours of communications. This most commonly refers to English and speech (oral communication) courses. The mixture of these courses will usually be English 101 and 102 and Speech 101. This will vary from college to college.

Comprehensive exams This term refers to exams that encompass materials from the entire course. If you are taking a history course and your instructor informs you that there will be a comprehensive exam, information from the first lecture through the last lecture will be included on the exam.

Continuing education Almost every college in the nation offers courses in continuing education or community education. These courses are not offered for college credit, but Continuing Education Units are awarded in many cases. These courses are usually designed to meet the needs of specific businesses and industries or to provide courses of interest to the community. Continuing education courses range from small engine repair to flower arranging, from stained glass making to small business management.

Co-op This term is used to refer to a relationship between business/industry and the educational institution. During a co-op, the student spends a semester in college and the next semester on the job. Some co-ops may be structured differently, but the general idea behind a co-op is to gain on-the-job experience while still in college.

Cooperative learning In cooperative learning, learning, exploration, discovery, and results take place in a well-structured group. Cooperative learning teams are groups that work together on research, test preparation, project completion, and many other tasks.

Corequisite A corequisite is a course that must be taken at the same time as another course. Many times, science courses carry a corequisite. If you are taking Biology 101, the lab course Biology 101L may be required as the corequisite.

Counseling Most colleges have a counseling center on campus. Do not confuse counseling with advising. Trained counselors assist you with problems that might arise in your personal life, with your study skills, and with your career aspirations. Academic advisors are responsible for your academic progress. Some colleges do combine the two, but in many instances, the counselor and the advisor are two different people with two different job descriptions.

Course title Every course offered at a college will have a course title. You may see something in your schedule of classes that reads: ENG 101, SPC 205, HIS 210, and so forth. Your college catalog will define what the abbreviations mean. ENG 101 usually stands for English 101, SPC could be the heading for speech, and HIS could mean history. Headings and course titles vary from college to college.

Credit Credit is money or goods given to you on a reasonable amount of trust that you can and will repay the money or pay for the goods. Credit can come in several forms; credit cards and loans are the most common. Credit can be very dangerous to a person's future if he has too much credit or does not repay the credit in time.

Credit hour A credit hour is the amount of credit offered for each class that you take. Usually, each class is worth three credit hours. Science courses, foreign languages, and some math courses are worth four credit hours because of required labs. If a class carries three credit hours, this usually means that the class meets for three hours per week. This formula may vary greatly in a summer session or mid-session.

Credit score Your credit score is calculated by the amount of debt you have, your salary, your payment history, your length of residence in one place, and the number of inquiries into your credit history, to name a few. Your credit score is used to determine if you will be extended future credit and the interest rate that you will be charged. A low score could mean that you cannot get credit or that you will pay a very high interest rate. Negative credit reports stay on your credit history for seven years.

Critical thinking Critical thinking is thinking that is purposeful, reasoned, and goal directed. It is a type of thinking used to solve problems, make associations, connect relationships, formulate inferences, make decisions, and detect faulty arguments and persuasion.

Curriculum   The curriculum is the area of study in which you are engaged. It is a set of classes that you must take in order for a degree to be awarded.

Dean   The word *dean* is not a name, but a title. A dean is usually the head of a division or area of study. Some colleges might have a Dean of Arts and Sciences, a Dean of Business, and a Dean of Mathematics. The dean is the policy maker and usually the business manager and final decision maker of an area of study. Deans usually report to vice presidents or provosts.

Dean's list   The dean's list is a listing of students who have achieved a GPA of at least 3.5 (B+) on a 4.0 scale (these numbers are defined under GPA). This achievement may vary from college to college, but generally speaking, the dean's list is comprised of students in the top 5 percent of students in that college.

Default   A default is when a person fails to repay a loan according to the terms provided in the original loan papers. A default on a federal government loan will result in the garnishment of wages and the inability to acquire a position with the government. Also, you will receive no federal or state income tax refunds until the loan is repaid. Further, a government student loan cannot be written off under bankruptcy laws.

Degree   When a student completes an approved course of study, she is awarded a degree. The title of the degree depends on the college, the number of credit hours in the program, and the field of study. A two-year degree is called an associate degree, and a four-year degree is called a bachelor's degree. If a student attends graduate school, she may receive a master's degree (approximately 2 to 3 years) and sometimes a doctorate degree (anywhere from 3 to 10 years). Some colleges even offer postdoctorate degrees.

Diploma   A diploma is awarded when an approved course of study is completed. The diploma is not as detailed or comprehensive as an associate degree and usually consists of only 8 to 12 courses specific to a certain field.

Distance learning   Distance learning is learning that takes place away from the campus. Distance learning or distance education is usually offered by a computerized platform such as Blackboard, WebCT, or Course Compass. Chat sessions and Internet assignments are common in distance learning.

Dropping   When a student decides that he does not enjoy a class or will not be able to pass the class because of grades or absenteeism, he may elect to drop that class section. This means that the class will no longer appear on his schedule or be calculated in his GPA. Rules and regulations on dropping vary from college to college. All rules should be explained in the catalog.

Ecstasy   Ecstasy, or "X," is a "club drug" that is very common at raves and dance parties. It produces a relaxed, euphoric state, which makes the user experience warmth, heightened emotions, and self-acceptance. It can cause se-

vere depression and even death among some users. Ecstasy is illegal to use or possess.

Elective   An elective is a course that a student chooses to take outside of her major field of study. It could be in an area of interest or an area that complements the chosen major. For example, an English major might choose an elective in the field of theatre or history because these fields complement each other. However, a student majoring in English might also elect to take a course in medical terminology because she is interested in that area.

Emeriti   This Latin term is assigned to retired personnel of the college who have performed exemplary duties during their professional careers. For example, a college president who obtained new buildings, added curriculum programs, and increased the endowment might be named President Emeritus upon his or her retirement.

Ethnocentrism   Ethnocentrism is the practice of thinking that one's ethnic group is superior to others.

Evening college   The evening college program is designed to allow students who have full-time jobs to obtain a college degree by enrolling in classes that meet in the evening. Some colleges offer an entire degree program in the evening; others only offer some courses in the evening.

Faculty   The faculty of a college is the body of professionals who teach, do research, and perform community service. Faculty members have prepared for many years to hold the responsibilities carried by this title. Many have been to school for 20 or more years to obtain the knowledge and skill necessary to train students in specific fields.

Fallacy   A fallacy is a false notion. It is a statement based on false materials, invalid inferences, or incorrect reasoning.

Fees   Fees refer to the amount of money charged by a college for specific items and services. Some fees may include tuition, meal plans, books, and health and activity fees. Fees vary from college to college and are usually printed in the catalog.

Financial aid   If a student is awarded money from the college, the state, the federal government, private sources, or places of employment, this is referred to as financial aid. Financial aid can be awarded on the basis of either need or merit or both. Any grant, loan, or scholarship is formally called financial aid.

Fine arts   Many people tend to think of fine arts as drawing or painting, but in actuality, the fine arts encompass a variety of artistic forms. Theatre, dance, architecture, drawing, painting, sculpture, and music are considered part of the fine arts. Some colleges also include literature in this category.

Foreign language   Almost every college offers at least one course in foreign languages. Many colleges offer degrees in this area. For schools in America, foreign languages consist of Spanish, French, Russian, Latin, German, Portuguese, Swahili, Arabic, Japanese, Chinese, and Korean, to name a few.

Fraternities   A fraternity is an organization of the Greek system whose members are male. Many fraternities have their own housing complexes on campus. Induction for each is different. Honorary fraternities, such as Phi Kappa Phi, also exist. These are academic in nature and are open to males and females.

Freshman   This is a term used by high schools and colleges. The term *first-year student* is also used. This term refers to a student in his first year of college. Traditionally, a freshman is someone who has not yet completed 30 semester hours of college-level work.

GHB, or gamma hydroxybutyrate   GHB is a club drug that comes most often in an odorless, liquid form but can also come as a powdery substance. At lower doses, GHB has a euphoric effect and can make the user feel relaxed, happy, and sociable. Higher doses can lead to dizziness, sleepiness, vomiting, spasms, and loss of consciousness. GHB and alcohol used together can be deadly.

GPA, or grade point average   The grade point average is the numerical grading system used by almost every college in the nation. GPAs determine if a student is eligible for continued enrollment, financial aid, or honors. Most colleges operate under a 4.0 system. This means that all A's earned are worth 4 quality points; B's, 3 points; C's, 2 points; D's, 1 point; and F's, 0 points. To calculate a GPA, multiply the number of quality points by the number of credit hours carried by the course and then divide by the total number of hours carried. For example: If a student is taking English 101, Speech 101, History 201, and Psychology 101, these courses usually carry 3 credit hours each. If a student made all A's, she would have a GPA of 4.0. If the student made all B's, she would have a 3.0. However, if she had a variety of grades, the GPA would be calculated as follows:

	Grade	Credit	Q.Points		Total Points
ENG 101	A	3 hours	× 4	=	12 points
SPC 101	C	3 hours	× 2	=	6 points
HIS 201	B	3 hours	× 3	=	9 points
PSY 101	D	3 hours	× 1	=	3 points

The total of 30 points divided by 12 hours would equal a GPA of 2.5 (or C+ average).

Grace period   A grace period is usually 10 days after the due date of a loan payment. For example: If your car payment is due on the first of the month, many companies will give you a 10 day grace period (until the 11th) to pay the bill before they report your delinquent payment to a credit scoring company.

Graduate teaching assistant   You may encounter a "teaching assistant" as a freshman or sophomore. In some larger colleges and universities, students working toward master's and doctorate degrees teach undergraduate, lower-level classes under the direction of a major professor in the department.

Grant   A grant is usually money that goes toward tuition and books that does not have to be repaid. Grants are most often awarded by state and federal governments.

Hepatitis   Hepatitis has three forms: A, B, and C. Hepatitis A comes from drinking contaminated water. Hepatitis B is more prevalent than HIV and can be transmitted sexu-

ally, through unsterile needles, and through unsterile tattoo equipment. Left untreated, hepatitis B can cause serious liver damage. Hepatitis C develops into a chronic condition in over 85 percent of the people who have it. Hepatitis C is the leading cause of liver transplants. Hepatitis B and C can be transmitted by sharing toothbrushes, nail clippers, or any item contaminated with blood. Hepatitis B and C have no recognizable signs or symptoms. Some people, however, do get flulike symptoms, loss of appetite, nausea, vomiting, or fever.

Higher education   This term is used to describe any level of education beyond high school. All colleges are called institutions of higher education.

Homophobia   Homophobia is the fear of homosexuals or homosexuality.

Honor code   Many colleges operate under an honor code. This system demands that students perform all work without cheating, plagiarism, or any other dishonest actions. In many cases, a student can be removed from the institution for breaking the honor code. In other cases, if students do not turn in fellow students who they know have broken the code, they, too, can be removed from the institution.

Honors   Academic honors are based on the GPA of a student. Each college usually has many academic honors, including the dean's list, the president's list, and departmental honors. The three highest honors awarded are Summa Cum Laude, Magna Cum Laude, and Cum Laude. These are awarded at graduation for students who have maintained a GPA of 3.5 or better. The GPA requirement for these honors varies from college to college. Usually, they are awarded as follows:

3.5 to 3.7 Cum Laude
3.7 to 3.9 Magna Cum Laude
4.0 Summa Cum Laude

Honors college   The honors college is usually a degree or a set of classes offered for students who performed exceptionally well in high school.

Humanities   The humanities are sometimes as misunderstood as the fine arts. Courses in the humanities include history, philosophy, religion, and cultural studies; some colleges also include literature, government, and foreign languages. The college catalog will define what your college has designated as humanities.

Identification cards   An identification card is essential for any college student. Some colleges issue them free, while some charge a small fee. The ID card allows the student to use the college library, participate in activities, use physical fitness facilities, and many times attend college events for free. They also come in handy in the community. Movie theatres, museums, zoos, and other cultural events usually charge less or nothing if a student has an ID. The card will also allow the student to use most area library facilities with special privileges. ID cards are usually validated each semester.

Identity theft   Identity theft is when another person assumes your identity and uses your credit, your name, and your Social Security number. Identity theft can't always be prevented, but to reduce the risk, always guard your credit cards, your address history, and most importantly, your Social Security number and driver's license number.

Independent study   Many colleges offer courses through independent study, meaning that no formal classes and no classroom teacher are involved. The student works independently to complete the course under the general guidelines of a department and with the assistance of an instructor. Many colleges require that a student maintain a minimum GPA before enrolling in independent study classes.

Internship   An internship involves working in a business or industry to gain experience in one's field of interest. Many colleges require internships for graduation.

Journal   Many classes, such as English, freshman orientation, literature, history, and psychology, require students to keep a journal of thoughts, opinions, research, and class discussions. Many times, the journal is a communication link between the students and their instructors.

Junior   The term refers to a student who is enrolled in his third year of college or a student who has completed at least 60 credit hours of study.

Late fee   A late fee is an "administrative" charge that lenders assess if a loan payment is late.

Learning style   A learning style is the way an individual learns best. Three learning styles exist: visual, auditory, and tactile. Visual means that one learns best by seeing, auditory means that one learns best by hearing, and tactile means that one learns best by touching.

Lecture   A lecture is the "lesson" given by an instructor in a class. The term usually refers to the style in which material is presented. Some instructors have group discussions, peer tutoring, or multimedia presentations. The lecture format means that the instructor presents most of the information.

Liberal arts   The liberal arts consist of a series of courses that go beyond training for a certain vocation or occupation. For instance, a student at a liberal arts college might be majoring in biology, but he will also have to take courses in fine arts, history, social sciences, math, "hard" sciences, and other related courses. The liberal arts curriculum ensures that the student has been exposed to a variety of information and cultural experiences.

Load   A load refers to the amount of credit or the number of classes that a student is taking. The normal load for a student is between 15 and 18 hours, or five to six classes. For most colleges, 12 hours is considered a full-time load, but a student can take up to 18 or 21 hours for the same amount of tuition.

Major   A major is the intended field of study for a student. The major simply refers to the amount of work completed in one field; in other words, the majority of courses have been in one related field, such as English, engineering, medicine, nursing, art, history, or political science. A stu-

dent is usually required to declare a major by the end of the sophomore (or second) year.

Meal plan   A meal plan is usually bought at the beginning of the semester and allows a student to eat a variety of meals by using a computer card or punch system. Meal plans can be purchased for three meals a day, breakfast only, lunch only, or any combination of meals.

Mentor   A mentor is someone whom a student can call on to help her through troubled times, assist her in decision making, and give advice. Mentors can be teachers, staff members, fellow outstanding classmates, or higher-level students. Mentors seldom volunteer to be a mentor; they usually fall into the role of mentoring because they are easy to talk with, knowledgeable about the college and the community, and willing to lend a helping hand. A student may, however, be assigned a mentor when she arrives on campus.

Methamphetamine   Crystal meth, as it is commonly called, is an illegal drug sold in pills, capsules, powder, or rock forms. It stimulates the central nervous system and breaks down the user's inhibitions. It can cause memory loss, aggression, violence, and psychotic behavior.

Minor   The minor of a student is the set of courses that he or she takes that usually complements the major. The minor commonly consists of six to eight courses in a specific field. If a student is majoring in engineering, she might minor in math or electronics, something that would assist her in the workplace.

Multiple intelligences   Multiple intelligences are the eight intelligences with which we are born. Howard Gardner, who believes that we all have one of eight intelligences as our primary strength, introduced the theory. The intelligences include Music/Rhythm, Logic/Math, Visual/Spatial, Naturalistic, Interpersonal, Intrapersonal, Verbal/Linguistic, and Body/Kinesthetic.

Natural and physical sciences   The natural and physical sciences refer to a select group of courses from biology, chemistry, physical science, physics, anatomy, zoology, botany, geology, genetics, microbiology, physiology, and astronomy.

Networking   Networking refers to meeting people who can help you (or whom you can help) find careers, meet other people, make connections, and "get ahead."

Online classes   Used in conjunction with distance learning or distance education, online classes use the Internet as a means of delivery, instead of a traditional classroom.

Orientation   Every student is requested, and many are required, to attend an orientation session. This is one of the most important steps that a student can take when beginning college. Important information and details concerning individual colleges and their rules and regulations will be discussed.

Plagiarism   This term refers to the act of using someone's words or works as your own without citing the original author. Penalties for plagiarism vary from college to college, but most institutions have strict guidelines for dealing with students who plagiarize. Some institutions force the student to withdraw from the institution. Your student handbook should list the penalties for plagiarism.

Prefix   A prefix is a code used by the Office of the Registrar to designate a certain area of study. The prefix for English is usually ENG; for Religion, REL; for Theatre, THE; for History, HIS; and so forth. Prefix lettering varies from college to college.

Preprofessional programs   Preprofessional programs usually refer to majors that require advanced study to the master's or doctoral level to be able to practice in the field. Such programs include, but are not limited to, law, medicine, dentistry, psychiatry, nursing, veterinary studies, and theology.

Prerequisite   A prerequisite is a course that must be taken before another course. For example, most colleges require that English 101 and 102 (Composition I and II) be completed before any literature course is taken. Therefore, English 101 and 102 are prerequisites to literature. Prerequisites are always spelled out in the college catalog.

President   A college president is the visionary leader of an institution. She is usually hired by the Board of Trustees of a college. Her primary responsibilities involve financial planning, fundraising, community relations, and the academic integrity of the curriculum. Every employee at the college is responsible to the president.

Probation   Many times, a student who has below a 2.0 GPA in any given semester or quarter will be placed on academic probation for one semester. If that student continues to perform below 2.0, suspension may be in order. The rules for probation and suspension must be displayed in the college catalog.

Professor   Many people believe that all teachers on the college level are professors. This is not true. A full professor is someone who may have been in the profession for a long time and someone who usually holds a doctoral degree. The system of promotion among college teachers is as follows:

    adjunct instructor
    instructor
    lecturer
    assistant professor
    associate professor
    full professor (professor).

Protease inhibitors   Protease inhibitors are a series, or "cocktail," of drugs used to fight HIV/AIDS and slow the destruction of the immune system. They have been instrumental in extending the lives of people living with HIV and AIDS. However, a new strain of HIV has arisen that is immune to the protease inhibitors presently used.

Provost   The provost is the primary policy maker at the college with regard to academic standards. He usually reports directly to the president. Many colleges will not have a provost but will have a vice president for academic affairs or a dean of instruction.

Racism   Racism occurs when a person or group of people believes that their race is superior to another race.

Readmit   When a student has "stopped-out" for a semester or two, he will usually have to be readmitted to the college. This term does not apply to a student who elects not to attend summer sessions. Usually, no application fee is required for a readmit student. He does not lose his previously earned academic credit unless that credit carries a time limit. For example, some courses in psychology carry a 5- or 10-year limit, meaning that if a degree is not awarded within that time, the course must be retaken.

Registrar   The registrar has one of the most difficult jobs on any college campus. She is responsible for all student academic records. The registrar is also responsible for entering all grades and all drops and adds, printing the schedule, and verifying all candidates for graduation. The Office of the Registrar is sometimes referred to as the Records Office.

Residence hall   A residence hall is a single-sex or co-educational facility on campus where students live. Many new students choose to live on campus because residence halls are conveniently located. They are also a good way to meet new friends and become involved in extracurricular activities. The college usually provides a full-time supervisor for each hall and a director of student housing. Each hall usually elects a student representative to be on the student council.

Residency requirement   Many colleges have a residency requirement, meaning that a certain number of hours must be earned at the "home" institution. For many two-year colleges, at least 50 percent of the credit used for graduation must be earned at the home college. For four-year colleges, many requirements state that the last 30 hours must be earned at the home college. All residence requirements are spelled out in the college catalog.

Room and board   If a student is going to live on campus, many times the fee charged for this service will be called "room and board." This basically means a place to stay and food to eat. Many students may opt to buy a meal plan along with their dorm room. These issues are usually discussed during orientation.

Root problem   The root problem is the main issue, the core of the situation at hand. Most troublesome situations have several problems, but usually one major "root" problem exists that causes all of the other problems.

Scholar   A scholar is usually someone who has performed exceptionally in a certain field of study.

Section code   At many larger colleges, many sections of the same course are offered. The section code tells the computer and the registrar which hour and instructor the student will have for a particular class. A typical schedule may look something like this:

English 101	01	MWF	8:00–8:50	Smith
English 101	02	MWF	8:00–8:50	Jones
English 101	03	T TH	8:00–9:15	McGee

The numbers 01, 02, and 03 refer to the section of English in which the student enrolls.

Senior The term *senior* is used for students in their last year of study for a bachelor's degree. The student must have completed at least 90 credit hours to be a senior.

Sexism Sexism is discrimination based on sex and social roles.

Sexual harassment Sexual harassment is defined as any type of advance that is unwanted by the receiver, including touching another person, taunting a person verbally, denying promotions based on forced relationships, and so forth.

Social sciences The social sciences are courses that involve the study or interface with society and people. Social Science courses may include, but are not limited to, psychology, sociology, anthropology, political science, geography, economics, and international studies.

Sophomore The term *sophomore* refers to students who are in their second year of study for a bachelor's degree. A student must have completed at least 30 credit hours to be a sophomore.

Sororities Sororities are organizations of the Greek system in which females are members. Many sororities have on-campus housing complexes. Initiation into a sorority differs from organization to organization and campus to campus.

Staff Personnel in the college setting are usually divided into three categories: administration, staff, and faculty. The staff is responsible for the day-to-day workings of the college. Usually people in admissions, financial aid, the bookstore, housing, student activities and personnel, and so forth hold staff titles. The people heading these departments are usually in administration.

Student Government Association (SGA) This is one of the most powerful and visible organizations on the college campus. Usually, the SGA comprises students from each of the four undergraduate classes. Annual elections are held to appoint officers. As the "student voice" on campus, the SGA represents the entire student body before the college administration.

Student loan Unlike a grant, a student loan must be repaid. The loans are usually at a much lower rate of interest than a bank loan. For most student loans, the payment schedule does not begin until six months after graduation. This allows the graduate to find a job and become secure in her chosen profession. If a student decides to return to school, she can get the loan deferred, with additional interest, until she completes a graduate degree.

Suspension Suspension may occur for a variety of reasons, but most institutions suspend students for academic reasons. While GPA requirements vary from college to college, usually a student is suspended when his grade point average falls below a 1.5 for two consecutive semesters. The college catalog contains the rules regarding suspension.

Syllabus In high school, you may have been given a class outline, but in college, you are given a syllabus. This is a legally binding contract between the student and the professor. This document contains the attendance policy, the grading scale, the required text, the professor's office hours and phone number(s), and important information regarding the course. Most professors also include the class operational calendar as a part of the syllabus. This is one of the most important documents that you will be issued in a class. You should take it to class with you daily and keep it at least until the semester is over.

Tenure You may hear someone call a college teacher a "tenured professor." This usually means that the professor has been with the college for many years and has been awarded tenure due to his successful efforts in research, publication of books and articles, and community service. Usually, tenure ensures the professor lifelong employment.

TOEFL TOEFL is an acronym for the Test of English as a Foreign Language. This test is used to certify that international students have the English skills needed to succeed at the institution or to become a teaching assistant. Some colleges allow international students to use TOEFL to satisfy English as their foreign language requirement.

Tolerance Tolerance is the ability to recognize and respect the opinions, practices, religions, race, sex, sexual orientation, ethnicity, and age of other people.

Transcript A transcript is a formal record of all work attempted and completed at a college. If a student attends more than one college, he will have a transcript for each college. Many colleges have a policy in which all classes, completed or not, remain on the transcript. Some colleges allow D's and F's to be removed if the student repeats the course with a better grade. Many colleges, however, leave the old grade and continue to count the D or F in the GPA. Rules regarding transcripts vary from college to college. Many employers now require that a prospective employee furnish a transcript from college.

Transfer This term may refer to course work or to a student. If a student enrolls in one college and then wants to go to another, she is classified as a transfer student. The course work completed is called *transfer work*. Many colleges have rules regarding the number of credit hours that may be transferred from one college to another. Most colleges will not accept credit from another college if the grade on the course is below a C.

Transient A transient student is someone who is attending another college to take one or two courses. If a student comes home for the summer and wants to enroll in a college near his home and maintain himself as a student at his chosen college, he is a transient student.

Transitional studies Many colleges have an open admission policy, meaning that the door is open to any student. In these cases, the college usually runs a transitional studies program to assist the student in reaching her educational goal. If a student has not performed well in English, math, or reading, she may be required to attend a transitional studies class to upgrade basic skills in certain areas.

Veteran's Affairs Many colleges have an Office of Veteran's Affairs to assist those students who have served in the military. Many times, a college will accept credit earned by a veteran while in the service. Most of the time, a veteran's financial packages will differ because of the GI Bill.

Many colleges have several vice presidents ⌐er the president. They are senior-level admin- ⌐o assist with the daily operations of the college. ⌐ges have vice presidents of academic affairs, fi- ⌐affairs, and student affairs, to name a few.

⌐nes   This term is used by most libraries in the nation. ⌐olume is a book or a piece of nonprinted material used to ⌐ssist the student in his studies. You may read that a college library has 70,000 volumes. This means that it has 70,000 books and other pieces of media. Many colleges have volumes that range in the millions.

WebCT   WebCT is a delivery platform for distance education courses taken over the web.

Who's Who   This is a shortened title for *Who's Who in American Colleges and Universities,* a nationally recognized grouping. Students are nominated by the college because of their academic standing and their achievements in cocurricular activities and community service.

Women's Studies   Some colleges offer majors and minors in Women's Studies. The curriculum is centered around the major contributions of women to art, literature, medicine, history, law, architecture, and sciences.

References

ACT, Inc. *National Dropout Rates, Freshman to Sophomore Years by Type of Institution.* Iowa City, IA: ACT, 2000.

Adler, R., Rosenfeld, L., and Towne, N. *Interplay. The Process of Interpersonal Communication,* 2nd ed. New York: Holt, Rinehart and Winston, 2001.

Advanced Public Speaking Institute. "Public speaking: Why use humor?" Virginia Beach, VA: Author, www.public-speaking.org/public-speaking-humor-article.htm.

American College Testing Program. *National Drop Out Rates.* ACT Institutional Data File, Iowa City, IA: ACT, 1995.

Amnesty International. Death penalty information, www.web.amnesty.org.

Anderson, D. *The Death Penalty—A Defence.* Sweden, 1998. Translated into English in 2001 at http://w1.155.telia.com/~u1550911 9/ny_sida_1.htm.

Armstrong, T. *Multiple Intelligences in the Classroom.* Alexandria, VA: Association for Supervision and Curriculum Development, 1994.

Astin, A. *Achieving Educational Excellence.* San Francisco: Jossey-Bass, 1985.

Bach, D. *The Finish Rich Notebook.* New York: Broadway Books, 2003.

Baldridge, L. *Letitia Baldridge's New Complete Guide to Executive Manners.* New York: Macmillan, 1985.

Barnes & Noble and the Anti-Defamation League. *Close the Book on Hate: 101 Ways to Combat Prejudice,* 2000. Available online at www.adl.org/prejudice/closethebook.pdf.

Beebe, S. A., and Beebe, S. J. *Interpersonal Communication: Relating to Others,* 3rd ed. Boston: Allyn and Bacon, 2002.

Benson, H. *The Relaxation Response.* New York: Caral Publishing Group, 1992.

Benson, H., and Stuart, E. *Wellness Encyclopedia.* Boston: Houghton Mifflin, 1991.

Benson, H., and Stuart, E. *The Wellness Book: The Comprehensive Guide to Maintaining Health and Treating Stress-Related Illness.* New York: Birch Lane Press, 1992.

Berenblatt, M., and Berenblatt, A. *Make an Appointment with Yourself: Simple Steps to Positive Self-Esteem.* Deerfield Beach, FL: Health Communication, 1994.

Beyer, B. *Developing a Thinking Skills Program.* Boston: Allyn and Bacon, 1998.

Boldt, L. *How to Be, Do, or Have Anything.* Berkeley, CA: Ten Speed Press, 2001.

Bosak, J. *Fallacies.* Dubuque, IA: Educulture Publishers, 1976.

Boyle, M., and Zyla, G. *Personal Nutrition.* St. Paul, MN: West Publishing, 1992.

Bozzi, V. "A healthy dose of religion." *Psychology Today,* November, 1988.

Brightman, H. Georgia State University Master Teacher Program: On Learning Styles, www.gsu.edu/~dschjb/wwwmbti.html.

Bucher, R. D. *Diversity Consciousness: Opening Our Minds to People, Cultures, and Opportunities.* Upper Saddle River, NJ: Prentice Hall, 2000.

Buscaglia, L. *Living, Loving, and Learning.* New York: Ballantine, 1982.

Business and Legal Reports, Inc. *Staying Safe on Campus.* Madison, CT: Author, 1995.

Cameron, J. *The Artist's Way: A Spiritual Path to Higher Creativity.* New York: Penguin Putnam, 1992.

Casperson, D. *Power Etiquette: What You Don't Know Can Kill Your Career.* New York: AMA Publications, 1999.

Cardinal, F. "Sleep is important when stress and anxiety increase." *The National Sleep Foundation,* April 10, 2003.

Cetron, F. "What students must know to succeed in the 21st century." *The Futurist,* July–August 1996, v. 30, No. 4, p. 7.

Checkley, K. "The first seven . . . and the eighth." *Educational Leadership, 55,* no. 1, September 1997.

Chickering, A., and Schlossberg, N. *Getting the Most out of College.* Boston: Allyn and Bacon, 1995.

Chopra, D. *The Seven Spiritual Laws of Success.* San Rafael, CA: New World Library, 1994.

Greger, J. *Nutrition for Living.* ...ity, CA: Benjamin/Cummings ...g, 1994.

...The color of death." *National Review Online.* ...11, 2001, www.nationalreview.com/ ...ntributors/clegg061101.shtml.

...ud, J. "The pioneer Harvey Milk." Accessed at www.time.com.

CNN Money. "More credit late fees paid." May 12, 2002. Accessed at http://money.cnn.com/2002/ 05/21/pf/banking/cardfees/.

Cohen, L. *Conducting Research on the Internet.* University of Albany Libraries, 1996a, www. albany.edu.

Cohen, L. *Evaluating Internet Resources.* University of Albany Libraries, 1996b, www.albany.edu.

Cojonet (City of Jacksonville, FL). "Consumer Affairs gets new tough law on car title businesses." Accessed at www.coj.net/Departments/ Regulatory+and+Environmental+Services/ Consumer+Affairs/TITLE+LOANS.htm, 2003.

Coldewey, J., and Streitberger, W. *Drama, Classical to Contemporary,* rev. ed. Upper Saddle River, NJ: Prentice Hall, 2001.

"Commonly Abused Drugs." National Institute on Drug Abuse. Accessed at www.nida.nih.gov/DrugsofAbuse.html.

Cooper, A. *Time Management for Unmanageable People.* New York: Bantam Books, 1993.

Cooper, M. "Alcohol use and risky sexual behavior among college students and youth." *Journal of Studies on Alcohol, 63*(2), 2002, p. S101.

Daly, J., and Engleberg, I. *Presentations in Everyday Life: Strategies for Effective Speaking.* Boston: Houghton Mifflin, 2002.

"Dan White." Accessed at www.findagrave.com/ php/famous.php?page=name&firstName= Dan&lastName=White.

Daniels, P., and Bright, W. *The World's Writing Systems.* England: Oxford University Press, 1996.

Donatelle, R., and Davis, L. *Health: The Basics.* Englewood Cliffs, NJ: Prentice Hall, 2002.

Eddlem, T. "Ten anti-death penalty fallacies." *The New American, 18*(3), June 3, 2002.

Eisenberg, D. "The coming job boom." *Time Online Edition,* April 29, 2002, www.time.com/time/ business/article/0,8599,233967,00.html.

Ellis, D., Lankowitz, S., Stupka, D., and Toft, D. *Career Planning.* Rapid City, SD: College Survival, Inc., 1990.

Elrich, M. "The Stereotype Within." *Educational Leadership,* April 1994, p. 12.

Equifax.com. "Glossary of terms." Accessed at www.econsumer.equifax.com/consumer/forward. ehtml?forward=credu_glossaryterms.

Equifax.com. "Identity theft and fraud." Accessed at www.econsumer.equifax.com/consumer/ forward.ehtml?forward=idtheft_howitstrikes, 2003.

Equifax.com. "Teaching students about money and credit." Accessed at www.equifax.com/ CoolOnCredit/parent1.html.

Facione, P. *Critical Thinking: What It Is and Why It Counts.* Santa Clara: California University Press, 1998.

Freshman Survey Data Report. Cooperative Institutional Research Program Sponsored by the Higher Education Research Institute (HERI). University of California, Los Angeles, 1999.

Fulghum, R. *All I Really Need to Know, I Learned in Kindergarten.* New York: Ivy Books, 1988.

Gardenswartz, L., and Rowe, A. *Managing Diversity: A Complete Desk Reference and Planning Guide.* New York: Irwin/Pfeiffer, 1993.

Gardner, H. *Frames of Mind: The Theory of Multiple Intelligences.* New York: Basic Books, 1983.

Gardner, H. "Reflections on multiple intelligences: myths and messages." *Phi Delta Kappan, 77,* no. 3, November 1995, p. 200.

Gardner, J., and Jewler, J. *Your College Experience.* Belmont, CA: Wadsworth, 2000.

Gay, Lesbian and Straight Education Network. "Just the facts." New York: GLSE, 2000. Synopsis found online at http://msn.planetout.com/ people/teens/features/2000/08/facts.html.

Gonyea, J. C. "Discover the work you were born to do." MSN.com Careers, 2002, http://editorial. careers.msn.com/articles/born.

Grilly, D. *Drugs and Human Behavior.* Boston: Allyn and Bacon, 1994.

Gunthrie, H., and Picciano, M. *Human Nutrition.* Salem, MA: Mosby, 1995.

Hales, D. *Your Health.* Redwood City, CA: Benjamin/Cummings Publishing, 1991.

Haney, D. "New AIDS drugs bring optimism." *The Las Vegas Review Journal,* February 12, 2003.

Hanna, S. L. *Person to Person.* Upper Saddle River, NJ: Prentice Hall, 2003.

Hickman, R., and Quinley, J. *A Synthesis of Local, State, and National Studies in Workforce Education and Training.* Washington, DC: The American Association of Community Colleges, 1997.

"Hidden menace: Drowsy drivers." Accessed at www.sleepdisorders.about.com/library/weekly/aa062902a.htm.

Jerome, R., and Grout, P. "Cheat wave." *People Magazine,* June 17, 2002, p. 84.

Kanar, C. *The Confident Reader.* New York: Houghton Mifflin, 2000.

Kirby, D. "The worst is yet to come." *The Advocate,* January 19, 1999, p. 57.

Kleiman, C. *The 100 Best Jobs for the 90's and Beyond.* New York: Berkley Books, 1992.

Konowalow, S. *Cornerstones for Money Management.* Upper Saddle River, NJ: Prentice Hall, 1997.

Konowalow, S. *Planning Your Future: Keys to Financial Freedom.* Columbus, OH: Prentice Hall, 2003.

Lecky, P. *Self-Consistency: A Theory of Personality.* Garden City, NY: Anchor, 1951.

Leinwood, D. Ecstasy–Viagra mix alarms doctors. *USA Today,* Sept. 23, 2002.

Lieberman, B. "1 in 5 new HIV cases is a drug-resistant strain, study finds." *The San Diego Tribune,* August 8, 2002.

Maker, J., and Lenier, M. *College Reading,* 5th ed. Belmont, CA: Thompson Learning, 2000.

Managing and Resolving Conflict, http://hr2.hr.arizona.edu/06_jcl/jobdesc/groundrules.htm.

Manisses Communications Group. *Alcoholism & Drug Abuse Weekly,* 13(36), September 2001, p. 7.

McGraw, P. C. *Life Strategies Workbook.* New York: Hyperion, 2000.

McKay, M., and Fanning, P. *Self-Esteem.* Oakland, CA: New Harbinger, 2000.

Moss, J. cited in Kates, W. "America is not getting enough sleep." *The San Francisco Chronicle,* March 30, 1990, p. B3.

National Association of College Employers. "Top ten personal qualities employers seek." *Job Outlook,* NACE, 2000.

National Foundation for Credit Counseling. "National Foundation for Credit Counseling announces study results on the impact of credit counseling on consumer credit and debt payment behavior." Press release, March 21, 2002. Accessed at www.nfcc.org/newsroom/shownews.Cfm?newsid=257.

Nelson, D., and Low, G. *Emotional Intelligence: Achieving Academic and Career Excellence.* Upper Saddle River, NJ: Prentice Hall, 2003.

Nevid, J., Fichner-Rathus, L., and Rathus, S. *Human Sexuality in a World of Diversity.* Boston: Allyn and Bacon, 1995.

Okula, S. "Protect yourself from identity theft." Accessed at http://moneycentral.msn.com/articles/banking/credit/1342.asp.

Ormondroyd, J., Engle, M., and Cosgrave, T. *How to Critically Analyze Information Sources.* Cornell University Libraries, 2001, www.library.cornell.edu.

Ormrod, J. E. *Educational Psychology: Developing Learners.* Upper Saddle River, NJ: Prentice Hall, 2003.

Pauk, W. *How to Study in College,* 7th ed. New York: Houghton Mifflin, 2001.

Paul, R. *What Every Person Needs to Survive in a Rapidly Changing World.* Santa Rosa, CA: The Foundation for Critical Thinking, 1992.

Popenoe, D. *Sociology,* 9th ed. Englewood Cliffs, NJ: Prentice Hall, 1993.

Powell, E. *Sex on Your Terms.* Boston: Allyn and Bacon, 1996.

Radelet, M. "Post-Furman botched executions." Accessed at www.deathpenaltyinfo.org/botched.html.

Rathus, S., and Fichner-Rathus, L. *Making the Most out of College.* Englewood Cliffs, NJ: Prentice Hall, 1994.

Rathus, S., Nevid, J., and Fichner-Rathus, L. *Essentials of Human Sexuality.* Boston: Allyn and Bacon, 1998.

"Retention Rates by Institutional Type," Higher Education Research Institute, UCLA, Los Angeles, 1989.

Rogers, C. *On Becoming Partners: Marriage and Its Alternatives.* New York: Delacorte Press, 1972.

Romas, J., and Sharma, M. *Practical Stress Management.* Boston: Allyn and Bacon, 1995.

Rooney, M. "Freshmen show rising political awareness and changing social views." *The Chronicle of Higher Education,* January 31, 2003.

263

Nurmi, J.E. "Uncertainty and interpersonal projects.
...es for social relationships and well-
...urnal of Social and Personal Relationships,
...996, pp. 109–122.

..., D. *The Seven Sins of Memory: How the Mind orgets and Remembers*. New York: Houghton Mifflin, 2001.

...ciolino, E. "World drug crop up sharply in 1989 despite U.S. effort." *New York Times,* March 2, 1990.

Seyler, D. *Steps to College Reading,* 2nd ed. Boston: Allyn and Bacon, 2001.

Shaffer, C., and Amundsen, K. *Creating Community Anywhere*. Los Angeles: Jeremy P. Tarcher Publishing, 1994.

Sherfield, R., Montgomery, R., and Moody, P. *Capstone: Succeeding Beyond College*. Upper Saddle River, NJ: Prentice Hall, 2001.

Sherfield, R. *The Everything Self-Esteem Book*. Avon, MA: Adams Media, 2004.

Silver, H., Strong, R., and Perini, M. "Integrating learning styles and multiple intelligences." *Educational Leadership,* 55, no. 1, September 1997, p. 22.

Smith, B. *Breaking Through: College Reading,* 6th ed. Upper Saddle River, NJ: Pearson Education, 2001.

Southern Poverty Law Center. *Ten Ways to Fight Hate*. Montgomery, AL: Author, 2000.

Syemore, R., and O'Connell, D. "Did you know?" *Chatelaine,* 73(8), August 2000, p. 30.

"Ten credit card management tips." Accessed at www.aol1.bankrate.com/AOL/news/cc/20021218 a.asp.

Texas A&M University. "Improve your memory." Accessed at www.scs.tamu.edu/selfhelp/ elibrary/memory.asp.

The Chronicle of Higher Education, 49(1), August 30, 2002.

The Motley Fool. "How to get out of debt." Accessed at www.fool.com/seminars/sp/index.htm? sid=0001&lid=000&ref=.

The World Almanac and Book of Facts, 2002. New York: World Almanac Books, 2003.

Tieger, P., and Barron-Tieger, B. *Do What You Are: Discover the Perfect Career for You Through the Secrets of Personality Type,* 3rd ed. Boston: Little, Brown and Company, 2001.

Uncle Donald's Castro Street. "Dan White: He got away with murder." Accessed at http://thecastro.net/milk/whitepage.html.

United States Department of Commerce. *2000 U.S. Census*. Washington, DC: U.S. Government Printing Office, 2001.

U.S. Bank. *Paying for College: A Guide to Financial Aid*. Minneapolis, MN: Author, 2002.

Warner, J. "Celebratory drinking culture on campus: Dangerous drinking style popular among college students." *Parenting and Pregnancy,* November 5, 2002.

Warnick, B., and Inch, E. *Critical Thinking and Communication—The Use of Reason in Argument*. New York: Macmillan, 1994.

Watson, N. "Generation wrecked." *Fortune,* October 14, 2002, pp. 183–190.

Wechsler, H., and Wuethrich, B. *Dying to Drink: Confronting Binge Drinking on College Campuses*. New York: Rodale Press, 2002.

Werner, R. *Understanding*. Newport, RI: TED Conferences, 1999.

Whitfield, C. *Healing the Child Within*. Deerfield Beach, FL: Health Communication, 1987.

Woolfolk, A. *Educational Psychology*, 8th ed. Boston: Allyn and Bacon, 2001.

Wurman, R. *Understanding*. New York: Donnelley & Sons, 1999.

Yale Study of Graduating Seniors. Yale University, New Haven, CT, 1953.

Young, J. "Homework? What homework?" *The Chronicle of Higher Education,* December 6, 2003.

Zarefsky, D. *Public Speaking: Strategies for Success,* 3rd ed. Boston: Pearson/Allyn and Bacon, 2001.

Zimring, F. *Capital Punishment and the American Agenda*. Cambridge, MA: Cambridge University Press, 1987.

Index